W9-ABR-812

ARTHURIAN LITERATURE

VI

Contents of previous volumes

ISSN 0261-9946

Arthurian Literature VI

EDITED BY RICHARD BARBER

Advisory editors

Tony Hunt
Toshiyuki Takamiya

WITHDRAWN

D. S. BREWER · BARNES & NOBLE

BURGESS
PN
685
.A68
v.6

© Contributors 1986

copy 1

First published 1986 by D. S. Brewer
240 Hills Road, Cambridge
an imprint of Boydell & Brewer Ltd
PO Box 9, Woodbridge, Suffolk IP12 3DF
and Barnes & Noble
81 Adams Drive, Totowa, NJ 07512, USA

ISBN 0 85991 226 4
US ISBN 0-389-20702-0

British Library Cataloguing in Publication Data

Arthurian literature VI.
   1. Arthur, *King* — Periodicals
   2. Arthurian romance — History and
   criticism — Periodicals   3. English
   literature — History and criticism —
   Periodicals
   820.9'351   PR149.A79
   ISSN 0261-9946
   ISBN 0-85991-226-4

The Library of Congress has cataloged this serial
   as follows:

Arthurian literature. — l- — Woodbridge, Suffolk:
D. S. Brewer; Totawa, N.J.: Rowman and Littlefield,
c1981-v; 24cm.
Annual.
l. Arthurian romances — History and criticism —
Periodicals.
PN685.A68   809'.93351 — dc19   83-640196
                          AACR 2   MARC-S

Printed and bound in Great Britain by Short Run Press Ltd, Exeter

B.C.
87-98906

CONTENTS

I

THE HISTORICAL VALUE OF
THE *HISTORIA BRITTONUM*

David N. Dumville

The *Historia Brittonum* is a work which has loomed large in the study both of early mediaeval British history and of early Welsh literature. It is a witness to the history of Latin writing in Wales and to various aspects of the vernacular literary tradition. In particular its early and datable testimony to the varied development of the Arthurian legend has made it a text of particular interest to a wide range of mediaevalists.

While the *Historia* has been widely used, there has been a large hiatus in the detailed study of the text as a whole. The controversies which engulfed the work in the century separating Joseph Stevenson's edition (1838) from A. W. Wade-Evans's translation (1938) seem largely to have exhausted the interested scholarly community. An uneasy consensus about how to approach the work has marked the scholarship of the last generation.

However, work towards a new edition has necessarily reopened many of the old issues. Since I took up this task in the late 1960s, I have been brought to very different conclusions from those adopted, however uneasily, by scholars of the previous thirty years. I have made these clear in a number of detailed papers published since 1974. The practical result is that many users of the *Historia Brittonum* must now expect to ask new questions of the text and employ its evidence in a different way. Publication of my edition of the *Historia* has just begun: it seems to me that at this moment a statement about the date, sources, and genre of this extraordinary text, and about the uses to which historians can hope to put it, may provide a helpful backdrop against which students of literature may reassess their own approaches to and employment of the *Historia Brittonum*.

To what extent can we rely on any direct statements made by the author of the *Historia* about the early history of the British Isles? And how much historical evidence can we deduce from the work about the milieu of the author himself? The second question, which seems to me to be by far the more profitable approach, has been largely ignored by historians. The former has consumed students of language, literature, history, and archaeology who have sought to employ the *Historia* as a prime source for the fifth, sixth, and seventh centuries; but the only thing which has united them has been an agreement that this work was indeed a suitable quarry for materials relating to the history of these centuries.

When the *Historia Brittonum* – under its all-purpose title of 'Nennius' – is presented to students of British history, it has customarily been accompanied by the words of Dr J. N. L. Myres, published in 1936 in his contribution to the *Oxford History of England*.[1] 'There remains', he says, after a survey of the other literary evidence for the period of the English settlements,

> the *Historia Brittonum*, a compilation composed or edited early in the ninth century by a Welshman Nennius or Nemnius, whose notion of historical method is best described in his own words. *Coacervavi*, he says, *omne quod inveni* – 'I have made a heap of all that I have found'. It is customary to treat this uncritical attitude of Nennius as a fatal objection to the *Historia Brittonum* as a source for the period. [I may interject here that in 1936 it was only English historians who thought so.] In fact, of course, it is the one thing which saves it from the contempt into which later writers such as Geoffrey of Monmouth and Henry of Huntingdon have fallen. Had Nennius used his sources with the same literary skill which they employed, he would have lost the interest of historians as completely as they have done. It is precisely his ignorance and his stupidity which caused him to jumble together good and bad materials without amalgamating them into a single whole, and each successive commentary on the evolution of his curious book makes it more possible to sort out the different elements of which it is composed. But while it may be agreed that some scraps in the heap are more valuable than others, that some indeed provide information unobtainable elsewhere, it is not from such material as this that a satisfactory history of the time can be made.

A few years later Sir Frank Stenton, again taking up the point about English historians' general hostility to the *Historia Brittonum*, wrote in his volume of the *Oxford History*:[2]

> At present there is no general agreement about the authority of the different parts of the work which passes under the name of Nennius .... Much that has been written about Nennius is hypercritical, but it is clear that no section of his work should be used without extreme caution and

---

[1] R. G. Collingwood and J. N. L. Myres, *Roman Britain and the English Settlements* (Oxford, 1936; 2nd edn, 1937), pp. 329-30. Cf. J. N. L. Myres, *The English Settlements* (Oxford, 1986), pp. 16-18.

[2] F. M. Stenton, *Anglo-Saxon England* (Oxford, 1943; 2nd edn, 1947), p. 684; (3rd edn, 1971), p. 694.

many reservations. For Anglo-Saxon history in the strict sense the most important feature of the work is a series of notes, mainly on Northumbrian history, which Nennius or another has added to a set of English royal genealogies. There are obvious mistakes in the notes, but they seem to represent an authentic tradition.

The combined authority of Myres and Stenton has carried the day, and insofar as one can speak of a generally accepted view of the *Historia Brittonum*, it has been theirs.

Anyone who is introduced to this work is generally offered two editions: that of Theodor Mommsen, published in 1894, often described as 'definitive'; and that of Ferdinand Lot, published forty years later, whose text is a degenerate reprint of Mommsen's with a thinned-out apparatus, but who for the first time prefixed to an edition of this work a detailed discussion of its content and an attempt at an assessment of its sources and its historical value. Lot's work is characterised by a fierce Gallic contempt for his author; in Myres's words,[3] Lot's edition is 'a characteristically original and lively work, of which the usefulness is somewhat marred by the editor's habit of dismissing statements of his text whose meaning is not self-evident as mere instances of Nennian imbecility'. In my opinion, both editions are unusable. Textually, Mommsen's edition is a conflate of a series of recensions, muddled together without any regard to the very varied times and places in which these versions were composed; and his introduction was devoted exclusively to distinguishing a series of families of manuscripts and to discussing the finer points involved in the restoration of allegedly corrupt passages. Lot's pioneering discussions of content and sources were made less valuable by his need to rely on Mommsen's incomplete textual investigations, and by his ignorance of Celtic philology, this last being a defect shared by all previous editors. And, as generally with the editors of mediaeval texts until recent years, those same editors had been trained in Classical Latin, with all the prejudices which that necessarily instilled. If I had today to recommend to students a text of the *Historia Brittonum*, pending completion of the new edition, my choice would fall on one of two books: the edition of Joseph Stevenson, *Nennii Historia Britonum*, published in 1838, remains an unpretentious conflated text (with a clear textual introduction) based securely on the primary 'Harleian' version; or, better, the

---

[3] Collingwood & Myres, *Roman Britain and the English Settlements*, p. 479; Myres, *The English Settlements*, p. 225, notes Lot's edition 'among the older commentaries ... worth a mention, if only as period pieces'.

3

text presented by Edmond Faral in the third volume of his great work of 1929, *La légende arthurienne*, gives a simple print of all the matter in Harley 3859 (including the Welsh annals and royal genealogies), with a parallel text – as far as it went – from the eleventh-century Chartres manuscript.[4]

The textual history of the *Historia Brittonum* is indeed rather complicated, and I shall mention it again at the end of this paper. For the moment, its chief relevance is that two quite contradictory views about its development have been repeated by eminent scholars, neither of which is well founded but both of which have extraordinary implications for the authorship and purpose of the *Historia*. The first, advanced by Rudolf Thurneysen and repeated on a number of occasions by Kenneth Jackson,[5] would have us believe that 'Nennius' was responsible for a series of recensions of his work, in the last of which alone – the so-called 'Nennian' recension – he added the prologue bearing his name; this view, which defers to the textual history just far enough to accept that the prologue does not belong to the primary text of the *Historia*, ignores the evidence regarding the dates and areas of origin of the various recensions and, in particular, the fact of their widely varying latinity. The second view, propounded particularly by Ferdinand Lot, wholly disregarded the textual history of the work, and invited us to believe – with an embarrassing lack of supporting testimony – that the prologue had somehow gone missing from the primary (and every other early) version, being perhaps associated with some abridgment of the work, and that the universal anonymity of the *Historia* in its early years was due to this unfortunate accident.[6]

The plain fact of the matter is that the attribution to 'Ninnius' is a secondary and late development in the textual history. I have discussed this fully elsewhere and have concluded, on a mixture of textual and linguistic evidence, that the writing of the prologue and

---

[4] *Nennii Historia Britonum*, ed. Joseph Stevenson (London, 1938); *Chronica Minora saec. IV. V. VI. VII.*, ed. Theodor Mommsen (3 vols, Berlin, 1891-8), III.111-222; Edmond Faral, *La légende arthurienne: Études et documents, Les plus anciens textes* (3 vols, Paris, 1929), III.1-62; Ferdinand Lot, *Nennius et l'Historia Brittonum. Etude critique suivie d'une édition des diverses versions de ce texte* (2 vols, Paris, 1934).

[5] R. Thurneysen (in a review of Mommsen's edition), *Zeitschrift für celtische Philologie* 1 (1896/7), 157-68, at pp. 163-6; Kenneth Jackson, *Language and History in Early Britain* (Edinburgh, 1953), p. 48, and 'On the northern British section in Nennius', in *Celt and Saxon. Studies in the Early British Border*, ed. Nora K. Chadwick (Cambridge, 1963; rev. imp., 1964), pp. 20-62, at 55.

[6] Lot, *Nennius*, especially I.6-7, 16-19, 145-6.

the general fashioning of the recension to which it belongs is to be assigned to the eleventh century.[7] The author of the primary recension, a Welsh Latin text assignable to the year 829/30 (the fourth year of King Merfyn of Gwynedd), remains anonymous. In itself, this might seem a trivial conclusion, but if we recall to mind the far-reaching impression of 'ignorance and stupidity', to use Myres's words, 'a dim-witted and muddle-headed person', to use Jackson's,[8] which the Nennian prologue has left in the minds of modern historians, and the impression that his lack of literary skill 'caused him to jumble together good and bad materials without amalgamating them into a single whole',[9] we shall observe that this has allowed historians of the post-War generation to believe that from this dolt's uncritical heap can be extracted a quantity of usable historical evidence for the fifth to seventh centuries, deriving from good early sources which he has largely left unaltered. This is not a small or trivial matter, and on this note we may now turn to the text, accepting it – I hope – on its own terms, without the preconceptions inspired by the bogus prologue.[10]

What we see is, in my view, a synchronising history – a form with which students of Irish history and literature are already quite familiar. The point about a synchronising history is that it attempts, though rarely with complete success, to provide a smooth account of a period of history by combining all the available, and often wildly contradictory, witnesses into a slick, coherent, and 'official' whole. The 'harmonisation' (in Old Irish, comuaimm 'a stitching together'[11]) is the important process. In Eoin MacNeill's words,[12]

---

[7] D. N. Dumville, '"Nennius" and the *Historia Brittonum*', *Studia Celtica* 10/11 (1975/6), 78-95. On the basis of new developments in the study of Leabhar na hUidhre and of Welsh manuscript-sources, I should now have sufficient confidence to assign this recension to a marginally earlier date than the mid-eleventh century.

[8] Jackson, 'On the northern British section', p. 57.

[9] Myres, *apud* Collingwood & Myres, *Roman Britain and the English Settlements*, p. 329.

[10] Professor Henry Loyn kindly reminded me, in discussion, that of course it is unnecessary to take the words of the prologue literally; the use of this topos of ignorance as a *captatio beneuolentiae* was perfectly common in mediaeval prefaces. However, the point here is that modern historians *have* taken it literally and, moreover, have built their views *of the original ninth-century text* on this reading.

[11] Cf. J. Carney, 'The Old Irish accentual poems', *Ériu* 22 (1971), 23-80, at pp. 51-2, for brief comment.

[12] *Celtic Ireland* (Dublin, 1921), pp. 37-8.

The probability is that after a certain amount of tentative history-building had gone on in a random way, the subject began to attract the attention of the schools. Once in their hands the work had to be done thoroughly and systematically. Stories could not pass for histories unless they fitted together, in time and in all other relations. The schools, therefore, set themselves to collect all the ancient traditions of the nation, weaving them into a single fabric, with dates and a regular succession and correlation of events. . . .

Along with the stories, it was necessary to harmonize the genealogies, which are the bone-work of the history . . . the whole general process was going on in the schools in the ninth century.

(We now know, in fact, that this work was in progress in Ireland much earlier than the ninth century.[13]) MacNeill went on to make the vital point that early efforts inevitably suffered from chronological confusion.[14] Rival views emanated from different schools, and were only gradually and with difficulty reconciled or harmonised.

In Ireland, the final scheme was that in the eleventh-century *Lebor Gabála Érenn* and the works of the eleventh-century poets – themselves 'synthetic historians' – Flann Mainistrech and Gilla Coemáin, plus – of course – the great collections of genealogies embodied in twelfth-century manuscripts, of which the surviving representatives are Oxford, Bodleian Library, MS. Rawlinson B.502 and the Book of Leinster.

I suggest that, in the *Historia Brittonum*, we have an early example, perhaps the earliest, of a Welsh attempt at constructing a similar synthetic history. It certainly does not represent the earliest work of harmonisation and synchronisation, for the secular men of learning, particularly concerned with genealogy, had already been at work, as Dr Molly Miller has so ably shown us. In 1968, Mr Bartrum asked 'Was there a British "Book of Conquests"?'[15] He does not seem to have considered the possibility that the *Historia Brittonum* was just such a book, but instead suggested that there perhaps was one in existence by the twelfth century. And I think that I have some evidence that, in twelfth-century Wales, a sort of super-*Historia Brittonum* was being written, again in Latin, of

---

[13] See, for example, J. Carney, 'Early Irish Literature: the state of research', in *Proceedings of the Sixth International Congress of Celtic Studies*, edd. Gearóid Mac Eoin *et al.* (Dublin, 1983), pp.113-30; cf. D. Dumville, 'Language, literature, and law in medieval Ireland: some questions of transmission', *Cambridge Medieval Celtic Studies* 9 (1985), 91-8.

[14] *Celtic Ireland*, p. 38.

[15] P. C. Bartrum, 'Was there a British "Book of Conquests"?', *Bulletin of the Board of Celtic Studies* 23 (1968-70), 1-6.

which we have some fragments preserved in a north English manuscript *ca* 1200.[16] There is, at any rate, a good deal of evidence to suggest that in Welsh learned circles in the earlier middle ages a fair amount of attention was being paid to genealogical work, to collection of stories, their reduction to order (as in the Triads),[17] and their harmonisation (for example within the increasingly avaricious Arthurian cycle). To my mind, the harmonisation and, above all, the synchronisation proper to such activity in Celtic literary circles is very apparent in the *Historia Brittonum*.[18] We must also reckon, I think, with the possibility of Irish influence, for an early version of *Lebor Gabála Érenn* (possibly in Old Irish rather than Latin) was available to the author and may have been an inspiration to him.[19]

The reaction of Irish scholars to this sort of attitude is now unequivocal. They reject wholly this material as the source of political history for the period with which it pretends to deal, for it is seen to be wholly fictional; its manipulation may, however, be studied with profit as evidence for shifting political attitudes and for developments in cultural activity. It has been recognised that there must be established an approximate date for what historians of illiterate and newly literate societies have come to describe as the 'historical horizon' of record.[20] Controversy about St Patrick and about the early recording of Irish annals has helped to clarify this issue; annal-writing in Ireland cannot be assigned to a period much before *ca* 550.[21] Living memory at that stage might have carried

---

[16] Cf. D. N. Dumville, 'Celtic-Latin texts in northern England, c.1150-c.1250', *Celtica* 12 (1977), 19-49.

[17] *Trioedd Ynys Prydein. The Welsh Triads*, ed. & transl. Rachel Bromwich (2nd edn, Cardiff, 1978).

[18] In my paper, 'Some aspects of the chronology of the *Historia Brittonum*', *Bulletin of the Board of Celtic Studies* 25 (1972-4), 439-45, at pp. 444-5, I have already made the point that the calculation of the date 428, for the *aduentus Saxonum*, was perhaps the first achieved in Wales by the author of the *Historia Brittonum* and under the influence of English concern about discovering a date for this 'event'.

[19] But, for doubts about this, see P. Sims-Williams, 'The evidence for vernacular Irish literary influence on early mediaeval Welsh literature', in *Ireland in Early Mediaeval Europe. Studies in Memory of Kathleen Hughes*, edd. Dorothy Whitelock *et al.* (Cambridge, 1982), pp. 235-57 at 246-7.

[20] For an essential qualification of this remark, see Donnchadh Ó Corráin in his notes to the second edition (1981) of MacNeill, *Celtic Ireland*, p. 190 (*ad* p. 57).

[21] See, for example, A. P. Smyth, 'The earliest Irish annals: their first contemporary entries, and the earliest centres of recording', *Proceedings of the Royal Irish Academy* 72 C (1972), 1-48; K. Harrison, 'Epacts in Irish chronicles', *Studia Celtica* 12/13 (1977/8), 17-32.

record back into the later fifth century.[22] Before that, nothing is clear. Further, a new generation of historians in Ireland has made great advances in the study of the early mediaeval manipulation for political purposes of genealogies and the associated origin-legends, and even of the annalistic chronicles – especially in their early stages. There is a growing recognition that these materials cannot be taken at face-value, especially where they deal with events which are beyond the historical horizon. If we accept that origin-legends, for example, could be orally transmitted to a mediaeval point of record, unaltered and with sufficient chronological data so as to render them available and useful to modern historians, we shall have deliberately ignored the fact that the *filidh*, the very means of preservation, the cultivators of *senchas* or native learning, were the people responsible for the harmonisation and synchronisation of these oral records and their adaptation for political motives.[23] We do not, of course, have to do with preservation of record by the early Irish equivalent of the man on the Clapham omnibus, with no particular axe to grind: the keeping of record was an aristocratic, and intensely political, business.

The implications of this Irish digression should be sufficiently obvious for the Welsh situation. The plentifulness of surviving Irish record in various spheres has been contrasted, *ad nauseam*, with the relative paucity of Welsh material. But there *is* a lesson here for us. If, with the abundance of Irish material and the checks and balances which derive from the inevitable discrepancies, it is still not possible to reduce to historical credibility the legends relating to the period before the historical horizon of native record, not to mention many referring to a later period,[24] how much less shall we be able to accept the small surviving percentage of Welsh learned legends when we lack most of its native intellectual context?[25]

Let us turn now to the treatment of the British fifth century by the author of the *Historia Brittonum*. There are five major issues,

---

[22] Compare the position in early Anglo-Saxon England: see, for instance, Frank Merry Stenton, *Preparatory to 'Anglo-Saxon England'* (Oxford, 1970), pp.116-22, reprinting a paper of 1926.

[23] On this subject see F. J. Byrne, 'Senchas: the nature of Gaelic historical tradition', *Historical Studies* [Irish Conference of Historians] 9 (1974), 137-59.

[24] Cf. D. N. Dumville, ' "Beowulf" and the Celtic world: the uses of evidence', *Traditio* 37 (1981), 109-60, especially pp.132-7.

[25] On the Welsh context see P. P. Sims-Williams, 'Some functions of origin stories in early medieval Wales', in *History and Heroic Tale. A Symposium*, edd. Tore Nyberg *et al.* (Odense, 1985), pp. 97-131.

comprising the whole central section of the *Historia*: (1) Hencgest and Horsa and the *primus aduentus Saxonum*, the colonisation of Kent, and the invaders' dealings with Gwrtheyrn and Gwrthefyr; (2) Gwrtheyrn and St Garmon (including the *dinnshenchas* of Foel Fenlli); (3) the *dinnshenchas* of Dinas Emrys; (4) St Patrick; and (5) Arthur. These groups of material are sometimes intertwined, sometimes laid end to end, but always with connecting passages. The result is a superficially continuous history, where the gaps have been glossed over; but this actually discontinuous record is occasioned by evident chasms in the author's sources of knowledge.

I think that the first point to be made is that the fifth century seems to be beyond the historical horizon of native British record. The thin line in literary record which allows us to travel from the Roman period to the later sixth century is the work of Patrick in the later fifth century and that of Gildas about the middle of the sixth, plus the series of more or less datable inscriptions on stone from those parts of Britain which remained in Celtic hands throughout much of the early middle ages.[26] If we consider the body of later Welsh legend, we seem to be part of a world which begins after the mid-sixth century; it is as if the plague (of 549) which we know to have been so disastrous in Ireland was even more so in Britain. But in Britain there is another factor.

The middle of the sixth century forms the major watershed in our post-Roman history. The century and a half during which the Celtic-speaking people of Britain held sway in their own island after the collapse of Roman authority seems to have formed little more than an anomalous interlude between the Imperial past and the barbarian future. The stubborn resistance of the Britons to English advance kept by far the greater part of the island – and, indeed, of what is now England – in Celtic hands. But after 550 came a rapid collapse. In 633 Cadwallon of Gwynedd may have thoroughly devastated Northumbria, but it was an English-settled Northumbria which he was attempting to destroy;[27] of the Britons of the north we hear nothing, and the year 638 – five years later – is supposed to see the fall of Edinburgh to the English and the

---

[26] *Saint Patrick: Confession et Lettre à Coroticus*, ed. & transl. R. P. C. Hanson & C. Blanc (Paris, 1978); *Gildas: The Ruin of Britain and Other Works*, ed. & transl. Michael Winterbottom (Chichester, 1978); R. A. S. Macalister, *Corpus Inscriptionum Insularum Celticarum* (2 vols, Dublin, 1945/49); V. E. Nash-Williams, *The Early Christian Monuments of Wales* (Cardiff, 1950).

[27] Bede, *Historia Ecclesiastica Gentis Anglorum*, II.20.

collapse of Gododdin.[28] Cadwallon was a Welsh king making a successful attack on England; with our hindsight, we can hardly see him as more than that. In the first half of the sixth century, Gildas was able to acquire a first-class Latin education which our professional latinists of today – Kerlouégan, Winterbottom, Lapidge – assure us is the Latin of the secular rhetorical schools. (The ninth-century and later stories about Gildas receiving his education from St Illtud are the window-dressing of mediaeval monastic hagiographers who were assuredly even more ignorant than we are about education in Britain *ca* A.D. 500.)[29] The surviving inscriptions show the use of Roman capitals. We have the evidence of Roman titles – *magistratus, medicus, protector, ciuis*, and perhaps *consul*: I hardly need to repeat the often rehearsed evidence. In the second half of the sixth century, however, the curtain comes down on literary activity. The next Latin writings belong to the end of the eighth century.[30] The script of stone inscriptions becomes vulgar – developments of the Insular script principally associated with Ireland. The titles which I mentioned just now disappear. Commemoration is for christian purposes only. And in Welsh sources we completely lose sight of England east of the Welsh marches and Devon. The heroic age of the North is with us, and it is of course that brief heroic age which comes to dominate much of the early Welsh literary tradition. We lose whatever record there may have been of the foundation of the post-Roman kingdoms in Wales, already in existence by Gildas's time, not to mention those which must have existed in what is now England. In the south we catch a fleeting glimpse of them in English sources in the mention of three kings in connexion with the battle of Dyrham in 577,[31] and in the

---

[28] For this hypothesis, see K. H. Jackson, 'Edinburgh and the Anglian occupation of Lothian', in *The Anglo-Saxons. Studies in Some Aspects of their History and Culture presented to Bruce Dickins*, ed. Peter Clemoes (London, 1959), pp. 35-42.

[29] See M. Lapidge, 'Gildas's education and the Latin culture of sub-Roman Britain', in *Gildas: New Approaches*, edd. Michael Lapidge & D. Dumville (Woodbridge, 1984), pp. 27-50 and references given there; on St Illtud, see pp. 32-3.

[30] For the intervening period, see now D. Dumville, 'Late-seventh- or eighth-century evidence for the British transmission of Pelagius', *Cambridge Medieval Celtic Studies* 10 (1985), 39-52.

[31] In the Anglo-Saxon Chronicle, *sub anno*; on Ceawlin's dates see D. N. Dumville, 'The West Saxon Genealogical Regnal List and the chronology of early Wessex', *Peritia: Journal of the Medieval Academy of Ireland* 4 (1985); in general see P. Sims-Williams, 'The settlement of England in Bede and the Chronicle', *Anglo-Saxon England* 12 (1983), 1-41.

North in the brief appearance in our sources of Ceredig, king of Elfed in south Yorkshire.[32]

I have hammered the point long enough. The mid-sixth century, or even a little later, is the horizon in Welsh historical record because the third quarter of the sixth century was a time of startling upheaval in Britain. It was the period in which England and Wales were really born. And when we come to look at how our Welsh writer of the early ninth century attempted to construct his own 'synthetic history' – to use MacNeill's term – we can understand his assumptions and his difficulties in relation to the period between 388 and 547.

These *termini* are deliberately chosen. For in the dark age of Welsh history between the cataclysm of the later sixth century and the more outward-looking Wales which emerged (after two centuries of near-isolation) in the later eighth, the native learned classes, secular and ecclesiastical, had been hard at work. A series of basic historical *dicta* had been developed. One of these was that Roman Britain had ended with the death of Magnus Maximus in 388, and that from the descendants of this last British emperor all legitimate post-Roman power flowed. The result was a series of genealogies relating existing royal pedigrees to Maximus by way of marriages to invented daughters of Maximus (as for Powys and Cornwall) or by claiming direct descent from him (as did the kings of Dyfed and, most importantly, the second dynasty of Gwynedd); in the process this gave some of the northern heroes Maximid ancestry.[33]

The author of the *Historia Brittonum* ends his Roman history with Magnus Maximus, and turns at once to his British successors. He offers us two of these. To one, Cunedda, we shall return very briefly, later on. To another, Gwrtheyrn (or Vortigern), is devoted a good deal of attention. He is presented as a king who holds sway over southeastern England, but there is never any attempt at a definition of his territories. The constituent parts of his story are five: a small section drawn from Bede; a narrative based on an English source, possibly oral but probably not, dealing with the wars between the English and the Britons; an account of his dealings with St Garmon of Powys, leading to his death; a folktale account of his troubles at Dinas Emrys; and a genealogy of a minor Powys dynasty which claimed descent from him and held the land

---

[32] Bede, *Historia Ecclesiastica*, IV.23 (21); *Annales Cambrie, s.a.* 172 = A.D.616.
[33] See D. N. Dumville, 'Sub-Roman Britain: history and legend', *History*, N.S., 62 (1977), 173-92, especially pp.179-81.

largiente Ambrosio – according to our author. All these have been woven together, fairly roughly, to form a continuous narrative. The only two sections which have been seen as offering historical information are (1) the English material which forms the framework of the Vortigern story and (2) the account of St Garmon. It is hardly necessary to say that the story of Gwrtheyrn and Garmon commands no historical credibility. Our author was a reader of Bede and knew that St Germanus of Auxerre was on the loose in Britain at approximately the right time. If the equation of Garmon and Germanus of Auxerre had not already been made by his source – and I rather doubt that it had – it was a simple one for him to make in the process of harmonising his sources. The equation is of course unacceptable[34] – even the philological equivalence of the two names has been challenged by a powerful authority.[35] In the Life of St Garmon, we see a statement of the dependence of the Powys dynasty on the church and cult of St Garmon *in the early ninth century*; the Pillar of Elise offers us the official secular statement of the same relationship.[36] For it is an axiom of Celtic hagiography that the alleged founder of a dynasty (Cadell in the *Historia Brittonum*, Gwrtheyrn on the Pillar-inscription) be shown to be dependent on the favour of the dynastic or territorial saint, in this case Garmon. Dr Myres's suggestion of 1960 that this story is a reflection of the Pelagian controversy in the fifth century is sheer fantasy.[37]

The English material is much more difficult to assess. The names of Vortigern and his sons are presented to us in Old Welsh guise. Were they in some form in the source, or are they a Welsh insertion? If the latter, the material becomes impossible to handle. But since the story ties up in outline with that told by Gildas and particularly Bede and the Anglo-Saxon Chronicle, and is fuller than theirs, we can probably accept it as representing more or less faithfully an English account current in the early ninth century.

[34] Myres, *The English Settlements*, p.17, n.1, sticks to the old opinion.
[35] Melville Richards, quoted by R. W. D. Fenn, 'Who was St Harmon?', *Transactions of the Radnorshire Society* 36 (1966), 50-5, at p. 55, n.15. Cf. M. Richards, 'Places and persons of the early Welsh Church', *Welsh History Review* 5 (1970/1), 333-49, at pp. 335, 348.
[36] P. C. Bartrum (ed.), *Early Welsh Genealogical Tracts* (Cardiff, 1966), pp.1-3; cf. Dumville, 'Sub-Roman Britain', pp.185-7.
[37] J. N. L. Myres, 'Pelagius and the end of Roman rule in Britain', *Journal of Roman Studies* 50 (1960), 21-36; it is astonishing to find him repeating this in *The English Settlements*, p.17. Cf. the remarks of R. A. Markus, 'Pelagianism: Britain and the Continent', *Journal of Ecclesiastical History* 37 (1986), 191-204.

The point to be emphasised about this circumstantial and detailed account, which depends in the story about the massacre of the British nobles on a literary play on the words *Saxones* and *saxas* also found in the work of Widukind of Corvey,[38] is that it is of English origin, and that even if it were served up to us in an eighth- or ninth-century English manuscript it would be unacceptable as historical evidence for the early or mid-fifth century. It is not the stuff of which history is made, but is instead saga-material of the sort plentifully attested for England and studied, for example, by C. E. Wright.[39]

Observe, nonetheless, how our author has used English source-material as the framework for his account. We shall meet this interesting circumstance again.

He continues, having tidily taken 'Germanus' back to Gaul, with St Patrick, alleged disciple of Germanus. The account of him is a collection of excerpts from the late seventh-century works by Muirchú and Tírechán, with some additional material now paralleled in the *Vita Tertia* and the Tripartite Life.[40] This section is of little importance for us at this stage.

After Patrick, we pass back to the Anglo-British wars, first to the descendants of Hencgest and then to Arthur. It was proposed many years ago by the Chadwicks[41] that this account of Arthur derived from a Welsh battle-catalogue poem such as those on Cynan Garwyn and Cadwallon, and this has (I think) received general acceptance.[42] The point here, of course, is that such catalogues – especially when composed centuries after the event, like that on Cadwallon – bear no particular relation to the historical circumstances of the period of the subject. Such a poem is evidence only for the extent of the development of the Arthurian

---

[38] Cf. H. Munro Chadwick, *The Origin of the English Nation* (Cambridge, 1907), pp. 41-2 (2nd edn, 1924, p. 39); see also M. O. Anderson, 'Dalriada and the creation of the kingdom of the Scots', in *Ireland in Early Mediaeval Europe*, edd. Whitelock *et al.*, pp. 106-32, at 116-17.

[39] *The Cultivation of Saga in Anglo-Saxon England* (Edinburgh, 1939).

[40] For the *uitae* of St Patrick, see Ludwig Bieler & F. Kelly (ed. & transl.), *The Patrician Texts in the Book of Armagh* (Dublin, 1979); *Four Latin Lives of St Patrick. Colgan's* Vita Secunda, Quarta, Tertia, *and* Quinta, ed. Ludwig Bieler (Dublin, 1971); *Bethu Phátraic. The Tripartite Life of Patrick*, ed. Kathleen Mulchrone (Dublin, 1939).

[41] H. Munro Chadwick & N. Kershaw Chadwick, *The Growth of Literature* (3 vols, Cambridge, 1932-40), I.154-5.

[42] But it was taken by our author from a written source, as is shown by his misinterpretation of Old Welsh *scuit*: cf. further R. Bromwich, 'Concepts of Arthur', *Studia Celtica* 10/11 (1975/6), 163-81.

13

legend by 830, and not for the historicity of Arthur or the alleged events of *ca* A.D. 500. In general, our ignorance of the political history of the British fifth century is almost total; in my view, it is not legitimate to seek to lighten this darkness by the use of unhistorical sources offered by a writer whose ignorance *was* complete and whose concept of history did not require him to distinguish between certain types of evidence, as we must do. We must seek alternative testimony which will introduce us to other areas of fifth-century culture.

From Arthur, with the connecting sentence 'Et reges a Germania deducebant ut regnarent super illos in Britannia, usque ad tempus quo Ida regnauit . . .' we leap straight to the other *terminus* of this murky period, A.D. 547. The date derives from another English source used by our author, and marks the beginning of a new stage in his History – what has been called the 'North British section' – which extends to 685 and deals exclusively with north British affairs. Its framework is provided by what I have called, in another connexion, 'the Anglian collection of royal genealogies and regnal lists',[43] a text which survives to us in English manuscripts. It is this section of the work which has *seemed* to possess most historical credibility and which has been most valued by historians of the early mediaeval North.

There are three vital questions. What were the Celtic sources of this section? What is their quality? And, finally, how does our author use these sources? The last question has often been answered in the light of the unhappy assumptions mentioned at the outset, which derive from a literal reading of the bogus prologue: the author has heaped up his sources and not attempted to manipulate them to any purpose; they are ripe for taking and using.

What, then, are these sources? The 'North British section' has always been the source of horrifyingly – and to my mind quite unnecessarily – complicated theories of development, the latest of which are Kenneth Jackson's and Molly Miller's.[44] Having published a detailed rebuttal of Jackson's theories, I do not wish to go into too much detail here. Let me concentrate instead on what I should

---

[43] *Anglo-Saxon England* 5 (1976), 23-50.

[44] Jackson, 'On the northern British section'; M. Miller, 'The foundation-legend of Gwynedd in the Latin texts', *Bulletin of the Board of Celtic Studies* 27 (1976-8), 515-32. For my reply to Jackson, see D. N. Dumville, 'On the north British section of the *Historia Brittonum*', *Welsh History Review* 8 (1976/7), 345-54.

regard as the minimum 'prehistory' of this part of the text. First, the latinity is of a piece with that of the rest of the work; this view was urged by Joseph Loth in 1932 and, after a detailed study, I should affirm it strongly.[45] I see no need for the assumption that an 'Original Northern History' ever existed, to be more or less bodily attached to the rest of the *Historia Brittonum*. The whole work seems to me to be built on the same synchronising pattern. I think that we need posit only two Celtic sources for this part of the text. We must remember that the amount of non-English material here is remarkably slight. The first is a set of north-British annals, related to that used as a source for *Annales Cambrie* but probably slightly fuller than their surviving record. We can document the existence of such a north-British chronicle also from its use in the Irish annals.[46] The few remaining items would be drawn from our author's knowledge of Welsh learned tradition about the Gwynedd dynasty and the figures of the Old North.

Dr Kathleen Hughes denied that our author's source was annalistic. 'If it was', she asked, 'why did the compiler of the *Historia* have to turn to an Anglo-Saxon king-list to provide his chronological structure?'[47] This is easily answered. If the author of the *Historia* had before him a set of laconic annals, perhaps (like the Harleian annals) with no absolute dates, although this is far from certain, he would have faced an insuperable task in attempting to construct even a skeletal history of the period. By adopting a Northumbrian regnal list as the basis of his account, however, he has gained a coherent and dated structure which he would otherwise have lacked. Also, it seems that he had more English than British material available concerning this period. There is no reason to believe in Dr Hughes's memoranda, or in Professor Jackson's 'Original Northern History'. Annals – which we know on other grounds to have existed – are sufficient for our purpose.

Let us examine the use to which our author put this source. For one thing, he had to synchronise its entries with his English framework, the Northumbrian regnal list. Let us first consider a case where we *know* him to have bungled the job. *Annales*

---

[45] J. Loth, 'Remarques à l'*Historia Brittonum* dite de Nennius', *Revue celtique* 49 (1932), 150-65 *and* 51 (1934), 1-31, at pp.153-65; cf. R. L. Thomson, 'British Latin and English history. Nennius and Asser', *Proceedings of the Leeds Philosophical and Literary Society (Literary and Historical Section)* 18 (1982), 38-53.

[46] Kathleen Hughes, *Celtic Britain in the Early Middle Ages. Studies in Scottish and Welsh Sources* (Woodbridge, 1980), pp. 70-2, 91-7.

[47] *Ibid.*, p. 71.

Cambrie put the death by plague of Cadwaladr of Gwynedd in the early 680s – rightly, as far as we can see. But our author has tied this up with the reign of Oswiu (642-670), mistakenly associating the plague with the great pestilence of 664 recorded by Bede.[48] There are errors too in his synchronisation of purely English affairs: by no known reckoning did Gregory the Great send Augustine to Kent in the reign of Frithuwald of Bernicia (579-585).[49]

Then there is the question of interpretative writing. *Annales Cambrie* give three successive entries: (1) *Strages Gaii campi*; (2) *Pantha occisio*; (3)*Osguid uenit et predam duxit*. This laconic series gives an acceptable version which can be reconciled with Bede's account.[50] The *Historia Brittonum* certainly had a fuller source which may indeed have included the phrase *edfryd Iddew*. I think that we must wonder if this 'restoration' or 'restitution' occurred in quite the circumstances suggested by our author; certainly Bede's account is rather different; and the *Annales* have as their *last* entry in the series, *Osguid uenit et predam duxit*. However we may try to rearrange the evidence, we are driven to Kenneth Jackson's conclusion that the account in the *Historia Brittonum* must be 'rearranged so as to remove the chronological contradiction'.[51] The fact is that our author's account, with its mangled chronology and its backward look, is a blatant piece of interpretative writing; it is itself an attempt to discover cause and effect – a historian's view of the situation, not (as old views of the text would have it) a heap of unsullied verities gathered together by a mere compiler.

Let us look at another item, which has particularly exercised students of Welsh literature, that dealing with the poets. After a brief account of Ida of Bernicia (547-559 by the official Northumbrian chronology), the author continues '*Tunc* Outigirn [Eudeyrn] *in illo tempore* demicabat contra gentem Anglorum.

---

48 *Historia Ecclesiastica*, III.27 and 30. Cf. the Annals of Ulster, *sub annis* 664-668.
49 The death of St Cuthbert at Lindisfarne during the reign of Ecgfrith, king of Northumbria (*ob.* 20 May 685), is also erroneous; Cuthbert died in 687. But the manuscripts' *obiit in insula* may be scribal error in their archetype for *abiit in insulam*, and refer to Cuthbert's acquisition of the see of Lindisfarne in March 685, or his first withdrawal to Farne as a solitary in about 676. For a parallel to the suggested corruption, see Paul Lehmann, 'Fuldaer Studien', *Sitzungsberichte der Bayerischen Akademie der Wissenschaften*, Philosophisch-philologische und historische Klasse, Jahrgang 1925, 3. Abhandlung, pp. 42-3.
50 Bede, *Historia Ecclesiastica*, III.24.
51 'On the northern British section', p. 37.

Tunc Talhaern Tat Aguen in poemate claruit; et Neirin et Taliessin
... simul uno tempore in poemate claruerunt.' The next section
deals with King Maelgwn and the Gwynedd origin-legend: 'Mailcunus
... regnabat' (his dates apparently being 534-549; note the imperfect tense). We must presume that our author's synchronisations
led him to believe that Ida, Maelgwn, and all these poets were
contemporaries. We should *perhaps* be careful about ascribing to
him too precise a view, for he is careful to leave an element of
imprecision in his expressions of time.[52] In the notice of the poets,
the verbs *claruit* and *claruerunt* particularly interest me. They are
part of the language of Late Latin annalistic writing. Could this
passage have derived from our Northern annals? The balance of
probability must, I think, be against it. The Latin annalists –
Jerome, Prosper, Isidore – whom our author used as sources in the
earlier, Roman, part of his work, used this terminology, and he
borrowed into the *Historia* a couple of examples of those who
claruerunt: Martin of Tours and St Jerome.[53] The Late Latin
annalists included in their chronicles notices such as 'Vergilius
claruit', and I think that our author must be seen consciously doing
the same thing for British poetry.

His chronology, then, could go seriously awry on account of the
difficulties of synchronising English and British material. He could
write like a historian, interpreting his sources, and so removing
them still further from the domain of readily usable evidence. But
his knowledge of Welsh literary tradition – of which we have seen
a concrete example in the use of the poem on Arthur – could also
have distorting effects. One has been captured by the eagle eye of
Kenneth Jackson:[54] no doubt because of the similarity of the written
forms of their names, Eda Glynfawr, a north-British hero apparently of the later sixth century, has been identified by our
author with the Northumbrian noble Eata, father of Eadberht,
king of Northumbria 737-758, a distortion of a century and a half.
Jackson has argued that the use of Brittonic epithets to describe
English kings of the sixth and seventh centuries speaks for a source

---

[52] On this question see D. N. Dumville, 'Early Welsh poetry: problems of
historicity', in *The Book of Aneirin and Early Welsh Poetry*, ed. B. F. Roberts
(Aberystwyth, forthcoming).

[53] These were drawn from Prosper, *Chronicon*, § 1175 (ed. Mommsen, *Chronica
Minora*, I.461), or Isidore, *Chronicon*, § 355 (*ibid.* II.469), and (Jerome)
Prosper, *Chronicon*, § 1186 (*ibid.*, I.462), or Isidore, *Chronicon*, § 358 (*ibid.*,
II.470).

[54] 'On the northern British section', pp. 43-4.

near to the time and place of their activities.[55] 'They could scarcely have been invented long after the time of their originals', he says. I should argue for the reverse: that the existence of the epithet implies a story about the character in question, and the use of the epithets in the *Historia* suggests our author's acquaintance with that item in the Welsh literary tradition. I submit that the mistaken identification of Eda and Eata, with the addition of the epithet in a standard formula (*Eatan ... ipse est Eata Glinmaur*), is precisely the proof required for my proposition. And to say that nicknames could not be invented (or, indeed, changed) long after the time of the character in question seems to me to defy the evidence of the genealogies (and, I daresay, of the Triads).

All this leads us to the question of the date of the source or sources used by our author. The matter turns essentially on the forms of three Welsh words – *atbret*, *Neirin*, *Cunedag* – to all of which Professor Jackson assigns a date much earlier than that of our author. I think that these are easily disposed of. Jackson assigns the first to the seventh century, because of the absence of vowel-affection. In a footnote to the same article, however, he rightly observes that this absence might be purely orthographic.[56] In 1953, in fact, he gave us examples of such absence in *tenth*-century sources.[57] *Neirin* he describes as 'very archaic';[58] but Ifor Williams[59] and Rachel Bromwich[60] have both taken this to be a standard Old Welsh form which develops into A*neirin* in Middle Welsh. If I read his *Grammar* aright, Simon Evans would be of the same view.[61] Certainly I can find no evidence to support the idea that this is an exclusively archaic Old Welsh form. Finally, *Cunedag*: Jackson says not later than about 750, and very probably earlier.[62] Again, there is the general argument from orthography to oppose to this; but, in addition, this, the last example of the retention of the -*g*, is little later than the first example of its loss – *Cinda* in the

---

[55] *Ibid.*, p. 45.

[56] *Ibid.*, p. 38 and n. 1.

[57] *Language and History*, pp. 606-7.

[58] 'On the northern British section', p. 47, n. 3.

[59] *The Beginnings of Welsh Poetry* (Cardiff, 1972), p. 76, reprinting a paper first read in 1950.

[60] *Ibid.*, p. 43, n. [7].

[61] D. Simon Evans, *A Grammar of Middle Welsh* (Dublin, 1964), p. 12.

[62] 'On the northern British section', p. 30. For a different emphasis, see *Language and History*, p. 458.

Chad-2 memorandum, allegedly of the late eighth century.[63] I hardly think that the margin is sufficient to enable us to say that our author's orthographic usage could not extend to (sporadic) retention of the -g.

In any case, I should not like to assert that any of these three words occurred in the annals used by our author; they would be likely, with the possible exception of *edfryd*, to derive from his knowledge of the Welsh literary tradition and need not therefore have been before him in a written source.

What, in general, can we conclude about the value of the annals which he used? For the seventh century, or part of it, they are likely enough to have been a contemporary record, although this requires further investigation unbiased by attitudes to the *Historia Brittonum*. Certainly in eighth-century Strathclyde annals were being kept which extended back into the seventh, and perhaps later sixth, century. But if we accept Molly Miller's attractive suggestion that whoever compiled the brief mnemonic series of entries (now preserved in *Annales Cambrie*), which deals with the heroic age of the late sixth-century North, was working on the basis of much knowledge rather than much ignorance of the period,[64] we may be sure that in their present form they constitute a retrospective record for that period. *Annales Cambrie* may perhaps for the seventh and eighth centuries be a reliable, even a contemporary, record – as far as their very brief entries go. But we must adjust to the fact the *Historia Brittonum* is not even a reliable – much less a contemporary – witness to the history of seventh- and sixth-century Britain. I cannot point to any item in it, other than material deriving from English sources already known, which is not open to serious question.

I have spent a great deal of time on the unpleasant task of debunking the work of an author with whom, over the years, I have come to feel a great deal of sympathy. This task I feel to be greatly necessary, since so much credence has, in the past generation, been given to his reconstruction (for that is what it is) of early north-British history; in particular, the considerable authority of

---

[63] *Ibid.*, pp. 42-7. On this source see further D. Jenkins & M. E. Owen, 'The Welsh marginalia in the Lichfield Gospels', *Cambridge Medieval Celtic Studies* 5 (1983), 37-66 *and* 7 (1984), 91-120. There may well be grounds, however, for assigning this memorandum to a much later date.

[64] 'The commanders at Arthuret', *Transactions of the Cumberland and Westmorland Antiquarian and Archaeological Society*, N.S., 75 (1975), 96-118, at p.117.

Kenneth Jackson has done much to reinforce the favourable view of our author's sources. And, in the past few years, there has even been a tendency to view sympathetically the *Historia*'s materials for the fifth century.

Let me stress that our author's sources, for the period of the late fourth to late seventh centuries – where scholars have hoped for the preservation of authentic early materials, are almost wholly legendary (as in the case of the English story of Hencgest and Horsa) or systematic (as with the Northumbrian regnal list which controls the chronology for 547-685; or the genealogies, Welsh and English; or the catalogue-poem on Arthur; or the hagiographical material about Garmon and Cadell, Garmon and Gwrtheyrn, and about Patrick) or folkloristic (as with the '*dinnshenchas*' of Dinas Emrys). In short, none of this can be taken at face-value, and little of it can be related to the period with which it purports to deal. In an ostensibly 'historical' source, we already see all the techniques of professional mediaeval Celtic scholarship being employed: hagiography; origin-legend; synchronisation; battle-catalogues; systematic pedigrees. We must turn to a later period to reap the value of our man's work, an invaluable source for Welsh intellectual history.

Much earlier, I stated what I thought his intentions to be, and where useful parallels could be found. Certainly I consider him to have made an intelligent attempt at a history of his countrymen from their origins down to the effective conclusion of the north-British wars at the end of the seventh century. By the standards of his day, he had performed a very difficult task – given the paucity and uneven quality of his materials – rather competently and in an up-to-date fashion. The synchronising history was not an easy genre to apply for the first time; I think that we may be fairly certain that his was the first Welsh attempt.[65] How effectively his successors felt him to have performed is amply demonstrated by the great amount of attention which they paid to his work, by the fact that it was not superseded until the twelfth or thirteenth century, by the stamp which it left on the mind of Geoffrey of Monmouth (whose historiography, if I may call it that, controlled Welsh historical thought until modern times), by its use by all the important Anglo-Norman historians, by its attribution in the twelfth century to 'Gildas Sapiens', and by its continuing circu-

---

[65] Cf. n.18 above; for aspects of the author's intellectual context see Sims-Williams, 'Some functions' (n. 25 above).

lation in England until the end of the middle ages. If brief, our author's work was nonetheless highly influential.

What does his work tell us of the milieu from which he emerged, and how does this tie in with other evidence for the period? I cannot write at length here on the evidence about the author himself.[66] But I conclude that he was a cleric, probably from the border-regions of southeastern Wales but working in Merfyn Frych's Gwynedd, perhaps even at his court. He may have been employed as an interpreter, in addition to his religious duties. And this brings me to my main point, his multilingualism. Apart from his native Welsh, and his natural and flowing – if *not* fluent – Latin, he seems to have had a good command of Old English, and there is just a suspicion of evidence that he may have known some Old Irish. He was, then, open to international influences, some of which I have already mentioned. But he was also a Welshman, sympathetic to and no doubt fairly knowledgeable in the Welsh learned traditions of his day. We know all too little about the organisation of the native learned orders in pre-Norman Wales, and of the relations of secular and ecclesiastical within those orders. We cannot therefore say if our author would have had any professional training in genealogy, place-lore, vernacular poetry, or hagiography. We can merely observe his work, and make our own deductions. My guess would be that he was fairly heavily dependent for his knowledge on written sources. He would have a certain amount of knowledge of native learning and traditional lore, as would any member of the aristocracy, but he would have to ask for specialist sources such as genealogies, and could not himself offer the repertoire of a professional.

He is nonetheless our earliest coherent and datable witness to the development of Welsh literature, and the value of his work to the historians of both oral and written literature *and* of professional antiquarian activity (with its many social implications) is immense. The Arthurian legend is an obvious consideration. Its development has been very thoroughly discussed and I shall not dwell on it here.[67] I should simply make two points. By 829/30, a battle-catalogue poem was available in written form, and the name

---

[66] A full study will appear in volume 8 of my edition: *The Historia Brittonum*, ed. David N. Dumville (10 vols, Cambridge, 1985-). Cf. also my *England and the Celtic World in the Ninth and Tenth Centuries* (O'Donnell Lectures: publication forthcoming).

[67] The classic study remains that of T. Jones, 'The early evolution of the legend of Arthur', *Nottingham Mediaeval Studies* 8 (1964), 3-21; cf. also Bromwich, 'Concepts of Arthur'.

of Arthur had taken sufficient hold on the keepers of place-lore (including natural marvels) that two episodes among the *mirabilia* which form the concluding portion of the *Historia* depend on knowledge of his exploits – his hunting of Twrch Trwyd and his killing of his son Amr.[68] I might add that the *mirabilia* (or at any rate the bulk of them) constitute a possible candidate for derivation from a pre-existing written source which was bodily incorporated by our author.[69]

We see the development of a learned etymological explanation for the name of Britain and the Britons. It is *possible* that our work provides its first expression, although that is made unlikely by the amount of detail about the eponym *Britto* or *Brutus*, and by the author's statement that he had *found* two explanations of the name.

The *Historia* presents our only explicit evidence that hagiography was practised as a genre in ninth- (and indeed eighth-) century Wales, as it was in Brittany and had long been in Ireland. He draws on what he calls the *Liber Beati Germani*, arguably written during the reign of Cadell ab Brochfael (*ob.* 808) of Powys. And he inserts among the *mirabilia* a miraculous episode from a Life of St Illtud, one which is paralleled in the extant eleventh- or twelfth-century Life.[70] Another episode, describing a miraculous tomb in Ceredigion, is probably another of our author's insertions, and looks very much as if it too may derive from a hagiographic source. (It is repeated centuries later by Giraldus Cambrensis.)[71]

The Life of Garmon appears to have been a peculiarly characteristic piece of Celtic hagiography, and I think that we may conclude from this that the practice of hagiography was widespread in Wales by *ca* 800. This should, I think, give an impetus to the critical study of the surviving *uitae* of *ca* 1100,[72] to see how ideas of the saints, and the claims of their churches, developed during this three-hundred-year period.

---

[68] It is worth noting that both episodes belong to eastern Wales (Buellt, Erging). On Twrch Trwyd, see Sims-Williams, 'The evidence' (n.19 above), p.239.

[69] This tentative conclusion depends on analysis of the evidence of Welsh language-forms in the *mirabilia*-section of the *Historia*: see K.H.Jackson, *apud* Dumville, *The Historia Brittonum*, vol.10.

[70] *Vita Sancti Iltuti* §22: ed. & transl. A.W.Wade-Evans, *Vitae Sanctorum Britanniae et Genealogiae* (Cardiff, 1944), pp.224-7.

[71] *Itinerarium Kambrie*, II.3 (*ad fin.*).

[72] Most of these have been edited and translated (if imperfectly) by Wade-Evans, *Vitae*. Cf. Michael Lapidge & R.Sharpe, *A Bibliography of Celtic-Latin Literature 400-1200* (Dublin, 1985), nos 32, 35, 37, 38, 56, 90-117, for a systematic listing of all known Cambro-Latin *uitae sanctorum*.

The *Historia* is important, too, in that it shows us a folktale-type of story, though used in the context of '*dinnshenchas*', about the boy-seer Emrys. This is a landmark of importance in the legend of Merlin; again, given the extent of published discussion, I shall not pursue the matter here.[73]

I wonder how important our author's witness is for the development of Welsh legend and systematic pedigree-work on the north-British heroic age. He knows of the poets, including at least one of whom we do not otherwise hear; there is at least a suggestion in his words that the King Eudeyrn whom he mentions was known to him from a poem, or poems, attributed to Talhaearn.[74]

The passage briefly relating the Gwynedd origin-legend – which may have been the creation of the genealogists for the newly established Second Dynasty – was fairly certainly drawn not from the north-British annals but from some other source. It reads like commentary on an entry about Maelgwn. From its wording and its discrepancies as compared with other sources we can learn much about the development of this origin-legend and of the pedigrees of the kings of Gwynedd.[75]

The account of the Lindisfarne confederacy of the four kings led by Urien, and ascribed by our author to the reign of Theodric of Bernicia (585-592) – although heaven only knows if that is an accurate synchronism[76] – seems to offer a little more than we might expect from a bare annalistic recital. Did our author know another poem ascribed to Taliesin which gave more detail than those which we know?[77] Or did he have access to the sort of ideas now embodied in the Llywarch Hen cycle?[78]

The story of Cadafael of Gwynedd, alluded to in the Triads, is unlikely, at least in part, to have derived from the annals; certainly the pun on his name seems unlikely to have done. It would appear

---

[73] See A. O. H. Jarman, *The Legend of Merlin* (Cardiff, 1960), for a brief but lucid introduction; cf. Bromwich, *Trioedd*, pp. 469-74, 559-60.

[74] M. Miller, 'Historicity and the Pedigrees of the Northcountrymen', *Bulletin of the Board of Celtic Studies* 26 (1974-6), 255-80, at p. 272.

[75] Dumville, 'Sub-Roman Britain', pp.181-3; M. Miller, 'Date-guessing and pedigrees', *Studia Celtica* 10/11 (1975/6), 96-109; Miller, 'The foundation-legend' (n. 44 above).

[76] I discuss this question in detail in a forthcoming paper, 'Some notes on the treatment of Northumbrian history 547-616 in the *Historia Brittonum*'.

[77] For the corpus currently attributed to him, with however much uncertainty, see Ifor Williams & J. E. C. Williams (edd.), *The Poems of Taliesin* (Dublin, 1968).

[78] For this see *The Poetry of Llywarch Hen*, ed. & transl. Patrick K. Ford (Berkeley, Cal., 1974). Cf. Bromwich, *Trioedd*, p. 70.

that the opprobrious story about him was already in circulation in our author's time.[79]

Here, then, are some indications – however vague – of the vernacular literary sources available to our author. They do not amount to a great deal, and we can hardly view him as a great repository of national literary tradition.

We must be grateful, however, for this very important, rare, early glimpse of Welsh literary activity. There is still a good deal of work which can be done on this material. For me, one of the most important points is the unobtrusive but quite certain importance which our text gives to Magnus Maximus, reflecting his commanding position in the national origin-legend. This has many ramifications which require to be worked out in detail.[80]

The *Historia Brittonum* is also a source for the general cultural history of the time. It fits in an interesting way into the broad pattern of Anglo-Welsh relationships in the approximate period 750 to 950.[81] Possible connexions with Ireland I have already briefly sketched in part; we know that early mediaeval Continental sources were reaching Wales in the ninth century – we can see the use of at least one in our text;[82] but the most important for present purposes (and the only ones on which I have space to dwell) are cultural relations with England. As far as we can make out, these were practically non-existent before the Easter-controversy was resolved in the later eighth century. The inevitable result of that resolution was the opening of Wales to more outside influences. (It is at precisely this period that annals begin to be kept at St Davids, into which Irish and north-British sources were incorporated.)[83] The *Historia Brittonum* is part of, and the most substantial evidence for, the development of English cultural influence in Wales. The

[79] K. Jackson, 'Brittonica', *The Journal of Celtic Studies* 1 (1949/50), 69-79, at p. 69, and 'On the northern British section', pp. 38-9; Bromwich, *Trioedd*, pp. 289-90, 546.

[80] For a beginning, see Dumville, 'Sub-Roman Britain', pp. 179-81. See also J. F. Matthews, 'Macsen, Maximus, and Constantine', *Welsh History Review* 11 (1982/3), 431-48; and M. G. Jarrett, 'Magnus Maximus and the end of Roman Britain', *Transactions of the Honourable Society of Cymmrodorion* (1983), 22-35.

[81] On this subject see my *England and the Celtic World* (n. 66 above).

[82] *Genealogiae gentium*: see W. Goffart, 'The supposedly "Frankish" table of nations: an edition and study', *Frühmittelalterliche Studien* 17 (1983), 98-130. The same conclusion might also be drawn from the study both of manuscripts from ninth-century Wales and of Asser's Life of King Alfred.

[83] Hughes, *Celtic Britain*, chapters 5 and 6.

alphabet of Nemniuus, part of a manuscript dated to the year 817, is an adaptation of the English runic futhorc with Welsh names; it is alleged by the text that this was done as part of a dispute between an English and a Welsh scholar.[84] For the date of this Welsh runic alphabet we have no precise information, but the half-century 768 x 817 is hardly likely to be wide of the mark. Our text, the *Historia Brittonum*, dates from 829/30.[85] About 840, there were Welsh monks apparently in residence at Lindisfarne;[86] their presence – or that of others like them – could help to explain our author's acquistion of Northumbrian materials. Finally, if the charters for the ninth century in the Book of Llandaf be in any sense trustworthy evidence, English personal nomenclature seems to have been becoming popular in Wales – at any rate in the south-east.[87] I think that the name 'Edwin' was borrowed at the latest in the ninth century (and, incidentally, that when Hywel Dda called his son Edwin, he was giving him an acceptable Welsh name!).[88]

Our author was very heavily dependent on English materials. Indeed, one might almost say that he had more English than Welsh sources. His account of the fifth to seventh centuries is controlled by three major English sources and a number of minor ones. In this and in his knowledge of Old English, we may see him as a representative of a new trend in Welsh culture, which was to be a feature of the ninth and tenth centuries. The relationship developed during the ninth century, being made closer, no doubt, by the viking-wars and by political cooperation (perhaps inaugurated by Offa of Mercia in the late eighth century[89] but most effectively practised by the West Saxon kings Alfred and Edward in the late ninth and early tenth). The work of Asser inaugurates a new phase, where the political dominance of Wessex is matched by a Welsh cultural superiority lasting for a century – a period in which

---

[84] Dumville, '"Nennius" and the *Historia Brittonum*', pp. 90-2, and the references cited there.

[85] Dumville, 'Some aspects of the chronology', pp. 439-40.

[86] Jackson, *Language and History*, p. 59.

[87] Cf. Wendy Davies, *The Llandaff Charters* (Aberystwyth, 1979), p.145, on the distribution of English names in the charters of *Liber Landauensis*. 'Chad 3' and 'Chad 4', Welsh charters of *saec.* ix/x in the Lichfield Gospels, have as a witness an ecclesiastic called *Cutulf*, which I take to be Old English Cuthwulf – not a very common Welsh name!

[88] In saying this I dissent from the frequently expressed opinion that this was an aspect of Hywel's pro-English toadying: see further D. P. Kirby, 'Hywel Dda: anglophil?', *Welsh History Review* 8 (1976/7), 1-13.

[89] But, on the evidence of recent archaeological work on Offa's Dyke, this now seems increasingly unlikely.

Wales (and Brittany and Cornwall) contributed a great deal to the cause of the revival of English learning (and ecclesiastical discipline).[90] Our author, in the early ninth century, was writing in a period of English cultural dominance; it is interesting that, just over a century later, a Welsh revision of his work was transmitted to England where the revival of learning was under way and where his History was rewritten in a less eccentric style to give us what is known now as the 'Vatican recension' of the *Historia Brittonum*.[91]

I do not propose to prolong this paper by considering at length the textual history of the work; yet this does give us a good deal of evidence for its later study in Wales, certainly up to and including the eleventh century; in Ireland, in the tenth and eleventh centuries; in England from the tenth century to the end of the middle ages, and in Normandy until the separation from England in the thirteenth century; in Brittany in the eleventh century at least; in the Low Countries in the twelfth; and elsewhere.[92] All this provides good historical evidence of cultural contacts.

The *Historia Brittonum* is certainly not one of the outstanding works of historical literature, but it does occupy an important place in Welsh history and culture, and is a major element in the developing picture of British historiography in the middle ages. If it does not serve to lighten the darkness of the fifth to seventh centuries, it nonetheless offers many unexplored possibilities when we come to consider the history and culture of the eighth and ninth centuries.[93]

---

[90] On all this, see Dumville, *England and the Celtic World*.

[91] See Dumville, *The Historia Brittonum*, vol. 3.

[92] For the principal versions, see the convenient list given by Lapidge & Sharpe, *A Bibliography*, pp. 42-5 (nos 127-34). All these are to be published separately by Dumville, *The Historia Brittonum*.

[93] This paper was first written for delivery to a Staff Colloquium of the Departments of Welsh in the University of Wales, held at Lampeter in July 1976. I owe the invitation to speak, and much kind hospitality, to Professor D. Simon Evans. For eventual publication this paper has been revised and updated but not substantially altered.

GEOFFREY OF MONMOUTH AND BEDE

Neil Wright

Perhaps the paramount problem posed by Geoffrey of Monmouth's immensely influential *Historia Regum Britannie*[1] is the question of the source or sources on which Geoffrey based the narrative of British history presented in his *magnum opus*. Geoffrey's claim that the *Historia* was a Latin translation of a very ancient book written in Breton or Welsh is, rightly in my view, not now generally accepted.[2] But denial of the existence of a single literary source in the vernacular raises the further problem of isolating the mass of material which Geoffrey reworked and transformed to create the *Historia*, but whose identity he effectively concealed behind his appeal to the authority of a *liber uetustissimus*. I hope elsewhere to examine the general question of the extent to which Geoffrey's known historical sources – chiefly Gildas, Bede and the *Historia Brittonum* – dictated the overall structure of the *Historia Regum Britannie* and in what ways they were combined with other literary and non-literary matter to produce a largely coherent whole. The present paper, which is intended as a preliminary step towards this more general investigation, concentrates on Geoffrey's

[1] The text used here is that of Neil Wright, *The Historia Regum Britannie of Geoffrey of Monmouth, I: A Single-manuscript Edition from Bern, Burgerbibliothek, MS. 568* (Cambridge, 1984).

[2] The search for a Welsh source never recovered from the discovery that the Welsh *Bruts* were translations of the *Historia* rather than *vice versa*. The hypothesis of a Breton source, first advanced by Arthur de La Borderie, *L'Historia Brittonum attribué à Nennius et l'Historia Britannica avant Geoffrey de Monmouth* (Paris & London, 1883), has recently gained support (see, for example, G. Ashe, '"A Certain Very Ancient Book": Traces of an Arthurian Source in Geoffrey of Monmouth's *History*', *Speculum* 56 [1981], 301-23). But, although Geoffrey may well have been influenced by Breton traditions, La Borderie's arguments rest on two *Latin* texts, which cannot for that reason themselves represent Geoffrey's vernacular source, and whose pre-Galfridian date has yet to be established with certainty; see further Wright, *The Historia Regum Britannie*, I. xvii-xviii.

use of Bede's *Historia Ecclesiastica Gentis Anglorum*[3] and is designed to complement two previous studies devoted to Geoffrey's debt to another important predecessor, Gildas.[4]

Geoffrey's use of Gildas's *De Excidio Britanniae* affords an excellent example of his methods of literary adaptation. Unlike his audience, who were generally unfamiliar with the *De Excidio Britanniae* at first hand, Geoffrey knew Gildas's work intimately. He borrowed from it verbatim in several passages and scattered verbal echoes of Gildas's prose liberally throughout the *Historia*. Significantly the vast majority of this imitation was effected without any acknowledgement of the debt to Gildas; when Geoffrey did cite Gildas as a source (which he did on seven occasions), all but two of the references were fraudulent.[5] Thus by silently incorporating Gildasian material into the *Historia* Geoffrey exploited his audience's ignorance of the *De Excidio Britanniae*, while at the same time he traded on their respect for Gildas's authority by using the latter's name to shore up more dubious elements of his narrative. The position regarding Bede's *Historia Ecclesiastica Gentis Anglorum*, however, was entirely different. The Anglo-Norman historians of the twelfth century looked to this work, completed in 731, as almost the single beacon illuminating the pre-Conquest history of Britain. William of Malmesbury, for example, begins his *Gesta Regum Anglorum* with the following admiring comments:[6]

> Res Anglorum gestas Beda, uir maxime doctus et minime superbus ab aduentu eorum in Britanniam usque ad suos dies plano et suaui sermone absoluit. Post eum non facile, ut arbitror, reperies qui historiis illius gentis Latina oratione texendis animum dederit.

Moreover, both William of Malmesbury and Henry of Huntingdon, who in the preface of his *Historia Anglorum* described himself as 'Bedae uenerabilis Ecclesiasticam, qua potui, sequutus Historiam',[7] saw the English historian as a spiritual precursor whose narrative was to be followed closely and extended down to their own time.

---

[3] Edd. (and transl.) Bertram Colgrave and R. A. B. Mynors, *Bede's Ecclesiastical History of the English People* (Oxford, 1969).

[4] N. Wright, 'Geoffrey of Monmouth and Gildas', *Arthurian Literature* 2 (1982), 1-40; and 'Geoffrey of Monmouth and Gildas Revisited', *Arthurian Literature* 4 (1984), 155-63.

[5] Wright, 'Geoffrey of Monmouth and Gildas', pp. 22-4.

[6] Ed. William Stubbs, *Willelmi Malmesbiriensis monachi de Gestis Regum Anglorum libri quinque: Historiae Novellae libri tres*, Rolls Series (2 vols, London, 1887-9), I.1.

[7] Ed. Thomas Arnold, *Henrici Archidiaconi Huntendunensis Historia Anglorum*, Rolls Series (London, 1879), p. 3.

Hence Bede's *Historia Ecclesiastica Gentis Anglorum* enjoyed great prestige and formed the basis of the accepted account of the early history of Britain. The question is immediately raised: to what extent did Geoffrey borrow from the *Historia Ecclesiastica Gentis Anglorum* and in what ways did the greater accessibility of Bede's work compared with that of Gildas cause him to modify his methods of literary adaptation?

Geoffrey's familiarity with Bede has long been recognised. A number of parallel passages was noted in the edition of San Marte (A. Schulz), which was the first to devote attention to the problem of Geoffrey's sources.[8] Geoffrey's use of Bede is also discussed sporadically in Edmond Faral's commentary[9] and by J. S. P. Tatlock.[10] Some parallel passages and verbal reminiscences have, however, so far gone unnoticed; nor has the body of Geoffrey's Bedan borrowings been examined as evidence for Geoffrey's attitude towards the *Historia Ecclesiastica Gentis Anglorum* as a literary and historical source. With this aim in view, the present study has been divided into three sections. The first of these deals with parallel passages between the *Historia Ecclesiastica Gentis Anglorum* and the *Historia Regum Britannie* and examines the extent to which Geoffrey integrates Bedan material into his *Historia*. The second section is devoted to Geoffrey's less extended verbal echoes of Bede. Finally, in a conclusion, the implications which both classes of borrowing have for Geoffrey's approach to – and manipulation of – Bede's *Historia Ecclesiastica Gentis Anglorum* are assessed.[11]

---

[8] *Gottfried's von Monmouth Historia Regum Britanniae mit literar-historischer Einleitung und ausführlichen Anmerkungen, und Brut Tysylio, altwälsche Chronik in deutscher Übersetzung* (Halle a.S., 1854).

[9] *La Légende arthurienne* (3 vols, Paris, 1929), II.68-340, *passim*.

[10] *The Legendary History of Britain. Geoffrey of Monmouth's Historia Regum Britanniae and its Early Vernacular Versions* (Berkeley, Cal., 1950); references to Bede are recorded in Tatlock's Index, p. 534.

[11] Unlike my first study of Gildas (pp. 24-30), no consideration has been given here to the use of Bede in the First Variant Version of the *Historia* since this question is discussed in detail in my forthcoming edition, *The Historia Regum Britannie of Geoffrey of Monmouth, II. The First Variant Version: A Critical Edition* (Cambridge).

I   Parallel passages between the *Historia Regum Britannie* and the
     Historia Ecclesiastica Gentis Anglorum

The very scope and structure of the *Historia Regum Britannie* in a
sense constitutes a challenge to the orthodox account of British
history found in Bede's *Historia Ecclesiastica Gentis Anglorum*.
Bede's narrative of the period prior to the *aduentus Saxonum* in
the fifth century forms little more than a preface to the main theme
of his work – the history of the English people. Moreover, Bede's
handling of the pre-Roman period and the Roman occupation is of
necessity neither detailed nor comprehensive when seen from the
native British perspective. Bede's initial remarks about the origin
of the British are sketchy – they arrive from Armorica at some ill-
defined prehistoric date. Bede was also hampered by the lack of
any native source for the Roman period except Gildas, whose
account of British history before the usurper Magnus Maximus is
anyway highly impressionistic. Bede was therefore forced to piece
together such information about Britain as was offered by Continental writers, primarily Orosius, and the resulting patchwork
narrative was with its Roman bias hardly flattering to the British.
Furthermore, after the arrival of the English, Bede for the most
part relegated the British to a subsidiary role and mentioned them
only when they impinged on the broader canvas of English politics
and church history.

The germ of an alternative version of British history had already
in the ninth century been given literary form in the anonymous
Historia Brittonum.[12] This text (later falsely ascribed to Nennius)[13]
recorded the Trojan origin of the British through their eponymous
progenitor Brutus as well as offering an episodic, but largely
British, version of events into the seventh century. In the twelfth
century, Geoffrey of Monmouth's contemporary Henry of Huntingdon had attempted to conflate the accounts of Bede and the
Historia Brittonum by incorporating the Trojan origin-legend and

---

[12] Ed. (and transl.) John Morris, *Nennius. British History and the Welsh Annals*
(Chichester, 1980). Although this is the most accessible text, it must be used
with caution; a comprehensive, critical edition is being prepared by David N.
Dumville, but as yet only one volume, *The Historia Brittonum, 3: The 'Vatican'
Recension* (Cambridge, 1985) has appeared.

[13] D. N. Dumville, '"Nennius" and the *Historia Brittonum*', *Studia Celtica* 10-11
(1975-6), 78-95.

other pseudo-Nennian material into the predominantly Bedan account of British history found in his own *Historia Anglorum*. Henry's experiment was not entirely successful, however; among the difficulties it raised was the problem of the long narrative gap between the arrival in Britain of Brutus (allegedly a contemporary of the High Priest Eli) and the invasions of Julius Caesar in the first century B.C. – a gap which the *Historia Brittonum* did almost nothing to fill.

Geoffrey's ambitious pseudo-history essentially solved this problem. Recourse to an alleged vernacular source enabled Geoffrey to present a continuous narrative of British history from the first British king, Brutus, to the last, Cadwaladr. In effect, Geoffrey offered not only an apparently authoritative account of the previously unknown period from Brutus to Caesar's invasions but also a supposedly authentic native version of events down to the seventh century. In this respect the *Historia Brittonum* was Geoffrey's most important source, since it provided him with much of the basic framework on which the elaborate construct of the *Historia Regum Britannie* rested.[14] The challenge which this Galfridian construct made against Bede's *Historia Ecclesiastica Gentis Anglorum* was two-fold: first, it contained an extensive account of pre-Roman British history of which Bede had known nothing; second, it offered an alternative native version of the Roman occupation and the arrival of the English which ran parallel to Bede's and invited comparison with it. This second challenge was particularly acute since, as R. W. Leckie Jr. has argued,[15] Geoffrey, by depicting seventh-century British kings, in particular Cadwallon, as exercising control over much of southern Britain and by delaying the final, successful English settlement of the island until the late seventh century, called into question the orthodox Bedan view that the passage of dominion from the British to the English had occurred at a much earlier date.

It is against this background that we must examine Geoffrey's extended verbal borrowings from Bede. Such borrowings are found in six separate episodes, as follows: the mission of St Augustine (*Historia Regum Britannie*, §188); the massacre of the monks of Bangor (§189); Cadwallon's reprisals against the English (§198); Oswald and the battle of Hevenfeld (§199); Oswy and the battle of

---

[14] Wright, 'Geoffrey of Monmouth and Gildas', p. 4.
[15] *The Passage of Dominion: Geoffrey of Monmouth and the Periodization of Insular History in the Twelfth Century* (Toronto, 1981).

Winwed (§ 200); the death of Cadwaladr (§ 205). As in my previous study of Gildas, the passages in question, which are discussed in detail below, have not been included in the body of the text, but are set out as an Appendix,[16] where each passage of the *Historia Regum Britannie* is followed by its Bedan model and the close verbal parallels indicated by italic type.

However, before examining each of these passages individually, some consideration of the disposition of Bedan borrowings in Geoffrey's narrative is in order. To this end, it is instructive to compare the way in which Geoffrey incorporated similar extended borrowings from Gildas into the framework of the *Historia Regum Britannie*, particularly as the conclusions of my previous study of these latter borrowings are in need of some refinement. Gildas's *De Excidio Britanniae*,[17] probably composed in the mid-sixth century, is not primarily a history, but its core, a twin attack on British kings and clergy, is preceded by a highly rhetorical and moralising account of British history (§§ 3-26). Prefaced by an elaborate description of Britain (§ 3), this narrative falls into four main sections: the Roman invasions (§§ 4-7); the coming of christianity, persecution and the martyrdom of St Alban (§§ 8-12); the expedition of Magnus Maximus and the Pictish wars (§§ 13-21); the arrival of the English, the *excidum* of Britain, and events down to Gildas's own time (§§ 22-26). If we compare Gildas's narrative with what was available to Geoffrey from his prime source, the *Historia Brittonum*, and also from Bede's *Historia Ecclesiastica Gentis Anglorum*, we find that much of its content up to and including the expedition of Maximus is also found, and treated in greater detail, in the latter texts. In particular, their accounts of the Roman invasions are markedly less hostile (even in Bede's Continental-based version) to the British than the moral vituperations of Gildas. For the period from the Pictish wars to Gildas's own day, the *De Excidio Britanniae* enjoyed greater authority and hence constituted Bede's main source in the relevant section of the *Historia Ecclesiastica Gentis Anglorum*; but the *Historia Brittonum* contains different native traditions about the *aduentus Saxonum*.

Despite the fact that a good deal of the content of the *De Excidio Britanniae* was duplicated in his other sources, Geoffrey made extended borrowings from Gildas in eight passages.[18] Three of

---

[16] Below, pp. 56-9.
[17] Ed. (and transl.) Michael Winterbottom, *Gildas. The Ruin of Britain and other Works* (Chichester, 1978).
[18] Wright, 'Geoffrey of Monmouth and Gildas', pp. 4-14 (and 34-40).

32

these – the description of Britain (*Historia Regum Britannie*, §5), the martyrdom of St Alban (§77), and the expedition of Maximianus (as Geoffrey, following the *Historia Brittonum*, calls the historical Maximus) (§86) – occur in the period prior to the Pictish wars. Since alternative versions of these passages are found in Bede or the *Historia Brittonum*, Geoffrey might have rejected Gildas in favour of another source – just as he did in fact replace the *De Excidio Britanniae*'s hostile account of the Roman invasions with a more favourable version loosely based on the *Historia Brittonum* and Bede. Geoffrey's decision instead to follow Gildas almost verbatim in these three passages was clearly motivated by admiration for Gildas's elevated, rhetorical prose-style and a desire to incorporate these purple passages, in modified form, into the *Historia*.[19] Of the remaining five Gildasian passages in Geoffrey's work, the most extensive is found in *Historia Regum Britannie* §§89-91, which deal with the Pictish wars; at this point in his narrative, Geoffrey clearly relied primarily on Gildas's account because it was the fullest of any of his sources, although he to some extent modified it under the influence of the *Historia Brittonum*.[20] The next borrowing, which occurs in *Historia Regum Britannie*, §§180-83, constitutes a cause célèbre: Geoffrey, using not the *historia*-section of the *De Excidio Britanniae*, but the subsequent attack on British kings in §§27-36 of that work, wilfully transformed four contemporary local rulers lambasted by Gildas into successive Kings of Britain (viz. Constantinus, Aurelius Conanus, Uortiporius and Malgo) whom he represented as reigning from Arthur's death (which, according to Geoffrey, fell in A.D. 542) until some unspecified date later in the sixth century. However, although he had now progressed beyond the chronological limits of Gildas's narrative, Geoffrey in three later passages – *Historia Regum Britannie*, §§184, 195 and 203 – returned to the *historia*-section to borrow details (respectively) of the *excidium* of Britain, of the corruption of the British, and of a disastrous plague. All these elements of the *De Excidio Britanniae* belong to the Pictish and English wars, which Gildas represented as taking place in the fifth and early sixth centuries; Geoffrey, however, assigned the final destruction of Britain to the later sixth and seventh centuries, beginning with the disastrous reign of Ceredig but separated by a British recovery from its final culmination in plague and Cadwaladr's death at Rome (supposedly in A.D. 689). Despite

[19] For Geoffrey's stylistic changes, see Wright, *ibid.*, pp. 6-7.
[20] *Ibid.*, p. 9.

these discrepancies of chronology, Geoffrey did not scruple to lift from the *De Excidio Britanniae* the three episodes already mentioned and fit them, along with a pronouncedly Gildasian note of moralising reproof,[21] into the completely different narrative framework of the post-Arthurian section of the *Historia Regum Britannie*.

The foregoing summary of the disposition of extended Gildasian echoes in the *Historia Regum Britannie* makes plain how eclectic were Geoffrey's methods of selection and recasting. In only one such passage – the Pictish wars – does Geoffrey's use of Gildas reflect the fact that the *De Excidio Britanniae* is the fullest source for the events in question. Elements of Gildas's narrative prior to the Pictish wars are included in Geoffrey's work primarily for their rhetorical impact. Later details of Britain's decline are repositioned in an entirely new historical setting. But a substantial portion of Gildas's impressionistic account of British history is nevertheless incorporated, in one guise or another, throughout Geoffrey's *Historia*.

The contrast with Geoffrey's extended borrowings from Bede is immediately apparent: all six such passages occur only in the last twenty chapters of the *Historia* (§§188-208). Although Bede's *Historia Ecclesiastica Gentis Anglorum* contained a narrative of British history from Caesar's invasions to the *aduentus Saxonum* and the battle of Badon, Geoffrey made extensive verbatim borrowings from Bede only in that section of his *Historia* dealing with the period from the mission of Augustine (A.D. 597) to the death of Cadwaladr. Furthermore, as Tatlock has noted, prior to Augustine's mission Geoffrey always refers to the English as *Saxones*; thereafter he also uses the term *Angli*, a shift in usage which reflects Bede's greater influence towards the end of the *Historia*. The question of why Geoffrey did not imitate or follow Bede closely in the earlier period (down to Badon) is one to which we shall return when considering shorter, verbal reminiscences of the *Historia Ecclesiastica Gentis Anglorum* in the *Historia Regum Britannie*;[22] the immediate problem is why extended passages from Bede are incorporated only in the closing chapters of the *Historia*. Once again, comparison with Geoffrey's alternative sources provides the probable solution. The narrative section of the *De*

---

[21] *Ibid.*, pp.11-14 and 20-21.
[22] Below, pp.45-52.

34

Excidio Britanniae ends, forty-four years after Badon,[23] at some point near the middle of the sixth century. The *Historia Brittonum*, whose narrative is frequently scrappy and discontinuous, does refer to Cadwaladr, Geoffrey's last British king,[24] but its account of the seventh-century events is opaque in the extreme and for practical purposes it ceases to be a useful source after the career of Arthur, whose death, as we have seen, Geoffrey assigned to A.D. 542. Both the *De Excidio Britanniae* and the *Historia Brittonum*, then, end effectively in the mid-sixth century. Although Geoffrey was able to cobble together from Gildas's denunciations an account of the reigns of four kings who immediately succeeded Arthur and anachronistically to incorporate other Gildasian material in the later post-Arthurian period, the only continuous narrative of seventh-century events available to him was that of Bede. Hence Geoffrey's reliance on the *Historia Ecclesiastica Gentis Anglorum* in the closing chapters of his work was in fact dictated by necessity.

In the concluding section of his *Historia*, then, Geoffrey was to some extent obliged to draw material from Bede; but we must now consider how, in the passages concerned, he manipulated that material in adapting it to its new setting.

1. The mission of St Augustine

In dealing with the arrival of St Augustine and his impact on the British church, Geoffrey assembles matter widely scattered in several chapters of Bede's text. Augustine's mission is first mentioned by Bede in *Historia Ecclesiastica Gentis Anglorum*, I.23; the verbal parallels in Geoffrey's reference to the same event (in *Historia Regum Britannie*, §188)[25] make it clear that he was directly influenced by that passage. However, Augustine does not come into contact with the British until *Historia Ecclesiastica Gentis Anglorum*, II.2, when at the conference of Augustine's Oak he invites the latter to join him in his efforts to convert the English. As a result, a second synod is held which is attended by

---

[23] This is the conventional interpretation of the controversial dating passage in *De Excidio Britanniae*, §26: for a general discussion of the problem, see Thomas D. O'Sullivan, *The De Excidio of Gildas. Its Authenticity and Date* (Leiden, 1978), pp.134-57; and, for a different view, Ian Wood, 'The End of Roman Britain: Continental Evidence and Parallels', in *Gildas: New Approaches*, edd. Michael Lapidge and David Dumville (Woodbridge, 1984), pp.1-25 (at 22-3).
[24] §64 (Morris, p.79).
[25] As set out below in Appendix, passage 1.

seven British bishops and by other clerics including Dinoot, abbot of Bangor-is-Coed. Augustine's offer is then finally rejected and Bede records a tradition that Augustine obliquely prophesied that divine retribution would ensue in the form of the massacre of British ecclesiastics (including Bangor monks) at the later battle of Chester. Finally, while reporting the events of that battle, Bede adds a parenthetical note on the size and internal division of the monastery at Bangor.

Geoffrey reorganises these elements in order to lend his version of events a more pro-British colouring. After Augustine's arrival, Geoffrey omits all discussion of his activities in converting the English, thereby shifting his audience's sympathy away from the Gregorian mission.[26] Instead, the organisation of the British church, its bishoprics and monasteries, is described at the outset so that Augustine by contrast seems a mere parvenu. Moreover, to the seven bishops whom he borrows from Bede, Geoffrey adds an archbishop – either, we must assume, of *Urbs Legionum* (Caerleon) or of Menevia[27] – and so recalls the division of Britain into three archbishoprics (of London, York and *Urbs Legionum*) which, Geoffrey alleged, was instigated after the conversion of the island by missionaries sent by Pope Eleutherius in the reign of King Lucius (*Historia Regum Britannie*, §72). Indeed, Geoffrey stresses the continuity of christianity among the British population by the comment (*Historia Regum Britannie*, §188): 'In parte autem Britonum adhuc uigebat christianitas que a tempore Eleutherii pape habita numquam inter eos defecerat'. These references add further authority to the sixth-century British church (as Geoffrey portrays it) and also implicitly underscore the novelty of Augustine's position as archbishop of Canterbury, since that see had no place in the Galfridian structure of the early British church. In this same context Geoffrey mentions Dinoot, the learned abbot of Bangor, and appends Bede's description of the thriving community of that monastery,[28] thus rounding off a coherent picture of a vigorous

---

[26] Cf. Leckie, *The Passage of Dominion*, p.106.

[27] An archbishop of *Urbs Legionum* (Kinocus) is last mentioned in *Historia Regum Britannie*, §179. The transfer of the archiepiscopal see to Menevia is forecast in the *Prophetie Merlini* (no.3, *Historia Regum Brittanie*, §112: 'Meneuia pallio Urbis Legionum induetur') among the events succeeding the Donation of Gormund (*Historia Regum Britannie*, §186); but it is unclear whether Geoffrey intended the reader to envisage this transfer as already having occurred by the time of the Augustinian mission.

[28] It is uncertain whether Geoffrey located the monastery (correctly) at Bangor-is-coed or in the see-city of Bangor (Carnarvonshire), although his references to

episcopal and monastic church in that part of the island occupied by the British. It should also be noted that Geoffrey suppresses any reference to the unorthodox paschal practices of the British church which, as Bede makes plain (*Historia Ecclesiastica Gentis Anglorum*, II.2), were an important point of contention between Augustine and the British clergy.

Only when he has completed this sketch of British ecclesiastical organisation, does Geoffrey pass on to the offer made by Augustine. While verbal echoes in this passage make it clear that Geoffrey is following Bede closely, he emends his source in one most important aspect: Bede records that Augustine attempted to persuade the British to aid him; Geoffrey prefaces this request with a demand for their subjection to his archiepiscopal authority, which Dinoot rejects on behalf of the Britons.[29] In the light of Geoffrey's preparatory description of the antiquity of the British church, this rejection of Augustine's offer, towards which Bede as an English church-historian is naturally unsympathetic, is made to seem entirely justified. Dinoot also demurs from joining Augustine in proselytising the English on the grounds of the hatred felt by the British towards the people which has dispossessed them. In fact, Dinoot's statement of contempt for the faith of the English and refusal in any way to commune with them constitutes a further, subtle borrowing from Bede, which has not so far been noticed. The same contemptuous attitude is ascribed to the British by Bede in *Historia Ecclesiastica Gentis Anglorum*, II.20, where he expresses his revulsion at the ferocious devastation of Northumbria by Cadwallon after the battle of Hatfield in A.D. 633. Bede explains that, because the British even up to his own day regard the English as no better than pagans, the latter's christianity was on this occasion no protection to them; hence the savagery of the British, who often play the villain's role in Bede's *Historia Ecclesiastica Gentis Anglorum*, is made to appear highly ungodly. Although Geoffrey follows Bede very closely, he makes Dinoot's assertion still stronger since, by substituting *canibus* for *paganis*, he dehumanises the English and equates them with dogs rather than

---

the *ciuitas* of Bangor (as opposed to Bede's *monasterium*) argue in favour of the latter interpretation; see Tatlock, *The Legendary History*, pp. 65-6.

[29] Geoffrey's attribution of the spokesman's role to Dinoot spawned a spurious Welsh version of the latter's epistolary reply to Augustine; see A. W. Haddan and William Stubbs, *Councils and Ecclesiastical Documents relating to Great Britain and Ireland* (3 vols, Oxford, 1869-78), I.122 and 149.

men (whether pagan or christian).[30] But by virtue of his careful repositioning of the Bedan borrowing, Geoffrey ensures that this increased virulence does not alienate his reader. In the *Historia Regum Britannie*, the events which immediately precede the Augustinian mission are the devastation of Britain by the African Gormund and the English, the retreat of the British into Wales and Cornwall, and the wholesale destruction of christianity in English-occupied Loegria (§§184-7). By assigning this *excidium* (largely inspired by Gildas) to the later sixth century, Geoffrey portrays Augustine's offer of a joint mission to convert the English as salt rubbed into a fresh wound; in the context of Dinoot's indignant rejection of this offer, British hatred of the English, which Bede saw as unchristian after the battle of Hatfield, seems rather a natural and spirited reaction against a deadly enemy. Geoffrey's manipulation of Bede's text in this way demonstrates his ready familiarity with the *Historia Ecclesiastica Gentis Anglorum* and imaginative skill in recasting a source to his own literary ends, traits which are also a keynote of his free adaptation of Gildas.[31]

2. The massacre of the monks of Bangor

Geoffrey next relies heavily on Bede when relating the massacre of the Bangor monks by the English (*Historia Regum Britannie*, §189); but, as comparison of the two relevant passages reveals, Geoffrey's clear verbal borrowings from his Bedan model are far outweighed by the contradictions in the two accounts. As we have seen, Bede (*Historia Ecclesiastica Gentis Anglorum*, II.2) reports the events of the battle of Chester (*circa* A.D. 616?)[32] out of their proper chronological place so as to demonstrate the fulfilment of St Augustine's prophecy. British clerics (including Bangor monks),

---

[30] In fact this change was necessitated by the new context to which Geoffrey assigned the Bedan borrowing, since at that period the majority of the English *were* pagans (and Geoffrey had supressed Augustine's missionary activities in Kent). While Dinoot's expression of British contempt for the *fides* of the English may refer only to their paganism, Geoffrey may also be alluding to the treachery which he imputes to the English (below, n. 40); if so, he adds another new resonance to the Bedan original.

[31] Wright, 'Geoffrey of Monmouth and Gildas', pp. 8 (St Amphibalus) and 16 (Guizelinus).

[32] On the date of the battle, see Charles Plummer, *Venerabilis Baedae Opera Historica* (2 vols, Oxford, 1896), II.76-7.

who accompany their army in order to pray for it, are – not with-out reason – seen by the pagan Ethelfrid, king of Northumbria, as legitimate targets for attack; at the first assault, the Briton Brocmail, to whom the task of protecting the monks has been entrusted, cravenly abandons them to be massacred, and the British army is annihilated. Geoffrey's version of this conflict again replaces Bede's English perspective with a markedly pro-British bias. Events in the *Historia* are further telescoped since the battle occurs immediately after Dinoot's rejection of Augustine's call for submission; the objective of the English is entirely to destroy the monastery of Bangor in retaliation for this snub and Ethelfrid is represented as the cats-paw of Ethelbert of Kent (and hence indirectly of Augustine himself). Brocmail is transformed into the *consul* of Leicester, at which city British anchorites and monks, including those from Bangor, congregate not, as Bede implies, to intercede with God for the defeat of the English, but more innocuously 'to pray for the safety of their people' ('ut pro salute populi sui orarent'). Far from deserting the monks, Brocmail dies bravely trying to protect his city after inflicting heavy losses on the English; and the Bangor monks are not killed during the battle, but slaughtered in cold blood after it – their death being more emotively portrayed as martyrdom.[33]

Clearly Geoffrey's prime motive for these changes was to secure his audience's sympathy for the British. However, other modifications were made for different reasons. The historical battle at which this massacre took place occurred at Chester, while Geoffrey places it at Leicester. Tatlock here accuses Geoffrey of an error, since Bede refers to Chester by its English name *Legacaestir*, a form confusingly close to *Legecestria*, the term which Geoffrey regularly uses for Leicester; Tatlock further argues that by locating the battle so far from the monastery (at whichever Bangor he intended this to be understood to be) Geoffrey shows considerable uncertainty as to the geographical position of Leicester.[34] However, it seems inconceivable that Geoffrey was

---

[33] Geoffrey's comment that the Bangor monks '*regni celestis* adepti sunt sedem' may be a typically ironic reflection of Bede's concluding remark (*Historia Ecclesiastica Gentis Anglorum*, II.20) that the massacre occurred long after St Augustine was 'ad *caelestia regna* sublato'. It is surprising that Geoffrey does not lay greater emphasis on the martyrdom – unlike the author of the First Variant Version (Jacob Hammer [ed.], *Geoffrey of Monmouth. Historia Regum Britanniae: A Variant Version* [Cambridge, Mass., 1951], p.255) – but monasticism is not altogether favourably treated in the *Historia*; see Tatlock, *The Legendary History*, pp. 267-8.

[34] *The Legendary History*, pp. 25-6.

ignorant of the location of this important borough;[35] and his ready familiarity with, and adaptation of, Bede's text also argue against Tatlock's assertions, particularly as Bede in the same passage makes the identification of *Legacaestir* with Chester unmistakeable by also referring to that place conventionally as *Ciuitas Legionum* and as *Carlegion* (its British name). It seems more likely, then, that Geoffrey's transfer of the battle to Leicester is wilful manipulation of his source and is not without purpose. After the *excidium* of Britain (*Historia Regum Britannie*, §§184-7), Geoffrey had represented the British as controlling only Cornwall and Wales. Yet by the terms of a settlement between Cadfan and Ethelfrid made shortly after the slaughter of the Bangor monks (*Historia Regum Britannie*, §190), Cadfan's sovereignty will extend over all the island south of the Humber. By shifting the massacre east to Leicester and by representing that town as under the control of a British *consul*, Geoffrey effectively paves the way for this otherwise startling reversal of the balance of power.[36] Furthermore, such opportunistic equation of Bede's *Legacaestir* with *Legecestria* is quite typical of Geoffrey's often whimsical recasting of his sources.

The Galfridian account of this massacre and its aftermath prepares the reader for the narrative dénouement of the *Historia* in one further way. After the *excidium* (*Historia Regum Britannie*, §§184-7), Geoffrey described the Britons as ruled by three tyrants – rulers, it seems, of North and South Wales (*Venedotia* and *Demetia* respectively) and Cornwall – with no one king exercising absolute control. However, this division does not, as it might, mark the end of the British as a united people, since they recover control over Southumbrian England under three successive kings: Cadfan, his son Cadwallon (who is depicted as a powerful ruler in Bede's *Historia Ecclesiastica Gentis Anglorum*), and grandson Cadwaladr (who is, according to Geoffrey, effectively the last in the line of British kings from Brutus). Historically these three kings belonged to the ruling dynasty of *Venedotia* (or Gwynedd), but up to this point in the *Historia* that region plays almost no part in the narrative; of the racially Celtic areas, Geoffrey is favourable

---

[35] Particulary in the light of its connection with one of Geoffrey's patrons, Waleran of Meulan (*ibid.*, p. 26).

[36] Geoffrey may also have suppressed Bede's reference to Chester (*Ciuitas Legionum*) to avoid any possible confusion with Caerleon (*Urbs Legionum*), since the latter plays an important role in the *Historia* as the metropolitan see of Wales, and as the scene of Arthur's sumptuous festival (in §§156-7).

to Brittany above all,[37] and also to Cornwall,[38] but regards the Welsh as degenerate and unworthy descendants of the British, so that his references to *Venedotia* (and *Demetia*) are infrequent and rarely favourable.[39] Geoffrey, then, had to explain how a Venedotian dynasty came to exercise control over the British: the battle at Leicester affords him the opportunity to do so. Departing from Bede's account entirely, Geoffrey represents Ethelfrid as advancing after his victory at Leicester against Bangor itself. He is opposed by a coalition of three British leaders – Cadfan of *Venedotia*, Margadud of *Demetia*, and Bledericus of Cornwall (evidently representing the successors of the three *tyranni* of *Historia Regum Britannie*, §187) – headed, significantly, by Bledericus of Cornwall 'qui ducatum in eisdem preliis prestabat' (*Historia Regum Britannie*, §189). In the ensuing battle Ethelfrid is defeated, but Bledericus is killed. Subsequently a council of British leaders is held at Leicester and Cadfan elected king to pursue the war against Ethelfrid in Northumbria (*Historia Regum Britannie*, §190). In this manner Geoffrey neatly accounts for the passing of overall control to a Venedotian dynasty and is also able to suggest that this transition occurred only when necessitated by the death of the Briton's existing Cornish leader.

3. Cadwallon's reprisals

The career of Cadfan's son, Cadwallon (called Caedualla in the *Historia Ecclesiastica Gentis Anglorum*) is so hugely magnified by Geoffrey that he becomes the last great king of the British. The early events of his reign – involving, according to Geoffrey, initial friendship with Edwin of Northumbria, flight to Brittany, and the elimination of a Spanish magician, Pellitus, who rendered supernatural aid to Edwin (*Historia Regum Britannie*, §§191-6) – unsurprisingly owe nothing to Bede's sober narrative. However, on his return from Brittany, Cadwallon kills Edwin and his son Osfrid at Hedfeld, ravages the English, and also kills Edwin's successor Osric (*Historia Regum Britannie*, §§197-8). Here Geoffrey draws on Bede's account of the battle of Hatfield (A.D. 633) and its aftermath (*Historia Ecclesiastica Gentis Anglorum*, II.20 and

---

[37] Tatlock, *The Legendary History*, pp. 397-8.

[38] O.J. Padel, 'Geoffrey of Monmouth and Cornwall', *Cambridge Medieval Celtic Studies* 8 (Winter, 1984), 1-27.

[39] Tatlock, *The Legendary History*, p. 400; in *Historia Regum Britannie*, §76, the *Uenedoti* barbarously slaughter Roman captives whom Asclepiodotus, the Cornish commander of the British, wished to spare.

III.1). In addition to borrowing historical names and details from Bede, Geoffrey also incorporates almost verbatim a passage describing Cadwallon's merciless harrying of the English after Hatfield. Geoffrey in no way hesitates to introduce such Bedan material into his own construct; he merely suppresses Bede's hostile description of Cadwallon as 'a savage in mind and character' ('animo ac moribus barbarus') and his reference to the latter's 'beastly cruelty' ('atrocitate ferina'). Indeed, in this new context, Cadwallon's attempt to exterminate the English, which Bede deplores, is made to seem a not-unmerited retribution for the efforts of the treacherous English (as Geoffrey regularly portrays them)[40] to dispossess the British. Moreover, it is immediately after this passage that Bede makes a disapproving reference to the ungodly hostility of the christian British towards their co-religionists, the English. We have already seen how Geoffrey turned this criticism on its head by transferring the remark to the quite different context of Dinoot's reply to St Augustine.[41] This constitutes a further illustration of Geoffrey's willingness to reshuffle his sources to his own literary ends.

Finally, before passing to the next borrowing, a word on Geoffrey's stylistic modifications of the *Historia Ecclesiastica Gentis Anglorum* is in order. As close comparison of the two passages discussed above will reveal, Geoffrey's adaptation of his Bedan original is limited to the transposition of some clauses (and of word order) and to the substitution for one word of its synonym (*abradere* for *eradere*). In other passages, stylistic changes are less extensive even than that.[42] Such minor tinkering is in no way comparable to the major recasting to which Geoffrey usually subjected the more difficult and flamboyant prose of Gildas.[43] Bede's simpler, but not unrhetorical, Latin style was more akin to Geoffrey's own; hence passages borrowed from Bede undergo in general only superficial reworking in the *Historia*.

---

[40] The *locus classicus* for a catalogue of English perfidy is Brian's speech to Cadwallon in *Historia Regum Britannie*, § 191, which is toned down in the Bern text; see Wright, *The Historia Regum Britannie*, I.lvi-lix.

[41] Above, pp. 37-8.

[42] As, for example, in Appendix, passage 4.

[43] See n.19, above.

4. Oswald and the battle of Hevenfeld

A heady mix of Bedan fact and Galfridian fancy continues to characterise the account of Cadwallon's reign presented in the *Historia*. Geoffrey next draws closely on Bede when describing the erection of a cross by Oswald of Northumbria at Hevenfeld before an impending battle (*Historia Regum Britannie*, §199). Oswald's pious speech is borrowed almost verbatim by Geoffrey, who makes no attempt to diminish the holiness of the English king and like Bede assigns his victory directly to his faith in God.[44] In all other respects Geoffrey's account runs counter to that of Bede. In the *Historia Ecclesiastica Gentis Anglorum* (III.1 and 2) Oswald's victory took place not at Hevenfeld, but at nearby Denisesburn where the Northumbrian defeated and killed Cadwallon himself. But according to Geoffrey, Cadwallon despatched the Mercian Penda north to deal with Oswald. Penda was then defeated (but not killed) by Oswald at Hevenfeld, the site of the raising of his cross. On hearing this, Cadwallon (whose death Bede has already recorded!) engaged Oswald at Burne – clearly mischieviously concocted by Geoffrey as a doublet of Bede's Denisesburn – where the Northumbrian is killed by Penda. In fact Oswald did die by Penda's hand, but some years later at Maserfelth (A.D. 642) as recorded in *Historia Ecclesiastica Gentis Anglorum*, III.9. The portrayal of these events in the *Historia Regum Britannie* constitutes a deliberate contradiction of their source; Geoffrey's version is irreconcilable with that of Bede.

5. Oswy and the battle of Winwed

Geoffrey's manipulation of Bede's account of the battle of Denisesburn is closely paralleled by his handling of that of Winwed. According to Bede (*Historia Ecclesiastica Gentis Anglorum*, III.24) Penda of Mercia attacked Oswy, Oswald's successor as king of Northumbria, but was defeated and killed at Winwed (A.D. 655). Thereafter Oswy established Peada, Penda's son, as king of Mercia; but on the latter's death, another son, Wulfhere, and the

---

[44] Geoffrey may have intended Oswald to serve as a foil to the British king Cadwaladr, on whose death at Rome in an odour of sanctity see below, pp. 44-5.

Mercian nobles Immin, Eafa, and Eadberht rebelled against Oswy. Geoffrey's version of events runs as follows. After Oswald's death, he is succeeded by Oswy who submits himself to Cadwallon. Oswy is opposed by his own son, Alfredus, and nephew, Orwald,[45] who are defeated and flee to Penda in Mercia. The latter dares not attack Oswy without Cadwallon's permission; at Cadwallon's Pentecost crown-wearing at London (the anachronism is Geoffrey's) he therefore accuses Oswy of treason *in absentia*. After some debate, Cadwallon gives Penda permission to attack Oswy, who after being harried by Penda, beats and kills him at Uunued (Winwed). On Penda's death, Cadwallon (usurping the role assigned by Bede to Oswy) creates not Peada but Wulfhere king of Mercia; Wulfhere and two Mercian nobles, Ebba and Edbert, rebel against Oswy, but are ordered by Cadwallon to make peace. Within this elaborate construct Geoffrey borrows verbatim from Bede an account of the prelude to the fight at Winwed as well as some historical names and details; his narrative is, however, so modified that the Briton Cadwallon, who in reality had died at Maserfelth, is represented as still alive, exercising supreme power over Britain and to a large extent stage-managing the civil wars of his English subjects.

6. Cadwaladr's death

Geoffrey's identification of Cadwaladr, the last important British king of the *Historia*, with Bede's Caedwalla, king of Wessex, who died at Rome in A.D. 689, is a problem which will be discussed in detail in the following section.[46] Here it is sufficient to note that, when describing Cadwaladr's journey to Rome, his confirmation by Pope Sergius, his fatal illness and death on 20 April 689, Geoffrey closely follows the passage in *Historia Ecclesiastica Gentis Anglorum*, V.7, where Bede relates Caedwalla's pious end.[47] Manipulation such as this is, as we have seen, typical of the freedom with which Geoffrey reinterpreted his other borrowings

---

[45] These rebels afford a further example of Geoffrey's easy familiarity with Bede, since they are taken from *Historia Ecclesiastica Gentis Anglorum*, III.14 (where their names have the forms Alhfridus and Oidilualdus).

[46] Below, pp. 50-52.

[47] Moreover, Cadwaladr's nephew Yni, who with Iuor attempts to revive British fortunes (*Historia Regum Britannie*, §§ 206-7), is modelled on Caedwalla's successor Ini mentioned in the same chapter (and also in *Historia Ecclesiastica Gentis Anglorum*, IV.15).

from Bede. Moreover, there cannot on this occasion have been any confusion in Geoffrey's mind about Caedwalla's true identity, since the Bedan passage expressly gives the Englishman's title as 'rex Occidentalium Saxonum' – 'king of the men of Wessex'.

II Verbal reminiscences of the *Historia Ecclesiastica Gentis Anglorum* in the *Historia Regum Britannie*

Despite the fact that extended verbal borrowings from Bede are restricted to the last twenty chapters of the *Historia Regum Britannie*, the structure of Geoffrey's narrative of the Roman period beginning with Caesar's invasions for the most part loosely corresponds to that of the *Historia Ecclesiastica Gentis Anglorum*. The contents of the first book of the latter down to I.12 – the point at which Gildas becomes Bede's primary source – may be briefly set out as follows:

Historia Ecclesiastica Gentis Anglorum

I. 1 Description of Britain
I. 2 Caesar's invasions
I. 3 Invasions of Claudius and Vespasian
I. 4 Conversion of Lucius
I. 5 Severus and the *uallum*
I. 6 Carausius, Allectus, and Diocletian's persecution
I. 7 St Alban
I. 8 Constantius and Constantine the Great
I. 9 Maximus [Geoffrey's Maximianus]
I.10 Pelagianism
I.11 Gratianus *municeps*; Constantine and Constans

With the single exception of the Pelegian heresy, which Geoffrey mentions only in passing,[48] all the above events and characters play a significant part in the *Historia*, although they are usually seen through the distorting mirror of Geoffrey's recasting (sometimes under the influence of Gildas or the *Historia Brittonum*).

One example will suffice to illustrate this general point. Bede (*Historia Ecclesiastica Gentis Anglorum*, I.11), using Orosius, gives the following details of the brief careers of the British imperial pretenders Gratianus *municeps* and Constantine and his son Constans (*circa* A.D. 407):

> ... apud Brittanias Gratianus municeps tyrannus creatur et occiditur. Huius loco Constantinus ex infima militia propter solam spem nominis sine merito

[48] *Historia Regum Britannie*, § 100.

45

uirtutis eligitur; qui continuo ut inuasit imperium, in Gallias transiit. Ibi saepe a barbaris incertis foederibus inlusus detrimento magis reipublicae fuit. Unde mox iubente Honorio Constantius comes in Galliam cum exercitu profectus apud Arelatem ciuitatem eum clausit, cepit, occidit; Constantemque filium eius, quem ex monacho Caesarem fecerat, Gerontius comes suus apud Uiennam interfecit.

Geoffrey's much expanded version of these events is found in *Historia Regum Britannie*, §§88-96. Gratianus *municeps*, despatched to Britain by Maximianus to counter barbarian incursions, seizes power on learning of the latter's murder. However, Gratianus's tyrannous reign is cut short when he is killed by his British subjects. Anarchy, further Pictish attacks, Roman intervention and eventual abandonment of the British ensue, mainly based on Gildas's account[49] (these latter events not being recounted by Bede until *Historia Ecclesiastica Gentis Anglorum*, I.12-13). Guizelinus, archbishop of London, then crosses to the newly established kingdom of Brittany, whence Aldroenus sends his brother Constantine to Britain with two thousand troops. Constantine defeats the enemy, is crowned King of Britain, and, after a successful ten-year reign, is murdered by a Pict. Of his sons, only Constans, now a monk at Winchester, is old enough to rule, his brothers Aurelius Ambrosius and Uther Pendragon being still in the cradle. Constans is persuaded to abandon his monastic vows by Vortigern, *consul Geuuisseorum*, who irregularly crowns him with his own hands. Later, manipulating the gullible Constans, Vortigern engineers his murder by a group of Pictish mercenaries and usurps the crown. The transformation of chronology and content which the Bedan material has undergone is typically Galfridian: for example, by representing Constantine as a member of the ruling dynasty of Armorica, Geoffrey gives a puff to Brittany;[50] by allotting Vortigern of Gwent, the paramount villain of the *Historia*, a role in these events and by representing the renegade monk Constáns as simple-minded, he also introduces a subtle note of anti-Welsh feeling[51] and a mild anti-monasticism[52]

---

[49] Wright, 'Geoffrey of Monmouth and Gildas', pp. 9-10.

[50] Indeed, such Breton aid to an endangered (or declining) Britain is a recurrent motif in the second half of the *Historia*: with Aldroenus's despatching of Constantine, compare the Breton cavalry which accompaniès Aurelius Ambrosius (and proves especially effective in §123); Arthur's request for Hoel's assistance (§144); Salomon's aid to Cadwallon (§§194-7); and Alanus's support for Cadwaladr's projected return to Britain (§205).

[51] See n. 39 above.

[52] See n. 33 above.

into his story. Nevertheless his ultimate debt to the *Historia Ecclesiastica Gentis Anglorum* remains apparent.[53]

Much, then, of Geoffrey's narrative of events after the Roman invasions, however elaborated and transmuted, runs parallel to that of Bede. We must now therefore consider to what extent Geoffrey incorporated verbal reminiscences of the *Historia Ecclesiastica Gentis Anglorum* in that section of the *Historia Regum Britannie* as well as that dealing with the pre-Roman period.

The first such reminiscences occur in the ornate description of Britain with which Geoffrey prefaces his account of British history proper (*Historia Regum Britannie*, §5). Geoffrey's description of Britain as 'Omni etenim genere *metalli fecunda*' is derived from Bede's observation that the island is 'Uenis *metallorum*, aeris ferri plumbi et argenti, *fecunda*' (*Historia Ecclesiastica Gentis Anglorum*, I.1); similarly Geoffrey's description of Britain as '*piscosis fluuiis* irrigua' echoes Bede's phrase '*fluuiis* quoque multum *piscosis*' (*Historia Ecclesiastica Gentis Anglorum*, I.1).[54] However, these two Bedan elements are buried within a far more extensive passage borrowed from Gildas.[55] It is clear that, these two echoes apart, Geoffrey largely rejected Bede's geographical sketch of Britain in preference for that of Gildas with the result that the reader who expected to find an orthodox Bedan (or pseudo-Nennian) description at the outset of Geoffrey's *Historia* encountered instead unfamiliar, Gildasian material.[56] This substitution of Gildasian for Bedan matter constitutes a snub of the same order as Geoffrey's later decision to base his account of the martyrdom of Alban (*Historia Regum Britannie*, §77) on Gildas rather than on the longer and far more complete version of that saint's passion found in *Historia Ecclesiastica Gentis Anglorum*, I.7.

Geoffrey next echoes Bede in his account of Caesar's invasions – at the very beginning, that is, of Bede's narrative of British history. In *Historia Regum Britannie*, §54, Caesar sights Britain for the first

---

[53] Cf. Tatlock, *The Legendary History*, p.159.
[54] The 'flumina piscosa' of Brittany (*Historia Regum Britannie*, §84) may constitute a further echo of Bede's phrase. From *Historia Ecclesiastica Gentis Anglorum*, I.1 Geoffrey also derived Britain's archaic name of Albion (*Historia Regum Britannie*, §21) and the outline of the Pictish origin-legend; on Geoffrey's use of the latter, see further N. Wright, 'Gildas's Geographical Perspective: Some Problems', in *Gildas: New Approaches*, pp.85-105 (at 96-8).
[55] Wright, 'Geoffrey of Monmouth and Gildas', pp.5-7.
[56] It was for this reason that in the First Variant Version the Gildasian passage was largely replaced by material drawn verbatim from Bede; see Hammer's edition, pp.23-4.

time and resolves to conquer its isolated inhabitants, whom he describes as '*inaccessi a Romano* populo ac intacti'. This phrase is clearly indebted to Bede's opening statement, itself derived from Tertullian,[57] that 'Britannia *Romanis* usque Gaium Iulium Caesarem *inaccessa* atque incognita fuit' (*Historia Ecclesiastica Gentis Anglorum*, I.2).[58] Thereafter, however, Geoffrey's treatment of Caesar's invasions owes most to the *Historia Brittonum* and, although his account shares characters such as Cassibellaunus, Androgeus and the tribune Labienus (*Historia Regum Britannie*, §56) with Bede's sober Orosian narrative, it is entirely differently handled. Yet when Geoffrey relates the blocking of the Thames in the following words (*Historia Regum Britannie*, §59), 'palis ferreis atque *plumbatis et ad modum humani femoris grossis* subter amnem infixit', he obviously echoes Bede's similar description of *acutissimae sudes* in the Thames '*ad modum humani femoris grossae et* circumfusae *plumbo*' (*Historia Ecclesiastica Gentis Anglorum*, I.2); but according to Bede, the Romans avoided this barrier, while the pro-British Geoffrey, following the *Historia Brittonum*,[59] reports that Caesar's ships were holed and many men drowned.

There are further indications that no matter how much Geoffrey diverged from the *Historia Ecclesiastica Gentis Anglorum*, the Bedan original remained steadily before his eyes. Geoffrey's account of the conversion of King Lucius chiefly comprises the establishment of twenty-eight bishoprics (based on the reference to twenty-eight cities of Britain first found in Gildas's *De Excidio Britanniae*, §3) and three archbishoprics; these were unknown to Bede or to any pre-Galfridian author. However, Geoffrey (*Historia Regum Britannie*, §72) describes Lucius's success in writing to Pope Eleutherius as follows, 'in amorem uere fidei anhelans *pie* petitionis *effectum consecutus est*'; Bede likewise says of Lucius's request 'et mox *effectum piae* postulationis *consecutus est*' (*Historia Ecclesiastica Gentis Anglorum*, I.4). Later Geoffrey treats the civil war between Geta and Bassianus (better known as Caracalla), the sons of Emperor Septimius Severus (who died at York), as a contest for the throne of Britain between Roman and British factions. Nevertheless, he begins this fantastic account with

---

[57] Plummer, *Venerabilis Baedae Opera Historica*, I.13.
[58] In *Historia Regum Britannie*, §55 (the succeeding chapter), a similar allusion to the Britons as 'extra orbem positos' (as well as the words 'ignoramus quid sit seruituti obedire') constitutes a further literary echo, in this case of Hegesippus, *Historia*, II.9; see J. Hammer, 'Les sources de Geoffrey de Monmouth, *Historia Regum Britanniae*, IV, 2', *Latomus* 4 (1940-45), 79-82.
[59] §20 (Morris, p. 64).

the words (*Historia Regum Britannie*, §75), '*Reliquit* ipse [viz. Severus] *duos filios Bassianum et Getam*', which reveal that his starting point was Bede's statement (*Historia Ecclesiastica Gentis Anglorum*, I.5) that Severus '*reliquit duos filios Bassianum et Getam*'. Similarly, although Geoffrey develops the story of Carausius quite differently from Bede's factual account, his description of '*iuuenis quidam* nomine *Carausius ex infima* gente creatus*' (*Historia Regum Britannie*, §75) clearly depends on that of Bede (*Historia Ecclesiastica Gentis Anglorum*, I.6), '*Carausius quidam*, genere quidem *infimus*'. In this case, Geoffrey's modification of 'genere infimus' to 'infima gente creatus' is an indication of his taste for poeticism, since the words *gĕntĕ crĕātūs* constitute the final cadence of a hexameter.[60] Geoffrey thus improves on Bede's phraseology by the insertion of a poetic tag.[61] A further Bedan echo occurs in Geoffrey's version of the *aduentus Saxonum* (*Historia Regum Britannie*, §§98-105). Although Geoffrey's account, largely based on the *Historia Brittonum*, could hardly differ more completely from that of Bede, at one point (*Historia Regum Britannie*, §101), Geoffrey includes amongst the arguments by which the Britons attempt to persuade Vortigern to expel the English the following complaint: 'Insuper tanta multitudo aduenerat *ita ut* ciuibus *terrori essent*'. There is nothing comparable in the *Historia Brittonum*; but Bede (*Historia Ecclesiastica Gentis Anglorum*, I.15) states that, after the arrival of the English, 'grandescere populus coepit aduenarum *ita ut* ipsis quoque qui eos aduocauerant indigenis *essent terrori*'. In this passage, then, despite Geoffrey's reliance on the *Historia Brittonum* as his primary source, his diction reflects rather the influence of Bede's treatment of the *aduentus Saxonum*.

All the reminiscences which we have so far examined are found in the same context in the *Historia* (no matter how altered by Geoffrey) as in Bede's *Historia Ecclesiastica Gentis Anglorum*. However, when relating King Arthur's invasion of Ireland (*Historia Regum Britannie*, §153), Geoffrey reports that the lightly equipped Irish were easily put to flight: 'gens eius *nuda et inermis* misere lacerata confugit'. Tatlock remarks on 'Geoffrey's knowl-

[60] Geoffrey's model may be *Aeneid*, X.543, '*Uulcani stirpe creatus*'; but the line-ending *gente creatus* is not uncommon in late-Latin and mediaeval poetry (see Otto Schumann, *Lateinisches Hexameter Lexicon: Dichterisches Formelgut von Ennius bis zum Archipoeta* [6 vols, München 1979-83], II.416) and Geoffrey may not be indebted to any one particular source.

[61] On Geoffrey's taste for poetic diction, see Wright, 'Geoffrey of Monmouth and Gildas', pp.6, 12, n.36, and 15, n.40; and 'Geoffrey of Monmouth and Gildas Revisited', p.162, n.27.

edge of the primitive weapons, lack of armour and scanty clothes of the Gaelic Irish'.[62] While he was right to compliment Geoffrey's accuracy, Tatlock failed to note an interesting verbal echo. In *Historia Ecclesiastica Gentis Anglorum*, II.2, Bede describes how the cowardly Brocmail abandoned the monks of Bangor, '*inermes ac nudos* ferientibus gladiis' – 'unarmed and naked to the swords that struck them down'. We have already seen that Geoffrey relied heavily on this very Bedan passage when dealing with the massacre of the Bangor monks; hence there can be little doubt that Geoffrey's inventive transference of the phrase 'inermis ac nudus' to the poorly armed Irish army of Gillamurius was directly influenced by Bede. It must be stressed, however, that this is the only case known to the present writer in which Geoffrey imitates the diction of the *Historia Ecclesiastica Gentis Anglorum* in a context entirely different from the Bedan original.

Geoffrey's final reminiscence of Bede again raises the question of why Geoffrey conflated the historical Cadwaladr of Gwynedd (*ob.* A.D. 682) with the English King Caedwalla of Wessex, who died in Rome in 689. Already in the tenth-century Welsh poem *Armes Prydein Vawr* Cadwaladr played a messianic role, but its precise nature remains uncertain.[63] Geoffrey's literary aim may have been to define this role more precisely by ascribing Caedwalla's saintly death in Rome to Cadwaladr, the last King of Britain – since, according to Geoffrey, the Britons would not recover the island until Cadwaladr's bones had been returned to Britain (*Historia Regum Britannie*, § 205); but our ignorance of Welsh traditions makes it impossible to determine the degree of Geoffrey's originality in so doing. However, Geoffrey had a further reason for this identification. He introduces Cadwaladr, Cadwallon's son, in the following manner (*Historia Regum Britannie*, § 202):

> Suscepit itaque regni gubernaculum Cadualdrus filius suus (quem Beda *Cheduallam iuuenem* uocat) .... Mater eius fuit soror Peande regis <ex patre tantum, matre uero diuersa>;[64] ex nobili *genere Gewiseorum* edita fuerat.

In this passage Geoffrey echoes Bede's first reference to Caedwalla of Wessex (*Historia Ecclesiastica Gentis Anglorum*, IV.15) as '*Caedualla iuuenis* strenuissimus de regio *genere Geuissorum*'.

[62] *The Legendary History*, p. 80.
[63] See further D. N. Dumville, 'Brittany and "Armes Prydein Vawr"', *Études Celtiques* 20 (1983), 145-59 (at 153-4).
[64] The bracketed clause (here restored from Faral, *La Légende arthurienne*, III.299) is erroneously omitted from the Bern text; see Wright, *The Historia Regum Britannie*, I.liv-lvi.

Bede describes Caedwalla as belonging to the royal dynasty of the Gewissi, an archaic term signifying the West Saxons;[65] however, Geoffrey in the *Historia* always uses the name Gewissei to denote the inhabitants of Gwent in south-east Wales.[66] Hence Geoffrey could have regarded Caedwalla as a British prince. He may also have been motivated by Bede's reference (in the preceding chapter) to a plague affecting British-occupied areas (*Historia Ecclesiastica Gentis Anglorum*, IV.14: 'multas Britanniae prouincias mortalitas saeua corripiebat'), since the historical Cadwaladr died in the plague of A.D.682 and Geoffrey represents a devastating pestilence – borrowed from Gildas – as the reason for Cadwaladr's flight to Brittany (*Historia Regum Britannie*, §203). Critics have maintained that Geoffrey's identification constitutes a slip; Fletcher called it 'a very careless mistake'[67] and Tatlock maintained that it 'can hardly have been done deliberately'.[68] Yet the ready familiarity with Bede's text which Geoffrey displays in other borrowings and the freedom of his adaptations flatly contradict this view. Moreover, as we have seen, in describing Cadwaladr's death at Rome Geoffrey borrows verbatim from another Bedan passage where Caedwalla is explicitly identified as an English king.[69] It seems highly unlikely, therefore, that Geoffrey was unaware of the arbitrary nature of his conflation.[70] The care with which Geoffrey explains Cadwaladr's Gewissean ancestry also argues strongly against Fletcher and Tatlock. Cadwaladr historically belonged to the ruling family of *Venedotia* (Gwynedd); hence the Gewissean background ascribed to him by Bede, even if understood as being Gwentian-Welsh, needed explanation. Geoffrey ingeniously solved this anomaly by giving Cadwaladr the following genealogy (*Historia Regum Britannie*, §202, quoted above):

---

[65] Plummer, *Venerabilis Baedae Opera Historica*, II.88-9.

[66] Tatlock, *The Legendary History*, pp.74-7.

[67] *The Arthurian Material in the Chronicles especially those of Great Britain and France* (Boston, 1906), p.65, n.2.

[68] *The Legendary History*, p.252.

[69] Above, pp.44-5.

[70] Tatlock's attempt to explain Geoffrey's supposed 'confusion' of the names Cadwaladr (*Cadualadrus* or *Cadualdrus*) and Caedwalla (*Caedualla*) by arguing that his manuscript of Bede may have contained the form *Ceduald* – as in London, British Library, MS. Harley 4978, (French, s.x), described by Plummer, I.xcviiii-c – is self-defeating since that reading is found only in *Historia Ecclesiastica Gentis Anglorum*, V.7, where Caedwalla's identity as king of Wessex is clearly stated.

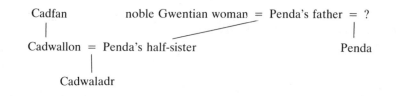

Geoffrey represents Cadwaladr, then, as on his father's side Venedotian, and on his mother's side half-Gwentian and half-English (in fact Mercian, through Penda's father).[71] This attribution of English blood to Cadwaladr may constitute, moreover, a typical piece of Galfridian whimsy because it implicitly reflects the fact that this character is compounded half of the historical ruler of Gwynedd and half of Bede's Caedwalla, English king of Wessex.

A further line of argument bears upon this question. When Geoffrey first mentions Cadwaladr, he refers to him as 'Cadualdrus ... quem Beda Cheduallam iuuenem uocat' (*Historia Regum Britannie*, §202). This citation, apart from an initial general reference to Bede as an historical authority (*Historia Regum Britannie*, §1), is unique in the *Historia*. As I have attempted to demonstrate in the case of Gildas, Geoffrey's appeals to an author by name provide useful evidence of his approach to that author as a source.[72] It is clear from the phrase 'Cheduallam iuuenem' that Geoffrey intended to recall *Historia Ecclesiastica Gentis Anglorum*, IV.15 ('Caedualla iuuenis'), rather than Caedwalla's death (*Historia Ecclesiastica Gentis Anglorum*, V.7). But did he really hope that the reader would not connect the Gewissean Caedwalla with the king of Wessex who died at Rome? If so, why risk calling attention to this discrepancy (among so many) by citing Bede at all? It seems more likely that Geoffrey deliberately chose to signal the contradiction between his *Historia* and the *Historia Ecclesiastica Gentis Anglorum* by making a cross-reference to Bede precisely at a point where the two works could not be reconciled. Geoffrey implies that Bede has misnamed Cadwaladr as Caedwalla; as to Cadwaladr's later career, is the account of the English historian or Geoffrey's version, supposedly based on a native source, to be believed? It is difficult to agree with Tatlock that 'Geoffrey did not deliberately contradict Bede';[73] rather, Geoffrey has thrown down the gauntlet and his reader must decide between them.

---

[71] Penda's half-sister is not entirely fictional, since Bede records the marriage of Cenwalh of Wessex to Penda's sister in *Historia Ecclesiastica Gentis Anglorum*, III.7.

[72] 'Geoffrey of Monmouth and Gildas', pp. 22-4.

[73] *The Legendary History*, p. 253.

Conclusion

To recapitulate, Geoffrey's approach to Bede differs in a number of ways from his use of Gildas. While passages based on the *De Excidio Britanniae* are spread not unevenly throughout the *Historia*, similar passages from the *Historia Ecclesiastica Gentis Anglorum* are clustered in the last twenty chapters of Geoffrey's work. In fact, Geoffrey makes extensive verbatim borrowings from Bede only when the *De Excidio Britanniae* and *Historia Brittonum* no longer constitute useful sources (viz. for the period from the mission of St Augustine). Nevertheless, although Geoffrey's account of British history from Caesar's invasions to the *aduentus Saxonum* does not make extended borrowings from the *Historia Ecclesiastica Gentis Anglorum*, the narrative framework of that section of his *Historia* unquestionably reveals the direct influence of Bede. Geoffrey's attitude towards Bede as a literary source is also significantly different from his evident appreciation of Gildas. Echoes of the rich and rhetorical Latin of the *De Excidio Britanniae* can be found almost everywhere in the *Historia*, most often in contexts entirely different (sometimes pointedly so) from their Gildasian originals.[74] By contrast, Geoffrey evidently had little regard for Bede as a stylist: he imitates Bedan phraseology only infrequently and in all cases (except one) these imitations are found in the same context as their models in the *Historia Ecclesiastica Gentis Anglorum*. In all other respects, however, Geoffrey reworked and transformed Bede's text as freely as he did that of Gildas. Indeed, the retention of verbal echoes of Bede in the *Historia* clearly demonstrates that Geoffrey's manipulations of the *Historia Ecclesiastica Gentis Anglorum* are entirely conscious. Furthermore, Geoffrey's one citation of Bede can be construed as a direct challenge to his English predecessor. In short, Geoffrey refused to make any concession to Bede's authority by modifying his customary free approach to his source; rather the *Historia* contradicts Bede at almost every turn.

Geoffrey's contemporaries were not unaware of the difficulties raised by the conflicting accounts of British history found in the *Historia Ecclesiastica Gentis Anglorum* and *Historia Regum*

---

[74] Wright, 'Geoffrey of Monmouth and Gildas', pp.14-21; and 'Geoffrey of Monmouth and Gildas Revisited', *passim*.

Britannie. Attempts to reconcile the two were made by Alfred of Beverley (*c*.1143)[75] and by the redactor of the First Variant Version of the *Historia*.[76] But the problem was most clearly stated by William of Newburgh, whose attack on Geoffrey of Monmouth in the preface of his *Historia Rerum Anglicarum* is well known.[77] What is often forgotten is the context of William's strictures. He contrasts Geoffrey with Gildas whom, because of his frank condemnation of his fellow Britons, William regarded as the true (though neglected)[78] native historian of the British. However, the real contest in William's eyes was between Geoffrey and Bede. After exposing Geoffrey's inventions, William concludes:[79]

> Ut ergo eidem Bedae, de cuius sapientia et sinceritate dubitare fas non est, fides in omnibus habeatur, fabulator ille [viz. Geoffrey] cum suis fabulisin-cunctanter ab omnibus respuatur.

For William, then, question of British history resolved itself into a straight fight between Bede and Geoffrey; and William was in no doubt on which side veracity lay.

William's counterblast came too late, however; Geoffrey's *Historia* had already been accepted by the majority of chroniclers and was not to be seriously questioned until the sixteenth century.[80] Why did Geoffrey succeed in outfacing Bede so completely? The appeal of the *Historia* to the Anglo-Norman and later mediaeval audience supplies one answer.[81] In the words of T. D. Kendrick: 'The British History rode majestically forward brushing quibblers and doubters aside'.[82] However, the role of Geoffrey's alleged vernacular source should not be minimised. Certainly a claim to be based on some 'lost' source is no more than a commonplace in mediaeval romance literature;[83] but such romances mostly postdate

---

[75] Leckie, *The Passage of Dominion*, pp. 86-92.

[76] *Ibid.*, pp. 102-109; the date and authorship of the First Variant Version is discussed in detail in my forthcoming edition (n. 11 above).

[77] Ed. Richard Howlett, *Chronicles of the Reigns of Stephen, Henry II, and Richard I*, Rolls Series (4 vols, London, 1884-9), I.1-II.500 (at I.11-19).

[78] Wright, 'Geoffrey of Monmouth and Gildas', p. 2.

[79] Howlett, *Chronicles*, I.18.

[80] On the acceptance of the *Historia Regum Britannie*, see Leckie, *The Passage of Dominion*, pp. 96-7 and (in the later middle ages) Laura Keeler, *Geoffrey of Monmouth and the Late Latin Chroniclers 1300-1500* (Berkeley and Los Angeles, 1946). The battle over Geoffrey's *Historia* in the Tudor period is entertainingly discussed by T. D. Kendrick, *British Antiquity* (London, 1950), especially pp. 65-133.

[81] See further Wright, *The Historia Regum Britannie*, I.xix.

[82] *British Antiquity*, p. 14.

[83] References are cited by Tatlock, *The Legendary History*, p. 424, n. 11.

the *Historia*. A closer parallel is afforded by the late-antique pseudo-history of Dares Phrygius, an allegedly eyewitness account of the Trojan war, which is lent specious veracity by an introductory letter, attributed to Cornelius Nepos, reporting to Sallust his recent discovery and translation of the autograph copy of Dares's history in Athens.[84] In much the same way, Geoffrey's appeal to the existence of a very ancient Breton- or Welsh-language book, of which the *Historia* was but a translation, was crucial to his challenge to Bede, since it implied that his source was older and more authoritative than the *Historia Ecclesiastica Gentis Anglorum*. Obvious points of similarity and divergence between the *Historia Regum Britannie* and *Historia Ecclesiastica Gentis Anglorum* might then be explained in terms of common reliance on (or, in the case of the Englishman Bede, manipulation of) native British traditions which, moreover, were more likely to be accurately reported in Geoffrey's supposed vernacular source. In this sense, the question of authority proves a key to Geoffrey's use of his sources: in the case of Gildas he adapted the *De Excidio Britanniae* freely, yet used Gildas's reputation to prop up his inventions; in that of Bede, he twisted, reshaped, and contradicted the previously accepted Bedan version of the British past while taking shelter behind the authority which the *liber uetustissimus* conferred on his *Historia*.[85]

[84] See further Wright, *The Historia Regum Britannie*, I.xviii, n. 30.
[85] I am deeply indebted to Dr J. A. Seeley and Dr D. N. Dumville for reading a draft of this paper and for much patient help, encouragement, and criticism. A version of this paper was read at the eighth Battle Conference on Anglo-Norman Studies, 1985; in this connection, the author would like to express his gratitude to Professor R. A. Brown and the other participants for a number of constructive suggestions.

APPENDIX

Parallel passages between
the *Historia Regum Britannie* and
Historia Ecclesiastica Gentis Anglorum

1. *Historia Regum Britannie*, §188: The mission of St Augustine.

Interea *missus est Augustinus* a beato *Gregorio* papa in Britanniam ut *Anglis uerbum Dei predicaret* .... Postquam ergo uenit Augustinus, inuenit in eorum prouintia *.vii. episcopatus* et archiepiscopatum religiosissimis presulibus munitos et abatias complures .... Inter ceteras erat quedam nobilissima in ciuitate Bangor *in qua tantus fuisse fertur numerus monachorum ut, cum in .vii. portiones esset cum prepositis sibi* prioribus *monasterium diuisum, nulla harum portio minus quam trecentos* monachos *haberet qui omnes labore manuum suarum uiuebant. Abbas* autem eorum *Dinoot* vocabatur miro modo liberalibus artibus eruditus qui Augustino petenti ab episcopis Britonum subiectionem et *suadenti ut secum genti* Anglorum *communem ewangelizando laborem susciperent* diuersis monstrauit argumentationibus ipsos ei nullam subiectionem debere nec suam predicationem inimicis suis impendere, cum et suum archipresulem haberent et gens Saxonum patriam propriam eisdem auferre perstarent. Unde eos summo habebant odio *fidemque et relligionem eorum pro nihilo habebant nec in aliquo Anglis magis quam* canibus *communicabant.*

Historia Ecclesiastica Gentis Anglorum, I.23, II.2, and 20.

I.23 ... *Gregorius* ... *misit* seruum Dei *Augustinum* et alios plures cum eo monachos timentes Dominum *praedicare uerbum Dei genti Anglorum.*

II.2 ... coepitque Augustinus eis fraterna admonitione *suadere ut* pace catholica *secum* habita *communem euangelizandi gentibus* pro Domino *laborem susciperent.* ... uenerunt, ut perhibent, *.vii. Brettonum episcopi* et plures uiri doctissimi, maxime de nobilissimo eorum monasterio quod uocatur lingua Anglorum Bancornaburg, cui tempore illo *Dinoot abbas* praefuisse fertur. ... Erant autem plurimi eorum de monasterio Bancor *in quo tantus fertur fuisse numerus monachorum ut, cum in septem portiones esset cum praepositis sibi* rectoribus *monasterium diuisum, nulla harum portio minus quam .ccc.* homines *haberet qui omnes* de *labore manuum suarum uiuere* solebant.

II.20 ... quippe cum usque hodie moris sit Brettonum *fidem religionemque Anglorum pro nihili habere neque in aliquo eis magis communicare quam* paganis.

2. *Historia Regum Britannie*, §189: the massacre of the monks of Bangor.

Edelbertus ergo rex Cantiorum ut uidit Britones dedignantes subiectionem Augustino facere et eosdem predicationem suam spernere, hoc graue ferens *Edelfridum* regem Northamhimbrorum et ceteros regulos Saxonum instimulauit ut *collecto grandi exercitu* in ciuitatem Bangor abbatem Dinoot et ceteros clericos qui eos despexerant perditum irent. Aquiescentes igitur consilio eius collegerunt mirabilem exercitum et prouintiam Britonum petentes uenerunt *Legecestriam* ubi Broohmais consul urbis aduentum eorum expectabat. Uenerant autem ad eandam ciuitatem ex diuersis Britonum prouinciis innumerabiles monachi et heremite et maxime de ciuitate Bangor ut pro salute populi sui orarent. Collectis igitur undique exercitibus Edelfridus rex Northamhimbrorum prelium iniuit cum Brochmail; qui pauciori numero militum resistens ad ultimum relicta ciuitate, sed prius maxima strage hostibus illata, diffugit. At *Edhelfridus* ciuitate capta *cum intellexisset causam aduentus* predictorum monachorum, *iussit in* eos *primum arma uerti et sic mille ducenti* eorum in ipsa die martirio decorati regni celestis adepti sunt sedem.

Historia Ecclesiastica Gentis Anglorum, II.2.

Siquidem ... rex Anglorum fortissimus *Aedilfrid collecto grandi exercitu* ad Ciuitatem Legionum, quae a gente Anglorum *Legacaestir*, a Brettonibus autem rectius Carlegion appellatur, maximam gentis perfidae stragem dedit. Cumque bellum acturus uideret sacerdotes eorum, qui ad exorandum Deum pro milite bellum agente conuenerant, seorsum in tutiore loco consistere, sciscitabatur qui essent hi quidue acturi illo conuenissent. ... Horum ergo plurimi [viz. the Bangor monks] ad memoratam aciem, peracto ieiunio triduano, cum aliis orandi causa conuenerant, habentes defensorem nomine Brocmailum qui eos intentos precibus a barbarorum gladiis protegeret. Quorum *causam aduentus cum intellexisset* rex *Aedilfrid*, ait: 'Ergo si aduersum nos ad Deum suum clamant, profecto et ipsi, quamuis arma non ferant, contra nos pugnant, qui aduersis nos inprecationibus persequuntur'. Itaque *in* hos *primum arma uerti iubet, et sic* ceteras nephandae militiae copias non sine

57

exercitus sui damno deleuit. Extinctos in ea pugna ferunt de his qui
ad orandum uenerant uiros circiter *mille ducentos* et solum .1. fuga
esse lapsos. Brocmail ad primum hostium aduentum cum suis terga
uertens, eos quos defendere debuerat inermes ac nudos ferientibus
gladiis reliquit.

3. *Historia Regum Britannie*, §198: Cadwallon's reprisals.

Habita igitur uictoria *Caduallo* uniuersas Anglorum *prouincias
peruagando* ita *debachatus est* in Saxones *ut ne sexui quidem
muliebri uel paruulorum aetati parceret; quin* omne *genus Anglorum* ex *finibus Britannie abradere* uolens quoscumque reperiebat
inauditis *tormentis* afficiebat.

Historia Ecclesiastica Gentis Anglorum, II.20.

At uero *Caedualla* ... adeo ... erat animo ac moribus barbarus *ut
ne sexui quidem muliebri uel* innocuae *paruulorum parceret aetati,
quin* uniuersos atrocitate ferina morti per *tormenta* contraderet,
multo tempore totas eorum *prouincias debacchando peruagatus*
ac totum *genus Anglorum Britanniae finibus erasurum* se esse
deliberans.

4. *Historia Regum Britannie*, §190: Oswald and the battle of
Hevenfeld.

At *Oswaldus* dum a predicto Peanda in *loco* qui *uocatur Heuenfeld*,
id est '*celestis campus*', quadam nocte obsideretur, *erexit* ibidem
crucem Domini et indixit commilitonibus suis ut suprema nocte in
hec uerba clamarent: '*Flectamus genua omnes et Deum omnipotentem*, unum *et uerum, in commune deprecemur ut nos ab*
exercitu *superbo* Britannici regis et eiusdem nefandi ducis Peandae
*defendat. Scit enim ipse quia iusta pro salute gentis nostre bella
suscepimus'. Fecerunt ergo omnes ut iusserat et sic incipiente
diluculo in hostes progressi iuxta meritum suae fidei uictoria potiti
sunt.*

Historia Ecclesiastica Gentis Anglorum, III.2.

... *Osuald* signum sanctae *crucis erexit* ... et ... proclamauerit:
'*Flectamus omnes genua et Deum omnipotentem*, uiuum *ac uerum,
in commune deprecemur ut nos ab* hoste *superbo* ac feroce sua
miseratione *defendat; scit enim ipse quia iusta pro salute gentis*

nostrae bella suscepimus'. Fecerunt omnes ut iusserat et sic incipiente diluculo in hostem progressi iuxta meritum suae fidei uictoria potiti sunt. ... *Uocatur locus* ille lingua Anglorum *Hefenfeld* quod dici potest latine *'caelestis campus'.*

5. *Historia Regum Britannie*, §200: Oswy and the battle of Winwed.

At Oswi *ad ultimum necessitate coactus promisit ei innumera regia ornamenta et maiora donaria quam credi potest* ut patriam suam *uastare desineret* et pretermissa inquietatione quam inceperat *domum rediret. Cumque* ille *precibus* eius *nullatenus assensum preberet,* rex *ille ad diuinum respiciens auxilium,* licet minorem *habuisset exercitum,* iniuit tum prelium cum illo iuxta *fluuium Uunued* et Peanda necnon et *.xxx. ducibus* peremptis uictoriam adeptus est.

Historia Ecclesiastica Gentis Anglorum, III.24.

[Osuiu] *ad ultimum necessitate cogente promisit* se *ei innumera et maiora quam credi potest ornamenta regia* uel *donaria* in pretium lucis largiturum, dummodo ille *domum rediret* et prouincias regni eius usque ad internicionem *uastare desineret. Cumque* rex perfidus *nullatenus precibus* illius *assensum preberet,* qui totam eius gentem a paruo usque ad magnum delere atque exterminare decreuerat, *respexit ille ad diuinae auxilium* pietatis. ... Osuiu ... perparuum, ut dixi, *habens exercitum* ... occurrit. ... Inito ergo certamine ... *duces* regii *.xxx.* paene omnes interfecti. ... Et prope *fluuium Uinued* pugnatum est.

6. *Historia Regum Britannie*, §205: Cadwaladr's death.

Tunc Cadualadrus abiectis mundialibus *propter Dominum regnum-que perpetuum uenit Romam* et a *Sergio* papa confirmatus, inopino etiam *languore correptus, .xii.* autem *die kalendarum Mayarum anno ab incarnatione Domini .dclxxxix. a* contagione *carnis solutus* caelestis *regni* aulam ingressus est.

Historia Ecclesiastica Gentis Anglorum, V.7.

Caedualla, rex Occidentalium Saxonum, ... relicto imperio *propter Dominum regnumque perpetuum uenit Romam.* ... pontificatum agente *Sergio* baptizatus est die sancto sabbati paschalis *anno ab incarnatione Domini .dclxxxviiii.*; et albis adhuc positus, *languore correptus, duodecimo kalendarum Maiarum die solutus a carne* et beatorum est *regno* sociatus in caelis.

59

III

THE *GESTA REGUM BRITANNIAE* OF WILLIAM OF RENNES: AN ARTHURIAN EPIC?

Rosemary Morris

In about 1182 there appeared a work which was destined to become one of the greatest scholarly sensations of the Middle Ages: the *Alexandreis* of Gautier de Châtillon.[1] The author's impeccable Latinity, polished versification and sound classical learning immediately made his work a favourite in the schools,[2] but the real secret of the book's success depended on its subject, Alexander, the most universally popular of all medieval hero-figures. Various accounts of Alexander were already circulating both in Latin and in the vernacular, but most of these were derived largely from the 'pseudo-Callisthenes' romance of Alexander and were extremely fanciful.[3] Beside them, Gautier's poem, while not lacking in colour and drama, must have seemed sober and reliable, based as it was on the stolid prose of Quintus Curtius. The *Alexandreis* gave a favourite figure historical respectability without detracting from his allure.

Such success invited emulation. A would-be rival to Gautier would need not only an equal mastery of his medium, but an equally attractive subject. Such a subject was ready to hand. For a late-twelfth-century writer, there was an obvious rival to Alexander as a popular and literary hero: King Arthur. (Charlemagne was another possible contender, but Arthur had the charm of novelty.) Like Alexander, Arthur was widely known through colourful but blatantly unhistorical stories, which in his case had circulated

---

[1] *Galteri de Castellione Alexandreis*, ed. M. L. Colker, Thesaurus Mundi 17 (Padua, 1978).

[2] Colker, p. xix; G. Cary, *The Medieval Alexander* (Cambridge, 1956), p. 62; H. Christensen, *Das Alexanderlied Walters von Chatillon* (Halle, 1905), pp. 165 ff.

[3] Cary, pp. 24-42.

orally, in French or Celtic vernaculars, and tended to be despised by the learned.[4] Like Alexander, Arthur was given respectability by a (comparatively) sober Latin prose account, though this time a recent one: the *Historia Regum Britanniae*.[5] An adaptation into Latin hexameters of this immensely successful work ought to have every chance of rivalling the *Alexandreis*. Such, at least, seems to have been the supposition of one William of Rennes, who shortly after 1236 composed just such a work.[6] He did not win the fame he sought, but his poem is of singular interest to students of Arthurian literature. It is the only attempt to clothe this quintessentially medieval hero in the prestigious mantle of a classical hero: to make him the rival not only of Alexander, but of Achilles, Caesar and Aeneas (see ll. 2976-85). However, the *Gesta* is not exclusively concerned with Arthur, as the *Alexandreis* is with its hero. William adapted the whole of Geoffrey's *Historia*, and the decision to do this was dangerous for one seeking literary fame. The author who at one moment aspires to equal Virgil and Lucan, at other times appears to be no more than a versifying chronicler, of a kind with which contemporary readers were only too familiar.[7] From this viewpoint the aptest comparison is not between William and Gautier de Châtillon, but between William and Wace. Both aspired to literary fame by adapting the whole of Geoffrey's Latin prose history into a more appealing mode; both oscillate between minute respect for the source and creative divergence from it. Here again, it was not William but his (putative) rival who won popularity, by aiming at a French-speaking, cultured but non-academic audience. It seems that William fell between two stools. Before we accept this, however, we must be sure what his real aims were. He may well have aspired to a unique distinction: that of becoming the Breton chronicler of the 'Breton hope'. For if William of Rennes was indeed a Breton, writing for a Breton

---

[4] For the early history of Arthurian story, see chapters 2-5 of R. S. Loomis (ed.), *Arthurian Literature in the Middle Ages* (Oxford, 1959), pp.12-63.

[5] Ed. E. Faral in *La Légende arthurienne*, 3 vols (Paris, 1929, reprinted, New York, n.d.), vol. 3, pp. 63-303. A full critical edition by N. Wright is in preparation, but only a single MS has so far been published (Cambridge, 1984). There is no evidence that William used the 'variant version' of the *Historia*.

[6] William of Rennes, *Gesta Regum Britanniae*, ed. F. Michel (Cambrian Archaeological Association, 1872). A critical edition by N. Wright is in progress. I am grateful to him for reading the present study and for eliminating many errors.

[7] F. Raby, *Secular Latin Poetry*, 2nd edn, vol. 2 (Oxford, 1957), pp. 67-72.

patron,[8] then his poem is the *only* direct evidence for what is generally believed to have been an enthusiastic cult of Arthur in medieval Brittany.[9] Though William eschewed the vernacular, the aptest comparison from this viewpoint would be with the Welsh *Bruts*, which sought to reintroduce the popular figure of Arthur to its (presumptive) creators in the new guise which Geoffrey had given him.

It is on the basis of these three comparisons that I wish to pursue this study of the *Gesta*.

William and Gautier

Gautier de Châtillon was aiming high when he wrote the *Alexandreis*. In the Prologue, under a becoming appearance of modesty, he claims equality with Virgil ('non enim arbitror me esse/ *meliorem* Mantuano vate', 19-20), and boasts that he has dared take up a subject which the poets of Antiquity feared to tackle (34-6). In his opening invocation to the Muse, he claims that this subject is superior to Virgil's: had Alexander not died young, his glory would have far outshone that of the whole Roman race (I,5-10). At the end of the poem, the author confidently looks forward to the immortality it will give him (X, 467-9). The subject itself, however, is strictly limited:

> Gesta ducis Macedum totum digesta per orbem,
> Quam large dispersit opes, quo milite Porum
> Vicerit et Darium, quo principe Grecia victrix
> Risit et a Persis rediere tributa Chorintum
>
> (I,1-4) (The events are listed in reverse order!)

He does not aim to produce a complete biography of Alexander; he in fact omits many episodes which were particularly popular and attested by history, such as the taming of Bucephalus and the

---

[8] Michel, 'Introduction' pp. vi ff. The name of William's patron, Cadioc of Vannes, is spelled out by the first letter of the ten books (CHADIOCCUS), just as Gautier's first letters spell GUILLERMUS. This shows that the dedication to Cadioc in *Gesta*, 4923, is not a spurious addition.

[9] On Breton attitudes to Arthur see R. S. Loomis 'The Oral Diffusion and the Arthurian Legend' in *Arthurian Literature in the Middle Ages*, pp. 54-63. No Breton vernacular literature whatever survives from before the fifteenth century.

marriage with Roxana.[10] Everything in Quintus Curtius which is not directly relevant to Alexander, or which is uncomplimentary to him, is ruthlessly excised, leaving the portrait of a noble, single-minded warrior king. Gautier makes no elaborate attempt to medievalise Alexander, as do the French Alexander-romances.[11] Though the hero's magnanimity, courage and generosity are calculated to appeal to a twelfth-century audience, he has none of the flamboyancy of a chanson de geste or vernacular romance hero. What Gautier does stress, however, is Alexander's role as the adumbration of an ideal Christian King, a proto-crusador: hence the exclusive concentration on his wars against the mighty alien power of the East, and the purple patches in which Gautier connects Alexander with Jewish prophecy and the coming of Christ.[12] It is this theme, Alexander as the warrior of God, which gives the poem a burning relevance to its own time, the time of the Third Crusade.

William of Rennes, like Gautier, approaches his task with a mixture of modesty and boldness. The assumption of modesty, while not going beyond the requirements of the standard modesty topoi,[13] is more insistent than Gautier's. The poem is a 'ludus' (1.17), an occupation for an idle hour, or a pleasant read for schoolboys (4910-1). The *Alexandreis* was, of course, a schoolbook, so there may be less modesty here than appears at first sight! The boldness lies in the vastness of the subject, for whereas Gautier avoids giving even a complete biography, William offers the destiny of a nation:

> Unde genus Britonum, que nominis hujus origo,
> Unde suos habuit generosa Britannia reges,
> Quis fuit Arturus, que gesta, quis exitus ejus,
> Qualiter amisit infelix natio regnum.
>
> (13-15)

Arthur is clearly the climax of this story (for so Geoffrey of Monmouth had made him), but he does not entirely dominate it. Whereas Gautier proposes Alexander as an epitome of the supra-national hero or crusader, William proposes his story as a national

---

[10] Cf. Christensen, *Alexanderlied*, pp.107 ff.

[11] P. Meyer, *Alexandre le Grand dans la littérature française du Moyen Age* (Paris, 1886), *passim*.

[12] Cf. Raby, *Secular Latin Poetry*, p. 76.

[13] See E. Curtius, *European Literature and the Latin Middle Ages*, trans. W. Trask (London, 1953), pp. 80-90.

epic, the exclusive property of the British race:

> Saxones hinc abeant, lateant mea scripta Quirites,
> nec pateant Gallis, quos nostra Britannia victrix
> sepe molestavit. Solis hec scribo Britannis ...
>
> (4911-14)

It is to remind them of their ancestors' virtue and stir them to emulation (4915-20). Thus, even while he seeks to rival Gautier's fame, William limits possible scope; and yet why, if he does not wish for a wider audience, does he write in classical hexameters? Perhaps his assertion of exclusiveness is only partly sincere and is another aspect of the modesty topos, as well as an assertion of national pride against competing races. We shall return to the problem later (p.111).

When he comes to Arthur's story, which occupies books VII, VIII and most of IX, William behaves as if he were beginning a new work, invoking the Muse, and protesting his inadequacy to the task, though he brackets Homer, Ovid, Virgil and (improbably) Cicero with himself in this, and claims that Virgil, Lucan and Statius would have preferred Arthur to their own heroes (2972-85). The claim is similar to Gautier's, and is probably based on it, but it is even bolder. William claims a place among the entire galaxy of the most admired classical poets, and claims for his British hero that international status which at the end of the poem he seems to reject. Writing in the 1230s, William would certainly be aware of Arthur's international fame: rather than limiting it, he wishes to secure the Britons' claim to the hero.

Unlike Gautier, William does not need to prune and reshape his source in order to focus on the hero and remove his less admirable qualities. Geoffrey's Arthur has no vices except a kind of hubris. The idea of using Arthur as *exemplum malum* is present in the French prose *Lancelot*,[14] the first redactions of which were probably contemporaneous with the *Gesta*, but William gives no sign of knowing this work. (If he did know of such denigration, he would certainly have combatted it – unless he simply ignored it, as Gautier did for Alexander). In presenting Arthur as an epic hero, William's problem was one of total scale. Because he hesitated to cut away material extraneous to Arthur as ruthlessly as Gautier had removed the excesses of Quintus Curtius, his work became

---

[14] See E. Kennedy, 'Social and Political Ideas in the French Prose *Lancelot*', *Medium Aevum* 26 (1957), pp. 91-106. On Alexander as *exemplum malum*, see Cary, *Medieval Alexander*, pp. 77-160, *passim*.

lost in the morass of dreary adaptations of the *Historia*.[15] He made the dangerous error of trying to work in two genres at once, and so did not receive the credit for the boldness of his original conception.

Both William and Gautier handle the hexameter competently, though William is more self-conscious about his mastery. Both display a range of styles and attitudes, ranging from simple versification of the source to independent purple patches.[16] William as versifier can be highly unpoetical and tedious, for he often follows Geoffrey even when the latter is employing his driest chronicle style in order to convince the reader of his veracity:

> Post illum autem Guithelinus diadema regni suscepit, quod omni tempore vitae suae benigne et modeste tractavit. Erat ei nobilis mulier, Marcia nomine, omnibus artibus erudita. Haec, inter multa et inaudita quae proprio ingenio repererat, invenit legem quam Britones Marcianam appellaverunt. (*Historia*, p.120).

> Guizelinus ei succedit; jura benigne
> regni, dum vivit, tractat; cui Marcia coniunx
> traditur, ingenio pollens, insignis et omni
> arte; novam legem statuit, de nomine eius
> nomen sortitur
>
> (*Gesta*, 1103-7)

There is nothing 'epic' here: William makes no effort to substitute poetic conviction for (apparent) factual accuracy. Apart from slight condensation, he makes only those alterations demanded by the metre. This passage also displays the most irritating aspect of William's style: the excessive enjambement, each *rejet* hitting the next line like a marble and knocking another word off the end. William is concerned to squeeze Geoffrey's meaning into as few lines as possible, and he does not seem to care if he destroys the poetic rhythm in the process.

William seems to derive some amusement from adapting Geoffrey's rebarbative nomenclature into hexameters:

> Post hunc Archinayl, Rodyon, Rodericus, Eldon,
> succedunt, Samul, Pennisel, Piz, Capeyrus,
> cui Dygoellus ...
>
> (1206-8; cf. *Historia*, p.124)

No name is omitted, and the correct order is maintained, with other words deftly inserted where the metre can no longer take the

---

[15] On which see R. H. Fletcher, *The Arthurian Material in the Chronicles* (Boston, 1910; reprint, New York, 1958).

[16] On Gautier as adaptor of Quintus Curtius see Christensen, pp.102ff.

strain even after maximum flexibility has been allowed with the quantity of the vowels! Even then a few names defeat William perforce. In such cases he takes a leaf out of Horace's book[17] and cheerfully admits the difficulty, as with Gratianus and Valentinianus 'quorum sunt nomina dissona metro' (1966). The same difficulty is adroitly turned to account in the matter of Merlin's prophecies. Many adaptors of Geoffrey simply omit them; a few, like Wace, apologise and excuse themselves for doing so. The Prophecies were generally popular,[18] so a simple omission might irk some readers; but to sceptical readers their insertion would mean an obscure and tedious digression. William, abusing his poetic licence, untruthfully declares the whole collection to be unadaptable ('quorum seriem difficile est committere metro', 2498) and so holds himself excused. In contrast, he does not shrink from the famous Anglo-Saxon interchange between Vortigern and Rowena, an incident which all Geoffrey's adapters make a point of retaining:

> Inquit: 'Laverd King wasail'. Rex ergo puellae
> conspecta facie stupet . . .
> Interpres dicit: 'Responde: Drinchail!' Ille
> 'Drinchayl' inquit ei.

(2233-4, 2236-7)

William apparently finds the contrast of classical form with violently non-classical content piquant. We should convict him of unique bad taste were it not that such contrasts are plainly relished by many of his contemporaries. Geoffrey delights in Celtic nomenclature; so, apparently, does Chrétien (though not his imitators). Chanson de geste authors are fond of weird Saracen names. The thrill of strangeness may indeed be necessary to any 'adventurous' genre. However, William's literary style is not modelled on contemporary writers of fiction, but on the Latin classics, and we should expect him to prefer elegance and sobriety to exoticism. Gautier certainly does so. Faced with a plethora of spicy Persian names, he omits as many as possible, and never juxtaposes them in quantity.

Another grave lapse from classical elegance is William's passion for *annominatio*. Of course, this did not count as an inelegance in

---

[17] Horace, *Satires* I.V.87; Neil Wright reminds me that this was a topos in Silver Latin and later poetry.

[18] Wace, *Roman de Brut*, ed. I. Arnold, Société des Anciens Textes Français, 2 vols (Paris, 1938-40), vol. I, ll. 7535-42. On the Prophecies see L. A. Paton, *Les Prophécies de Merlin*, 2 vols (New York and London, 1926-7); J. S. P. Tatlock, *The Legendary History of Britain* (Berkeley and Los Angeles, 1959), pp. 403-21.

his day: it was recommended by all poetic authorities.[19] Gautier is not immune to it. William is a hopeless addict: scarcely a page of his work is exempt. Rarely does the *annominatio* contribute more than decoration for its own sake. Once or twice William may be trying visibly to outshine Gautier. For example, Gautier's

> et labi sine labe fuit non cedere cedi
> cedereque et cedi dum non cedantur inulti
>
> (III, 324–5)

may have prompted William's

> Caesar, qui ceso nomen trahis istud ab hoste,
> ne quia cederis, sis Cesar, cede Britannis
>
> (1242–3)

A hint from Gautier ('vincite iam victos', II.470) may have produced this coruscation:

> hos quos victores feci me reddere posse
> victos; quos vici, versa vice, reddere posse
> victores
>
> (1412-14)

William particularly loves to ring the changes on a single lexeme, and thus he may drive home the key idea of a passage:

> gratus ades gratis, cape sceptrum quod tibi grates
> ut capiatur agit; populo gratare Quirito,
> qui tibi gratatur . . .
>
> (1781-3)

Thus speak the Roman envoys begging Constantine to rule over them. The tone of obsessive self-abasement is flattering to a British ear – or to a thirteenth-century clerkly ear tired of hearing the insistent demands of the Roman Curia. At other times, the word-play may be reduced to a mere echo of sound: 'dum *res si*nit ipsa, *resis*te' (4131: to Mordred, that he should resist the temptation to treachery). Such echoes nag at the modern reader's mind and distract him from the meaning of what he reads. Such distraction is all too common, and it predictably increases when the narrative reaches an emotional height – normally in a set speech, where, of course, rhetorical devices come most readily to the author's pen. Obvious cleverness and emotional intensity do not go well together, and many an epic moment is, to later taste, ruined by William in this way.

Well-placed cleverness can contribute to aesthetic enjoyment, however, and some of William's efforts may be commended. The

---

[19] Curtius, *European Literature*, pp. 378-80.

most elaborate is his explanation of the name 'Angle', round which he creates an intricate web from the threads 'angulus', 'anglus', 'anglicus' and 'angelicus':

> Respondet sic Musa mihi: 'Dat patria nomen
> illud, id eventus nomen facit angulus Anglum;
> Anglicus angelicus tamen exponi solet: hujus
> nominis expositor et dictus apostolus Angli
> Gregorius populi respexit ad exteriorem
> candorem vultus, cum quondam dixerit Anglos
> angelicos; tamen angelico perversa nitore
> mens caret. Angelus est sathane hujus nominis auctor,
> forte vel interior determinat angulus Anglos
> in quo cauda riget, vel id ex ui gloria nomen
> composita exponit, sine qua gens illa futura est.

(4874-84)

He is, of course, adapting Pope Gregory's famous pun (he says so) but he first contradicts it and then inverts its meaning. William asks the Muse for the correct derivation, the Muse being (presumably) a more reliable authority than the Pope for a classical poet. 'Anglus', the Muse says, derives from 'angulus', because the Angles are crooked both physically (they notoriously have tails) and mentally. Alternatively (she says obscurely) it is because their race is destined to be inglorious: here she seems to be thinking of the genitive plural 'An-glorum', as in the title of Bede's history. Gregory was deceived by the angelic appearance of the Angles; their minds are far from angelic. In these lines, the mocking resentment of Breton for Englishman is effectively expressed in and through a display of superior mental agility.

In a more serious vein, William's word-play succeeds in giving ritual solemnity to an important moment in the poem. Writing for an episcopal patron, William wisely (and sincerely) heightens the importance of Christianity in the *Historia*. The first Christian King is Lucius, who is

> orto
> Lucifero praelucidior, nam lucet in eius
> tempore vera fides, errorum nube fugata

(1564-6)

Here, the effect does not depend solely on the clever pun, for the simile is apt: Lucius is the 'morning star' of British Christianity, and like the unfallen Lucifer he is closer to God than any of the (British) host. The 'cloud of errors' metaphor, commonplace as it is, develops the simile. We move on from the morning star to the Sun of righteousness whose rising disperses those clouds.

At best, the *annominatio* engenders a vivid, unusually antithetical, epigram, as when William describes the repeated collapse
of Vortigern's tower:

> quicquid *luc*ente *luc*erna
> *Phoe*bi *fund*atur, *Phe*bes con*fund*itur hora

(2370-1)

The balance of sound and meaning in line 2371, and the opposition
of Sun and Moon by simple alteration of the ending, are very
satisfying. The lines recall the story of Penelope and her weaving,
which William knew from Hyginus.[20] The reminder is apt, because
the reason for the collapse of the tower is as mysterious to
Vortigern as that for Penelope's lack of progress was to her suitors.

With such ornaments does William seek to enliven his narrative
and put his own stamp on it. That stamp is of the competent
craftsman rather than the inspired poet, and William's aesthetic
judgement remains inferior to Gautier's. But it is infinitely
superior to that of almost any other *Brut* adapter. Only Geoffrey
himself brought to bear on the Arthurian material as much
learning, as much determination to make use of the resources of
scholarship.

Geoffrey is a medieval writer. William, as his translator, and as
an accomplished rhetorician, is also profoundly medieval. But the
source of William's creative impulse is classical, and it is when he
imitates the classics that he achieves his best effects. Geoffrey
himself knows his standard authors, and occasionally uses the
vocabulary of classical poetry; it may be this which attracted
William to him in the first place. William, however, goes much
further. Like Gautier[21] (and like any other aspiring Latinist of the
high medieval 'Renaissance'), William fills his work with echoes
from the great Roman poets, though (again like Gautier) he
seldom borrows whole lines. Occasionally William does make
mischievously ingenious use of a familiar line in a new context.
Thus Imogen, Brutus's newly (and reluctantly) married wife, looks
back on her native shores and

> 'me miseram! quid id est? Pater, o pater! auferor', inquit

(224)

The second half of the line is borrowed from Ovid, *Ars Amatoria*
II.91, in which Icarus, having flown too near the sun, cries out as

---

[20] M. Grant, ed. and trans., *The Myths of Hyginus* (Lawrence, Kansas, 1960),
p.106.
[21] See Christensen, pp. 76-101, and footnotes in Colker's edition.

69

he falls into the sea. Imogen, like Icarus, is leaving her home, and like him, she fears danger from the sea, as she explains in the following lines ('est mihi latum/ pro tumulo pelagus', 225-6). But whereas Icarus really is about to drown, Imogen's danger is imaginary. On the other hand, Icarus is not being 'carried off' as literally as is Imogen, whom Brutus is taking on his wild search for an unknown land. The appeal to the father (Daedalus or Pandrasus) is apt in both cases, though Icarus's father is sharing his flight and can respond to the cry for help, whereas Imogen's is being left behind, and the cry is one of despair. In such cases we derive pleasure from recognising the borrowing, and admire the ingenuity of the transference.

Such momentary satisfactions are outclassed by the passages in which William sustainedly combines classical echoes with creative adaptation of Geoffrey's text. It is at such times that a touch of genuine epic magnificence can be felt. One example is Arthur's flight with the giant of St Michael's Mount, where the hero gains mythical stature as the fated slayer of a monster as awesome as Polyphemus or Cacus.[22] Another even more significant one is the last battle between Arthur and Lucius, the greatest of all the innumerable battles of the *Historia*, all of which William retells with marked enthusiasm. Battle is the epic scene par excellence, and in battle William's Arthur has the best chance of rivalling Gautier's warrior king, Alexander. However, it is not always straightforward *victory* in battle which marks the epic hero. Magnificence in defeat moves us more; or we may be asked to view with pity and terror the consequences of the hubris and nemesis which victory brings. Such is Alexander's case: his very success in war alarms nature and the infernal powers, who conspire to bring him a humiliating death by poison (*Alexandreis*, X). This idea of hubris exists in embryo in Geoffrey. Arthur wins a complete victory over Lucius, but the fruits of it are snatched away by Mordred's rebellion. No overt connection between the two events is made, and Arthur is not accused of presumption. The possibility of the connection is obvious, however, and William with his epic pretentions could not avoid making it. The chance to rival Gautier was particularly evident, too, because there is every reason to believe that Geoffrey himself had modelled Arthur's war with Lucius on Alexander's with Darius.[23] Both Gautier and Geoffrey

[22] See Morris, *The Character of King Arthur in Medieval Literature* (Cambridge, 1982), p. 78.
[23] Tatlock, *Legendary History*, pp. 312-19.

adapted the original Alexander story in order to give their hero the prestige of a crusader, defending Christian (or proto-Christian) civilisation against the infidel hordes. Such an interpretation would be doubtly attractive to the pious William.

William does not merely develop ideas culled from Geoffrey and Gautier, however. He introduces a new and potent idea of his own. This is territorial hubris, connected to spiritual hubris. If Arthur is to be a 'crusader', he must crusade for the heavenly, not the earthly, Kingdom. Territorial aggrandisement is intrinsically wrong. This conviction transcends William's own national pride:

> contenta Britannia fine
> debuit esse suo
>
> (3890-1)
>
> quis furor, o fortes! pro regno deperituro
> perdere perpetuum regnum. Perdetis utrumque
> excedendo modum
>
> (3888-90: addressed to both sides).

Geoffrey has no such idea: he is in favour of unlimited British expansion. Gautier does not stress it either: his Alexander, paving the way for Christ, follows the ruling of his tutor Aristotle, 'parce humili, facilis oranti frange superbum' (I,105). William's Arthur is in a more tragic position. He is setting up his will against that of the divine power which rules the world and assigns all things their limits. In such a contest the very world itself may be shaken. The hero cannot win, but he may be so terrifying and magnificent in his fall that we ourselves almost wish the eternal law to be suspended for his sake.

So large a concept seems at first sight beyond the scope of the genial academic we have seen so far in William. Is he not merely playing with the commonplace ideas of the folly of pride and the vanity of earthly glory? One might reply that these ideas are commonplace only because they are important. In any case, William has guarded himself against the accusation. He has called on the aid of one of the most passionate of epic poets, whose poem does indeed tell of the shattering of a world: Lucan and his *Pharsalia*. To strengthen the effect of his creative imitation of Lucan, William extends it over Arthur's next and last battle, with Mordred, thus linking the two ominous battles in a single literary construct and emphasising their conceptual unity: Siesia seals Arthur's fate, Camlann consummates it.

William's imitation of Lucan begins before the battle itself, in the rhetorical outburst at the end of book VII in which he accuses both Britons and Romans of presumption. The tone of impassioned personal concern is very like Lucan's tone throughout the *Pharsalia*. Lucan's sympathies are with Pompey, but he sees madness on both sides: *'quis furor, o cives, quae tanta licentia ferri?'* (I.8; cf. *Gesta* 3888, *'quis furor, o fortes, pro regno deperituro ...'*). Indignant horror at this madness pervades the *Pharsalia*. By adopting the same tone, William proclaims his (temporary) literary allegiance. He was, of course, not unique in this allegiance: Lucan, with his crashing rhetoric, was inevitably a medieval favourite.[24] Gautier was not immune to the attraction, and while drawing on Lucan, William is occasionally able at the same time to throw down the gauntlet to his rival.

The climax of *Pharsalia* is book VII, the battle. William is inevitably attracted by the famous opening lines (VII.1-5), describing the sun's reluctance to rise over the battlefield. Gautier had used them twice: once for the occasion of Darius's death (VII,1-16) and once for Alexander's (X,356-64). Though the basic idea is the same in all four passages, the detail is different. In Lucan, Titan disobeys the 'lex aeterna' of the universe by climbing the sky late and reluctantly; he covers himself in clouds 'ne Thessaclico purus luceret in orbe'. In Gautier's first adaptation, the whole notion is reversed: it is the moon ('Latonia ... virgo', 4-5) which is reluctant to rise, for Darius's murder is to take place treacherously by night; the sun is reluctant to set. The idea of an eternal law is retained and Christianised: 'et sacer orbis amor, quo cuncta reguntur, utrumque/ corripuit iussitque vices explere statutas' (2-8). For Alexander's death-day, Gautier inverts the commonplaces of the medieval dawn-song: the birds refuse to sing, the morning star is reluctant to shine (360-4). Once again, Fate compels the reluctant sun to rise; the Fate which rules the world is here identified with the personal fate of Alexander, who also aspires to rule the world, and the glory of the sun is compared with Alexander's: 'Extinguet Macedum tua, Phoebe, lucerna lucernam' (374). Thus Gautier sensitively enhances two dramatic moments.

William, in comparison, is melodramatic. His adaptation is more elaborate than Gautier's, for it involves three borrowings, not one. The disastrous dawn is preceded by an ominous night:

> Visibus humanis, premissa nocte, cometes
> Luciferum capud exercuit, tot regibus omen
> triste; stringes noctis aves cecinere propinquas

---

[24] M. Bendena, *The Translations of Lucan and their Influence on French Medieval Literature* (Ann Arbor, Michigan, 1976), pp.12-31.

tot procerum strages, ululantum rixa luporum
latratusque canum . . .

(3928-31)

The inspiration for this seems to be the nightmarish scene in
Pharsalia VI (687-95), in which the Thessalian witch consulted by
Sextus Pompeius speaks in the voices of beasts and natural
phenomena. For those who recognised the borrowing, the night-
mare feeling might be projected into William's scene, enhancing it.
William then uses a Virgilian borrowing whose meaning he cleverly
inverts (see e.g. *Aeneid* IV.585, IX.460). The image of Dawn
leaving the couch of Tithonus is in Virgil a gracious cliché ex-
pressing the relief and beauty of a new day. William changes the
relief to horror by playing on the legend of Tithonus's decrepitude:

Aurora maritum
decrepitum fugiens, confuso sanguine vultu,
obtusis radiis lacrimisque fluentibus orta
prestitit instantis presagia certa ruinae.

(3933-6)

Here, Dawn is personified as a *mal mariée* who seeks consolation
for her own misery by inflicting misery on the world. The horror of
the night is not relieved by dawn. Only then does William describe
the tardy appearance of Phoebus (3937-41), who, as in Lucan,
veils himself in cloud rather than look on the carnage. The three
borrowings create an impression of brooding horror which makes
up in intensity for what it lacks in subtlety. William is as well able
as Gautier to make intelligent creative use of a classical model.

In his description of the battle proper, William is unable to
follow Lucan closely, for he has to take account of his primary
source, the *Historia*. Whereas Lucan describes Pharsalus im-
pressionistically, Geoffrey describes Siesia in detail, after the
pattern of a chanson de geste: a display of the forces, a series of
single combats inspired by personal rivalry, a final attack by the
leader, and victory (pp. 267-73). Geoffrey's style is lively but
objective: he reports the emotional reactions of his characters, but
never attempts to share or direct them. William makes no radical
changes, but he alters the focus just enough to maintain an
overtone of cosmic doom. Thus, while Geoffrey, as a 'historian'
should, gives exact battle positions, William takes them for granted
and diminishes their importance by putting the whole field under
supernatural control:

dispositis igitur Laciis hic, inde Britannis,
in medium Bellona venit, gladisque ministrat
telaque militibus

(3942-4)

Lucan uses the Bellona concept – as a simile only, for he disbelieves in the direct intervention of the gods – for the worse moments of Pharsalus (VII.567-9). Lucan borrowed it from Virgil (*Aeneid* VII.703), and Gautier uses it freely (III.135; IV.411; V.206). Commonplace as it is, however, it helps William to maintain the sombre loftiness of classical epic, in which gods and humans interact, and to maintain the idea that Arthur is now subjected to a cruel and superior power. Bellona is in charge of the battle from the start, instead of representing the height of the carnage, as she normally does. Bellona has no purpose save war itself: thus William emphasises that Siesia is an unnecessary battle.

The image of Bellona is followed by that of Chaos come again:

> Strepitus et clangor et Echo
> omnia confuse reboant finguntque supremum
> advenisse diem. Rediise elementa putares
> in Chaos antiquum, rerum compage soluta
>
> (3947-50)

This is a direct Lucanian borrowing:

> sic, cum compage soluta
> saecula tot mundi suprema coegerit hora
> antiquum petens iterum chaos, ignea pontum
> astra petent, tellus extendere litora nolet
> excutientque fretum . . .
>
> (I.72-7, excluding a possibly spurious line)

For Lucan, the simile covers the whole civil war. He is referring to the Stoic cycle of destruction and renewal: the convulsion of the war is the ending of the old world. Gautier used the same image for the last great battle with Darius (IV.589-94), and William certainly has Gautier in mind as well as Lucan. It is a favourite with William, who uses it twice more (2590-1; 4188-90). The idea of a final cosmic catastrophe was consonant with Christian belief as shaped by Revelation, so its terror can be authentically felt by the medieval audience. Its force is rather diminished, however, if it is merely used to describe the clash of two armies meeting, as it is by Gautier. At William's Siesia, it is enhanced by its context. The general 'confusion' includes the confusion of morality: an unjust war provokes chaos in human souls.

After this ominous introduction, the narrative of the battle begins. William emphasises the equality and the ferocity of the struggle: 'dant vulnera mutua . . . utraque pars patitur et agit . . . sternuntque viros, sternuntur et ipsi . . . mille cadunt Britonum, perimuntur mille Quiritum' (3956-99 *passim*). The 'overall views' of the battlefield, commonplace in a chanson de geste narrative (and doubtless necessary to any account of a battle) become more prominent because the individual combats are recounted briefly: the excitement of heroic deeds never overcomes the horror of carnage.

As in the *Historia*, the climax of the battle is Arthur's attack. In Geoffrey, he exultantly exhorts his men to ferocity: 'Ne abscedat ullus vivus ... ne abeat ullus vivus, ne abeat!' (p. 272). William, significantly, omits this; his Arthur gives only a generalised encouragement. There must be no joy in this battle. He does retain Geoffrey's comparison of Arthur with a starving lion (a comparison surely borrowed by Geoffrey from classical poetry, possibly *Aeneid* X.339 or X.723). For Geoffrey's Arthur, whose physical courage and successful aggression seem to transcend human morality, it is an apt simile. It is less so for William's doomed king, but William can never resist a chance for classical allusion. He therefore tones down the force of Geoffrey's simile, ironically by expanding it. To the lion he adds an eagle: 'Veluti Jovis ales/ dispergit volucres' (4026-7). This is not a bloody image, though the King of birds is an apt symbol for this earthly king of kings.[25] As for William's lion, it is still starving and 'avidus cruoris' (4029), but it is filled not just with undiscriminating hunger, as in Geoffrey, but also with 'nobilis ira' (4027). The phrase is borrowed from Lucan (VI.487 'nobilis ira leonum'). Though the lion is savage, the verbs describing its depredations, like those of the eagle, are bloodless: 'rapit hos [tauros] et dissipat illos' (4030). Thus William, who elsewhere shows a predilection for sanguinary spectacle, here makes Arthur into an elemental, almost an abstract force, as irresistible as nature itself – but about to undergo the common lot of mortals.

The classical borrowings in this passage, especially those from Lucan, are thus used to transform Geoffrey's meaning, but only up to a point. The Britons still win a famous victory. However, the rapidity of William's condensed narration and the continuing nexus of borrowings from Lucan cause this battle to coalesce with the war against Mordred in an uninterrupted progress of Doom. The details of the last battle are far less prominent than William's comments on it, and his comments are inspired by *Pharsalia*. Once Mordred has rebelled, the situation indeed becomes intrinsically Lucanian, a 'plus quam civile bellum'. (William calls it 'bella

---

[25] The direct inspiration is probably Ovid (*Metamm.* VI.517 or *Ars Am.* III.420). William has transferred the image from an amorous to a heroic context!

intestina', snatching the phrase from Sallust *Catilina* V, having already used Lucan I.i for Brennius and Belinus, 934-5. Fratricidal warfare is a recurrent theme in the *Historia*.) Lucan sees the whole civil war as the impious conflict of 'gener' (Pompey) and 'socer' (Caesar). For 'gener' and 'socer' William substitutes 'avunculus' and 'nepos', but he slyly drives home the parallel by bidding Mordred remember the treachery of Hengist:

> nescisque quod olim [sc. Vortegirno]
> fecerat Engistus, *genero socer* impius?
>
> (4127-8)

Mordred is cast in the role of Caesar, Lucan's 'rabies populis stimulusque fuorum' (VII.557), the suppressor of liberty, the ruin of a mighty people, the consort of infernal powers. The analogy is not exact, since in Lucan it is Pompey who has foreign aid (274-83), whereas in William it is Mordred who consorts with heathen Saxons. However, it is Pompey to whom Rome looks for salvation (369-76), just as, in William, Arthur is the defender of British liberty (IX.4124-7). Rome, Lucan laments, will not even have the consolation of receiving Pompey's tomb (36ff). Similarly, Arthur will have no tomb in Britain, for 'mortis ianua clausa/ creditur Arturo' (4209-10). Pharsalia involves patricides and fratricides ('turba ... quae patrum iugulas, quae pectora fratrum/ sperabat', VII.181-3) (Lucan, 180-4), and the horror of the battle is like the collapse of nature (134-7). Arthur's last struggle is no less horrible:

> In jugulum fratris intendit frater, anhelat
> filius in patrem; victa pietate paterna,
> inminet exicio nati pater: omnia jura
> nature confusa jacent ...
>
> (4107-10)

Arthur, like Pompey, impresses on his men the justice of their cause, the former invoking the 'pia causa ... patriam defendere nostram' (4181), the latter 'patriam carosque penates' (346). All their efforts are in vain, however, for fate is against them. Pompey 'sensit ... fata suae contraria menti' (86), and William remarks of his battle 'fatorum contra decreta venire/ nulli permissum est' (4158-9). Both battles mean the downfall of a nation which had virtually achieved world domination (Lucan, 415-27; William, 4138-55, where Arthur's conquests are reviewed to show Mordred his apparent invincibility).

One of Lucan's major themes, in book VII as throughout, is the Romans' loss of liberty. Similarly, British liberty is William's major theme of all, and although it is not stressed at this particular point, it dominates the rest of the poem (see further below, pp.105-9). The Lucanian echoes in the battles of Siesia and Camlann ('Canibula') set the tone for the concluding books, and they accord excellently with Geoffrey of Monmouth's notion that Arthur's reign was the Britons' last success before they plunged into irreversible decline.[26] This double inspiration allows William to unite 'historical' sobriety with something of epic grandeur.

One aspect of William's narrative here is contrary to Lucan's. Lucan sees the disaster of Pharsalia as the final proof that 'mortalia nulli/ sunt curata deo' (VII.454-5). As a Christian author, William is concerned to emphasise God's continual intervention in human affairs. Throughout his poem he accentuates Geoffrey's already insistent idea that the Britons are a chosen people, finally (like the Jews) rejected by God because of their sins. Arthur has divine favour, but loses it through his excessive ambition when he marches on Rome: 'Deus opposuit tantis sua numina votis' (4062). Mordred, unbeknown to himself, is guided by the devil, who seeks consolation for his own fall by involving Mordred in a similar one:

> Cedere te regi [i.e. be reconciled with Arthur]
>   vetat angelus ambicionis,
> et memor ipse sui casus causeque ruinae,
> consimile capiens te crimine tollit in altum
> ut te deiciat lapsum graviore ruina.
>
> (4133-6)

'Solamen miseris socium habuisse doloris'! Thus the war between Arthur and Mordred (his most trusted counsellor, as Lucifer was once closest to God) becomes an echo of the cosmic conflict. Not even the Grail writers were to bring out this idea so clearly again. William would need no other source for it than Geoffrey's text and his own imagination, but he may also have had *Alexandreis* in mind. Though Alexander is pre-Christian, his vast success could not occur without God's favour, and it alarms Nature and Lucifer, who agree to put an end to him (X.108ff) by the instrument of Proditio's willing tool, 'meus Antipater' (150). At the same time, Alexander, like Arthur, merits his own downfall by limitless ambition (191-204). If Gautier's pagan Alexander is part of God's universal designs, then of course William's Christian Arthur must be.

His treatment of the story of Arthur's downfall shows that by creative imitation of the classics, William is capable of increasing

---

[26] See R. Hanning, *The Vision of History in Early Britain* (New York, 1966), pp.137-40.

the power and variety of at least part of Geoffrey's narrative. His poetic talent is not adequate to sustaining such grandeur throughout; he can descend to verbal cleverness, and often he merely versifies. The purple patches are too obviously sewn in, whereas Gautier (for all his frequent aridity) does make his seem part of the fabric, forcing a unity of style and conception on sometimes unpromising source-material. William could equal Gautier *en petit*, but not overall.

To be fair to William, however, we must not compare him exclusively with Gautier. Rivals they were, but not on exactly the same ground. To estimate more truly how well William succeeded in adapting Geoffrey, we must compare him with another successful adapter. The obvious candidate is Wace. Wace has no epic pretensions; down-to-earth, cheerfully ironic, he gives his public their 'history' in easily digestible form. Will William's 'epic' qualities shine the brighter by contrast?

William and Wace

If William knew any of the numerous vernacular Arthurian works which had appeared between Geoffrey's time and his, he gives no sign of it in his writing. Certainly he shows no knowledge of Wace, and would have thought of him (if at all) as being of a different literary world. We may therefore consider their works as independent adaptations of a common source. Indeed, they are polar opposites in many ways. Wace is a kind of popular historian, encouraging the bright but unlearned layman to understand 'history' from the perspective, and in the vocabulary, of his own day, attributing motives, commenting perceptively but often irreverently, always trying to imbue the narrative with life, variety and colour.[27] William, in contrast, is scholarly, self-assured, not scorning a wide public but refusing to descend to its level. They may be compared as adaptors, as story-tellers and in their personal attitude to the *Historia*.

Both William and Wace are adaptors, not 'translators'. Their rendering must be acceptable in the terms of its new medium. Obviously Wace, working in a vernacular which lacks many of the syntactic resources of Latin, and in short rhymed verses, has further to go than William. William, however, is working within a

---

[27] Cf. Arnold, *Roman de Brut*, Vol. I., pp. lxxxviii-xc.

poetic convention defined by centuries of expert practice, and may be as hampered by this as Wace is in his own medium. As an example of their methods let us take the brief encounter between Gawain and the Emperor at the battle of Siesia (*Historia*, 271-2; *Gesta*, 4007-16; *Brut*, 12829-68). Geoffrey stresses the eagerness of the two young men for combat and glory, and the extent to which they are evenly matched. The incident occupies only four sentences: it is one of those indecisive clashes which often occur in hand-to-hand battle. William has three sentences whose narrative content is virtually identical with Geoffrey's, but the two versions have scarcely a word in common:

Historia	*Gesta*

Walwanius turmas, ut praedictum est, infestans invenit tamen aditumque petebat, et in imperatorem irruit, et cum illo congressus est. At Lucius, prima juventute florens, multum audaciae, multum vigoris, multum probitatis habebat, nihilque magis desiderabat quam congredi cum milite tali, qui eum coegisset experiri quantum in militia valuisset. Resistens igitur Walwanio, congressum ejus inire laetatur et gloriatur, quia tantam famam de eo audierat. Commisso diutius inter se proelio, dant ictus validos et clypeas ic tibus praetendendo uterque neci alterius imminere elaborabat.	porro Galganus, quo nil ardencius optat Caesaris impetui velox, velocis ad instar fluminis occurrit, et eum stricto
	        impetit ense.
	Lucius exultat, quia cum tam milite forti,
	
	cum tam magnanimo potuit certamen inire Ambo pares etate, pari probitate chorusci, viribus equales, equali mente superbi, mutua bella gerunt, crebros dant
	        ensibus ictus.

William, as so often, has condensed, and some of the colour has gone from his account. However, he has abstracted the essentials and his words render them with forceful dignity. The juxtaposition of the river simile with word 'ardencius' may seem incongruous, but is probably a deliberate play of ideas designed to keep the reader on the alert. The shock of Gawain's drawn sword against Lucius's 'impetus' gives an almost physical impression of their perilous meeting. William's second sentence makes Geoffrey's look verbose. The chiasmic structure of lines 4012 and 4013 conveys in itself what Geoffrey conveys in many more words, the equal merit of the combatants. Line 4016 is colourless in comparison with Geoffrey's final sentence, but it presents the scene with unimpeachable clarity. William's lines would score full marks as a school exercise in abstraction, but they also have balance, elegance and even a degree of epic weightiness.

Wace's inclination is all against brevity and abstraction, but on analysis his spreading octosyllabics often turn out to contain little new detail. He tells us at the start that Gawain was tireless in battle (12829-82), but we can deduce this anyway from his vigorous attack on Lucius. Gawain's determined search for the emperor is revealed in

> Tant ad alé et tant ad fait
> et tant enpeint et tant retrait
> l'empereur ad rencuntré
>
> (12837-9)

Geoffrey says the same in the vivid word 'turmas *infestans*'. William has lost this detail, but we may ask (in his defence) whether it was worth Wace's three extra lines, especially as the actual attack is then related baldly:

> De grant vertu s'entreferirent,
> Mult furent fort, pas ne chaîrent.
>
> (12843-4)

Modern-minded Wace is, of course, thinking of a joust, whereas the Latinists (like their classical predecessors) envisage a combat on foot. Another new idea slips in with Lucius's hopes of boasting of the encounter afterwards. The Latinists say rather that he wanted to put himself to the test, to prove something to himself. Wace has coarsened the idea, perhaps deliberately. In describing the fight, Wace passes automatically into a standard chanson de geste description, lightly inspired by Geoffrey's shock of shields:

> des escuz volent les asteles
> et des aciers les estenceles
>
> (12859-60)

He ends with another extrapolation:

> S'il eussent le champ commun,
> tost fust la fin faite de l'un
>
> (12863-4)

– though if they are so evenly matched, how is it that one or the other would succumb 'tost'? Does he mean that the emperor would have been the one to succumb ('por poi ne l'orent ja perdu', 12865)? It seems that Wace allows himself to be carried away by the story, and for a moment it develops freely in his imagination. The suspicion that the 'translator' may at any moment escape from his model's control does, in fact, make one of the charms of Wace's *Brut*. When reading the *Gesta*, we admire rather the controlled and analytical reading of his model which enables William to highlight its essentials. Both authors serve their original well in their way, but it must be admitted that, where neither has a particular interest in the current narrative, they find it extremely difficult to beat Geoffrey on his own ground, for he is a master story-teller.

As an example of the rival merits of all three authors as story-tellers we may take an episode which Geoffrey himself seems particularly to have enjoyed. This is the story of Corineus, the bluff giant-killer and eponymous hero of Cornwall whose adventures savour of folklore, more strongly than anything else in the sophisticated *Historia* except Arthur's own giant-killing activities. Behind folklore there often lurks myth, and the myth of the monster-slaying hero is universal and can be narrated on any level. Here, then, is a theme which can appeal both to Wace, familiar with contemporary European legend, and to William, connoisseur of classical mythology.

Geoffrey introduces Corineus thus:

> ... vir modestus[!], consilii optimus, magnae virtutis et audaciae. Qui, si cum alio gigante congressum faceret, ilico obruebat eum, acsi cum puero contenderet. (p.85).

William simply adapts this description to his metre (306-9). Wace, either deliberately or through hasty reading, distorts the vital point:

> Corineus esteit mult granz,
> hardis et forz *come gaianz*.
>
> (781-2)

Geoffrey makes it clear later that Corineus is exceptionally large and strong, but the fact remains that Wace has failed to tell us about his special talent, which is to prove so useful!

Corineus immediately becomes Brutus' strongest ally. His first exploit is to pick a quarrel with the Aquitanians, in whose preserves he is caught trespassing while leading a foraging expedition:

> Quibus cum Corineus respondisset licentiam huius rei nequaquam debere haberi, irruit unus ex illis, Imbertus nomine, et curvato arcu sagittam in ipsum direxit. Vitavit eam Corineus cucurritque ocius in Imbertum et arcu, quem tenebat, caput ei in frusta contrivit. (p.86)

Corineus's brutal dexterity – justified because he was not the aggressor – is entirely typical of him. Evan Geoffrey's severely 'factual' narrative conveys excitement. It inspires both William and Wace to transfer the quarrel into direct speech and to expand the narrative. William makes it into a clash of Virgilian heroes.

81

Corineus is not just on a practical foraging expedition, he is 'apros/ insectans aliasque feras in montibus altis' (323-4). 'Hymbertus' addresses him with powerful and lofty scorn:

> O stolidi miserique viri, mortique propinqui,
> que vos in saltus regis dementia duxit?

(326-7)

The packed 'i' sounds of line 326 convey angry disdain, which Corineus takes 'placide' (330), and he replies with the calm logic of an advocate doubled with a philosopher:

> 'Lex veterum commune facit genus esse ferarum;
> sic hic nulla tuo facta est injuria regi.'

(331-2)

This is not Geoffrey's hot-tempered hero, but a steadfast thinker aware that his cause is just. Corineus only uses violence as a last resort, after Hymbertus is seen (in a happy phrase) 'utens pro lege sagitta' not once but three times (334-6). At this, the hero 'frangit caput eius, eumque/ destinat at Stigios (336-7). The last expression is common enough in classical poetry (William has innumerable variations on it), but it maintains the mythic dignity of the scene. We might be looking at figures on a Grecian urn.

Wace, as we should expect, gives the conversation a colloquial turn. The Aquitanians speak collectively, with the authority of the king's verderers confronting a poacher:

> Li reis, ço dient, ad fait vié
> qui'il n'i ait bersé ne chacié
> ne adesee veneisun
> en la forest, se par lui nun ...

(819-22)

Corineus replies with simple defiance, not (as in William) with justification:

> 'se vostre reis l'ad defendu
> de sa defense rien ne sai,
> ne jo neiient ne l'atendrai'

(826-8)

The rest of the incident is briefly told, and Corineus's slaying of Humbert is described in chanson de geste style: 'parmi le chief tant l'embati,/ que la cervele en espandi' (833-4). Wace adds nothing save a little liveliness in the quarrel; William sets it in a new, grave, heroic dimension. Which version one prefers is a matter of taste, but William here shows the greater skill and attention.

Corineus also dominates the ensuing battle between Trojans and Aquitanians. In Geoffrey's Latin the notions, and even some of the idioms, of the chanson de geste are perceptible. Corineus, with the confident individualism of a Roland, turns the whole tide of battle by his unaided efforts. Losing his sword, he seizes a double-headed axe 'cum qua quemcumque attingebat a summo usque ad imum disjungebat' (p.86), to the wonder of his allies. He boastfully chides the enemy, and provokes an opponent to single combat; the opponent is forthwith cloven in twain, after which the enemy turn and flee. Though classical heroes are equally given to vigour and boastfulness in battle, Geoffrey's spirit here is wholly medieval. It is perhaps for that reason that Wace makes no attempt to gild the lily, but confines himself to translation and summary. Indeed, some vigour is lost. In Geoffrey, Corineus's onrush causes picturesque carnage: 'huic brachium cum manu amputat; illi scapulas a corpore separat; alii caput uno ictu truncat; alteri crura a summo dissecat'. Wace ignores this, even though it is easily translatable into the anaphoric style which he favours ('tant fist ... tant fist ...' etc.). He substitutes the outworn simile of the lion pursuing sheep (912).

William, without altering the sequence of events, transforms the style of the narrative. Geoffrey and Wace bring us close to the action: we, with Brutus, wonder at the vivid, tumultuous ferocity of Corineus. With William, we are at such a distance that the living figure is almost hidden under a cloak of metaphor. Corineus is in turn a torrent sweeping down from a mountain-side, a wolf among sheep, a starving lion among the herds (349-55). None of the metaphors is original; William uses all three elsewhere, and Wace lights independently on the second. They are expressed here with a touch of vision, however:

> torrentis and instar
> qui de monte cadit horrendo turbine, mentis
> irate ductus ...
>
> (348-50)

The patterned *r*s, *n*s and *t*s help to convey the sense of a rushing and turbulent stream, and the striking phrase 'horrendo turbine', emphasised by the rhythm of the line, makes this more than an echo of the Virgilian original (*Aen.* X.603), where the torrent and the whirlpool are separate comparisons.

William has the advantage over Wace of being able to use Geoffrey's actual words. (It is not, of course, always an advantage!) In this episode he takes a phrase which already has a classical ring: '[soleo ...] ternos ac quaternos ad Tartara detrudere' (notice that Geoffrey has carefully broken the poetic cadence by substituting 'ac' for 'atque'). In Geoffrey it is said by Corineus in reference to giants he has killed elsewhere. William puts it in the narrative with reference to Corineus's present victims:

> quemcumque bipenni
> quam tenet assequitur, divisum *in Tartara trudit.*

(356-7)

Again the phrase is far from original – it is more striking, because less usual, in Geoffrey – but it makes a vigorously alliterative conclusion to the hexameter, while dissociating us, again, from the bloody immediacy of the battle. Foes are not cloven ('disjungebat' is Geoffrey's word) 'a summo usque ad imum', but 'divisi', an equally complete but more formal operation! The idea of Tartarus is taken up shortly afterwards in a far more imaginative phrase:

> callis qui ducit ad Orcum
> quamvis sit latus, strictus tamen esse videtur
> hiis quos occidet Corineus.

(372-4)

This is austere humour here, but one's mental picture of a vast throng of disembodied souls is an impressive one. It contrasts absolutely with Geoffrey's very physical vision of flying limbs!

Some would say that William's version lacks the liveliness of Geoffrey's/Wace's and adds nothing very original of its own. In context, however, it is framed within two almost ritualistic evocations of full battle (345-9, 277-81), and (again) has the combination of energy and stillness of the figures on a Grecian urn. The generalising phrases, the extended similes, recall the battle-scenes in the last books of the *Aeneid*, though as usual there is little direct imitation. Doubtless William, like Virgil himself, preferred to contemplate battle from a safe and literary distance, but that does not make their descriptions less worth reading.

The climax of Corineus's career is inevitably his fight with a giant, Goemagog (*Historia*, pp.81-2). This foreshadows Arthur's fight with the giant of Mont Saint-Michel. Wace takes his cue from Geoffrey's 'instat Corineus, instat gigas', and builds his whole description on the contention of equal forces (1116ff, especially 1116-30). The result is an excellent evocation of a wrestling match, given immediacy by the jongleresque 'es ... vos' (1119), 'dunc veïssez' (1113). Each limb contests with its rival, 'braz a braz ... piz contre piz, lez contre lez ... pied avant et pied ariere ... des dos ... des peitrines ... des jambes'. We can almost feel the terrific effort, hear the grunts for breath, and we certainly sympathise as we view their empurpled faces on which even the eyebrows twitch with agonised effort (1136). The second phase of the combat is more lively: a torrent of verbs replaces the balanced pairs of nouns (1133-50). Something has to give: in the end it is three of Corineus's ribs (1150). All of this is built up from two sentences in Geoffrey. In Geoffrey, as in Wace, the combat culminates in the magnificent horror of Goemagog's fall from the clifftop. It is an exciting moment, but Geoffrey slackens it somewhat by adding a calculation: 'Corineus [carrying Goemagog] ... *quantum* velocitas *pro* pondere sinebat, ad proxima littora cucurrit'. The apparent concern for accuracy and verisimilitude is commendable in a (pseudo) historian, but much better judged in Wace's:

> ovri ses mains, lascha ses braz,
> cil fud pesanz, si prist tel quaz ...
> n'i remist os a depescier

(1161-2, 1164)

There is an instant of horrid suspense as Corineus relaxes his grip, before the weight of the giant topples him towards the rocks far below. Here, Wace's pictorial imagination and rich vocabulary give us the thrill of a *chose vue*.

This combat is far less congenial to William. He succeeds with Arthur's giant because he gives him a mythic dimension; the basically onomastic legend of Goemagog does not strike William as expansible with the same heroic *gravitas*. An avalanche of enjambements (485-509: only five of these lines are end-stopped) betrays his uneasiness, as does his word-play, which is even denser than usual. By a kind of convergent evolution, William's play on lexemes produces an effect slightly similar to Wace's as the enemies contend 'pectore pectus/ frontem fronte' (490-1). There is a slight imaginative projection as Corineus *feels* his ribs breaking (478), but there is none of the thrill of Wace's account, or even the coloured vocabulary of Geoffrey's 'letabile monstrum' falling 'per abrupta saxorum' and staining the sea red with his blood. In William he simply(!) falls to pieces: 'preceps in frusta cadit'. We must admit that William could have made far more of the story had he wished. Classical models were not lacking, Virgil's Cacus, for example; Corineus is certainly a good approximation to Hercules.

It is, in fact, hard to predict which incidents will inspire William, apart from battles and political discussions. Wace, on the other hand, seldom fails to respond to the emotional or the picturesque. A good example of this, in which Wace indisputably scores over William, is the little-known but touching story of Tonvenna, who reconciles her sons Brennius and Belinus on the field of battle

(*Historia*, pp.114-15). Her appeal to Belinus in Geoffrey is a textbook example of persuasory rhetoric. She prefaces it by baring her breasts to him – a kind of appeal which is actually quite common in classical literature.[28] Her decrepit appearance and hobbling gait are meant to arouse pity in the reader, and doubtless do in Belinus and the armies between which she passes (p.114, l.13). They certainly inspire Wace, who adds the dramatic (and, to a twelfth-century audience, presumably shocking) gesture by which Tonvenna tears away her bodice to reveal the withered bosom of age (2721-4). Her speech in Wace (2729-816) is peppered with incremental repetition, and is as rhetorical in its way as Geoffrey's, but the naturalistic rhythm of the octosyllables, the greater expansiveness (the speech is twice as long as Geoffrey's, though it adds no new arguments), the emphatic *tutoiement*, the frequent exclamations, all concur to give it a tone of genuine passion. Wace has appreciated a point which Geoffrey repeatedly makes: that the course of history is largely decided by the *passions* of those who are in a position to influence it. As befits an author with a close affinity to the romance, and who was probably working for a female patron,[29] Wace takes a special interest in the passion felt or inspired by women, analysing their psychology in more detail than Geoffrey ever does. William (except, perhaps, in the case of Imogen) thinks differently. His treatment of the Brennius and Belinus story is symptomatic of an essential difference from Wace. If William is to follow Geoffrey at all, he cannot deny the importance of passion, but he likes it to be channelled as narrowly as possible to political ends, and he likes it to be masculine. Thus he expands the speeches in which Brennius's counsellors urge him to indulge his jealousy and ambition by rebelling against his brother (893-901; *Historia*, p.109). He turns the challenge from Brennius to Belinus into direct speech to emphasise the former's possessiveness and ferocity (924-30; reported speech in *Historia*, p.109). But Tonvenna's intervention, playing on gentler emotions, is reported in only three lines (1006-8).

We may generalise these comments. William does not like women at all. He cannot avoid the pathetic story of Estrildis, but he tells it in his driest style (545-96). The story of Cordilla is much abbreviated (669 ff). The story of Igerna inspires a couple of nice

---

[28] The original inspiration was probably the *Little Iliad*, in which Helen apparently won Menelaus's mercy at the sack of Troy by baring her breasts.

[29] Arnold, *Brut*, p.xxviii.

touches: Uther at his great feast 'fieri Gorlosius optat' (2905), which he is actually about to do with Merlin's help; three days and three nights are required for the begetting of Arthur, an apposite borrowing from the classical legend of Hercules. Apart from that, William's account is deeply disappointing, especially in comparison with Wace's.[30] Ronwen is of some interest to William, not for her feminine charm but for her political importance, and above all for her paganism, which turns Vortigern into a black traitor against the Faith:

> nam mas et femina cultus
> disparis esse pares divina lege vetantur.
> Non tibi [sc. Vortegirno] sed regno virgo Germanica nubit.
> (2246-8)

Wace also condemns this betrayal (6993-6), but unlike William he is concerned to convey the strength of the sexual temptation: the smile, the kiss, the fair face, the alluring body, appearing to the King through a drunken haze (6972-88). With Wace, we enjoy the scene even while we disapprove; William reports the facts with the distasteful accuracy of a police witness.

Two of William's rhetorical set-pieces do depend on female emotion: Imogen's farewell to her native land (224-34; cf. p. 69 above) and the anguished farewells of a Roman maiden to her lover, who is about to go off to fight Arthur's army (3560-87). However, although these speeches are meant to express the deepest feelings of the speaker, the reader's reaction is, and is meant to be, purely intellectual. In the first we are delighted(?) by a clever conceit on the idea of death-in-life and of the assorted ways to death offered by the classical ocean:

> predulci me voce vocant syrenes edendam;
> Scilla suis canibus promittit ferre frequenter
> exequias vive, si recte vita vocari
> talis vita potest, que pejor morte videtur ...
> (228-30)

In the latter, William flatters one of his favourite models, Ovid, by imitation of the *Heroides*. His maiden, like Ovid's Ariadne, is driven by despair to the wildness of a Bacchante (3370-3; *Heroides*, X.47-8). Like Ovid's Laodamia, she tells her beloved that this war does not concern him (3757-9; *Heroides*, XIII.77-8), and she shudders at the very sound of the enemies' names (3582-3; *Heroides*, XIII.53-4, with place-names instead of personal ones).

---

[30] On Wace's handling of it see my article in *Arthurian Literature* IV, esp. pp. 76-7; on the Hercules borrowing, *Character of Arthur*, pp. 24-5.

Laodamia is particularly terrified by Hector (6506), as the Roman maiden is by Arthur (3580-1). William lacks Ovid's urbane skill in weaving a tissue of feminine apprehensions, but he fully shares the latter's indifference to genuine sentiment. The implied comparison of Arthur's war with the Trojan war is of more value to William than any feminine emotion: he is, after all, trying to do for Arthur what Homer did for Achilles (see 2976, 2978-80). William, in fact (doubtless with his clerkly patron well in mind) seems to think that the importance of women in a work is in inverse proportion to its status as a respectable piece of literature, and certainly to its status as an epic. He is by no means alone in this view. His epic model and rival, Gautier de Châtillon, banishes female complications from the *Alexandreis* – save for the brief visit for breeding purposes of the Amazon queen, who with her single breast and 'barbara simplicitas' (VIII.22-3, 28) is as unromantic an object as can well be imagined. In this respect William is in the same position vis-a-vis Wace, Chrétien and their school as is Gautier vis-a-vis the Alexander romances. This distancing must be deliberate in each case. The same distance exists between the original *Roland*, with its bare mention of Aude, and the thirteenth-century and later retellings which wallow in sentiment on her behalf.[31] It exists between the Lavinia of the *Aeneid* and the Lavine of the *Eneas*. Is it simply the difference between 'epic' and 'romance' versions? If one is seeking easy definitions, one can say that it is. But the epic genre is not without memorable female characters, beginning with Helen, culminating perhaps in Dido, resuming in the immortal Guiborc of the Guillaume cycle. Nor is the romance genre wholly dominated by women, and certainly not by women who participate in the main action. By banishing women as far as possible from his epic world, William narrows it and unnecessarily impoverishes its emotional range, for unlike Gautier and (most particularly) the *Roland*, he fails to channel into man-to-man relationships the feelings of passion and tenderness which he is reluctant to acknowledge between man and woman. Dignity and austerity, if too evenly sustained, begin to look like empty posturing. In this domain we must judge Wace to be not merely different, but superior.

Any adaptor of Geoffrey's *Historia* ultimately stands and falls by his treatment of Arthur. Most certainly this is true of William, by his own claim. It is also true of Wace, whose attitude to Arthur is vital to the future literary development of that hero. Now, *Brut*

---

[31] On retellings of the *Roland* see W. W. Kibler, 'The *Roland* after Oxford: The French Tradition', *Olifant* 6 (1978-9), pp. 275-92.

authors who wish to set their own stamp on the Arthurian material always find themselves in a dilemma. Geoffrey's narrative framework is closely woven, his time-scheme is strict and he keeps Arthur almost permanently on a war footing. Outside Geoffrey's work, however, and contrasting with it, there was from the beginning another source of Arthurian information, which, all the indications go to show, was loosely organised, timeless, and depended on keeping Arthur in a basically peaceful realm: 'romance' narrative, available orally at first, and in written form from Chrétien's time onward. Any new material injected into the *Historia* was almost bound to come from 'romance' sources, and was equally bound to ruin the balance of the original, but without such injections a retelling of Geoffrey would become stale and flat. In other words, any creative adaptor of Geoffrey was bound to ask himself what could be done with the Arthur of peacetime.

At first sight, we should not expect William to be much perturbed by the question. Epic is always concerned with fighting, and a warlike Arthur will most easily qualify to rank with Achilles or appeal to a 'Lucanus gravis' (2980-3). If William knew either Breton Arthurian legends or French vernacular romance (whose development was at its height in the early thirteenth century)[32] he gives no sign of it. He could no more include such exuberances than Gautier could take on board the fantasies of the Alexander romance. As a fervently nationalistic Breton/Briton (see 4911-20) he can also be expected to banish from his work anything which would savour of the frivolity and untruthfulness for which Breton conteurs were denounced by the Latinate literary establishment.[33] However, William is aware that if Arthur is no different in kind from the other warriors of the *Gesta* then his unique status as epic hero will be threatened. If he is seen only as a conqueror and destroyer, then the portrait will turn out to be negative, even distasteful, in the end, since the conquests are not destined to endure. Some thought must be taken for Arthur's peacetime establishment.

Wace seems to arrive by a different route at a similar conclusion. Though he can describe a battle competently enough (no twelfth-century story-teller could fail in such an elementary duty) he is more interested in the clash of human emotions and interests than

---

[32] Loomis, *Arthurian Literature*, pp. 52-63.

[33] See Loomis in *Arthurian Literature*, 52-71 *passim*. References to the stupidity of the Bretons (and insular Britons), especially because of their belief in Arthur's return, abound in Provençal as well as Latin literature: see Lejeune, *ibid.*, p. 396.

that of swords. He likes to observe the comedy of human society with an alert, and at times mildly sardonic, eye. His inclinations, in fact (and doubtless those of his audience) incline him towards a 'romance' attitude. Later romancers were not slow to realise this.[34] Wace, however, has no desire to be a romancer himself: his job is to popularise history, not to fictionalise it. He is indeed, at great pains to avoid the latter charge, for he refuses to repeat even the most credible of the 'aventures' and 'merveilles' of which he has heard told of Arthur's reign (9987-98). (We, as literary historians, may lament his reticence, but we must also acknowledge that without it Arthur might never have attained the respectability which made him so universally acceptable as a theme for vernacular literature). What Wace can do, however, is to create a background for the peacetime Arthur against which other authors, not bound to the chronicle mode, can set stories which will be colourful, credible, and firmly attached to the accepted Arthur of history. And Wace, in seeking to do this, struck gold; he brought in (or invented) the Round Table, an artefact of unimpeachable credibility which an infinite number of tales could be brought to focus. William of Rennes hit on no such inspired symbol, but his description of Arthur's peacetime court is no less interesting than Wace's.

Beate Schmolke-Hasselmann has pointed out that Wace's own interpretation of the significance of the Round Table is that it imposed equality on those who sat around it, an idea which was not adopted by most of Wace's successors. Wace probably imposed this meaning for political reasons.[35] It is interesting to find that William, without mentioning the Round Table (and without giving the smallest sign that he knew Wace), also imposes an ideal of equality on Arthur's court:

> nobilium interea de quantumcumque remotis
> partibus adveniunt. Juvenes rex letus honorat,
> Neoptolomosque facit, et equis armisque decorat,
> muneribusque datis ditat. Venientibus eius
> omnibus aula patet, nec queritur unde vel qui
> quis veniat. Nichil propruim, communia cuncta
> Rex regum tantum servat sibi nominis usum.

(3276-83)

---

[34] See M. Pelan, *L'Influence de Wace sur les romanciers de son temps* (Paris, 1931).
[35] 'The Round Table: Ideal, Fiction, Reality', *Arthurian Literature* II, pp. 41-70, especially 49-68.

It is the last four lines which are startling. Up to this point William has followed Geoffrey (p. 238), though with an increased emphasis on Arthur's kindness to young knights. The use of 'neoptolomus' ('tyro, novus miles' in Ducange) in line 3278 is particularly felicitous here, conveying that Arthur, the modern Achilles, loves these young men as his sons. This is in accordance with the romance tradition, in which Arthur is consistently seen as a father-figure,[36] but it need not be inspired by that tradition: to be 'fathered' at a strange court was normal experience for a young thirteenth-century nobleman. Thus far, William reproduces Geoffrey's aristocratic and monarchistic ideal. But that the court should be open to *all*, without any distinction of rank, that possessions should be held in common, and that Arthur should keep only the name of King: this is in violent contrast with both the literature and the practice of the age. It is also in conflict with the rest of the *Gesta* account of Arthur, in which he behaves just as autocratically as he does in the *Historia*. It may remind us of Wace's Round Table, but the spirit is quite different. Wace's Arthur apparently does not sit at the table, and his aim in instituting it is to keep the quarrelsome barons in their places, which are well below his.[37] William's Arthur is barely *primus inter pares*, and in this he is unique in Arthurian literature. In many romances Arthur is a far from commanding figure, but he does not renounce his right to command. And while the Arthurian knights are supposed to be a brotherhood ('supposed' being often the operative word), nowhere else to my knowledge is it suggested that they held property in common. It is possible that William had in mind the contemporary court of St Louis, who did admit humble folk to his court, and whose way of life was so simple that he scarcely looked like a King.[38] In his youth he did indeed have only the name of king, but by the 1230s he was already exercising that vigorous control which was to make him the most powerful and respected monarch in Christendom.[39] However, not even his own barons seem to have approved of his sobriety, in an age when magnificence was a political weapon.[40] It is not perhaps

[36] *Character of Arthur*, p. 108.
[37] Schmolke-Hasselmann, 'Round Table', p. 66.
[38] See Joinville, *Histoire de Saint Louis* (ed. N. Corbett, Quebec, 1977), §22, p. 87; §667, p. 223; Guillaume de Saint Pathus, *Vie de Saint Louis*, ed. H. Fr. Delaborde (Paris, 1899), p. 79.
[39] See E. Hallam, *Capetian France* (London and New York, 1980), pp. 211-15, 262.
[40] Even Joinville, §95, p. 103, remarks disapprovingly on Louis's precocious sobriety of dress.

very likely that a Breton of this time would hold Louis up as a model. William may instead be remembering classical descriptions of the Golden Age, when the bountiful earth provided all that was necessary and there was no strife among men.[41] Closest to his Arthurian ideal, however, is a kind of community which would have been familiar to him. In a Benedictine monastery, all property was held in common, guests were always welcomed, and the abbot, while holding undisputed authority, was elected by the monks and was in a way *primus inter pares*.[42] If Arthur was able to maintain this sacred ideal in a secular society, his must indeed have been a Golden Age.

Thus William, like Wace, emphasises the uniqueness of Arthur's peacetime establishment. In Wace, the uniqueness is absolute. Only Arthur has a Round Table: it is his emblem. William's Arthur is uniquely, that is quintessentially, excellent, but within parameters established by the text itself. The basic idea of Arthur's peacetime court holding possessions in common and so abolishing covetousness and strife – is in harmony with the entire *Gesta*, for all its insistence on warfare. William castigates the Gauls, whose 'auri argentique fames' (1297-8, with an eye to *Aeneid* III.57) tempts them into yielding to Caesar. He criticises Arthur's later thirst for aggrandisement, which he shares with his Roman enemies, and generally he always disapproves of those who lust after others' property (who are a permanent feature of Geoffrey's Britain). By combining the ideals of the classical past and the monastic present, William sets up a powerful counter force to the aggressiveness of the *Historia*, and then brings the two forces together in Arthur, who thus becomes ideologically and structurally central to the poem, its true 'hero'. And he becomes a hero with a political message, which is as relevant to William's day as that of the Round Table was to Wace's, a theme to which we shall return (p.108 below).

The other crucial point in the Arthurian section of the *Historia* is Arthur's death. While Arthur's peacetime establishment was the

---

[41] See e.g. Ovid, *Metamm.* I.89-112; Virgil, *Georgics*, I.125-8.
[42] *Rule of St Benedict*, ed. A.J.McCann (London, 1952), pp.18, 84, 120, 126, 144-6.

starting point for the great vernacular verse romances, the mystery of his end was a vital inspiration of the romances in prose.[43] Geoffrey's deliberately ambiguous account (p. 278) invites investigation and comment from adaptors. Wace certainly feels that comment is needed, but he tackles the necessity with a deal of canny Norman scepticism. As with the oral stories of Arthurian adventure, he admits the existence of data other than the *Historia* (namely the 'Breton hope')[44] but refuses either to elaborate on it or to pass outright judgement of its trustworthiness (ll.13275-84). Instead, he transfers from earlier in the *Historia* the comment 'exitus eius dubius erit' (p.191; Wace 1384-6). Originally, this was one of Merlin's prophecies, which Wace did not translate. It is easy to find reasons for Wace's reticence over Arthur's end. As one who worked in and for Henry II's court, he would not want to antagonise either Breton or Norman opinion. The Bretons (and British) could, it was said, wax violent if their belief in Arthur's return was challenged;[45] the Normans (and Angevins) would have no wish to see such a belief – let alone the actual return of Arthur! – foment an insurrection in Brittany. A historian, however, ought always to decide on the most certain answer to a question. In this case, the most 'certain' answer, one backed up by a widely credited prophetic authority, is paradoxically one of doubt – so Wace happily opts for doubt. However, he does make one significant final comment: 'Damage fud qu'il n'ot enfanz' (13294). It seems an anodyne remark prompted by sympathy, and regret for the loss of so much excellence. But it may hint at something else. If there is no real possibility of Arthur's return, *and he had no heir*, then there can be no-one in the world today who has a right to Arthur's political heritage. Therefore there are no grounds for disputing the Angevin claim on Brittany, which was being forcibly made by Henry II just at the time when the *Brut* was being written.[46] Some years later Henry, and then Richard I, were to preside over the 'discovery' of Arthur's bones at Glastonbury and so put paid (they

---

[43] For its development see F. Bogdanow, 'The Changing Vision of Arthur's Death', in J. H. M. Taylor (ed.), *Dies Illa: Proceedings of the 1983 Manchester Colloquium* (Vinaver Studies in French I, Manchester, 1984), pp.107-23.

[44] On which see Loomis, *Arthurian Literature*, pp. 64-71.

[45] *Ibid.*

[46] The *Brut* is dated c.1155; Henry's campaigns in Brittany began in 1154. See E. D. de Saint-Sauveur, *Histoire de Bretagne* (Rennes/Paris, 1935), pp.124 ff.

hoped) to any expectations of his return.[47] Wace could not antici-
pate the discovery, but he did not put documentary obstacles in its
way, and in this he doubtless read his patron' mood aright. His
comments on Arthur's death, like those on the Round Table, are
political.

William's reaction to the narrative crux is strangely different.
Hitherto we have watched him adapting his source with caution,
though not without the use of creative imagination. He has
commented freely, adapted and interpreted, but he has never
added extraneous material. Now he throws caution to the winds
and becomes the only high medieval *Brut* adaptor to include the
legend of Arthur's *survival* on a paradise island – thus laying
himself wide open to the charge of Breton fatuity which hitherto
he has seemed anxious to avoid (2400-34). This was not a sudden
impulse, however. In the proemium to the *Gesta* he had promised
to tell 'quis fuit Arturus, que gesta, *quis exitus eius*'(14) the very
question which Wace, on Merlin's authority, declares to be
unanswerable. But why should a would-be epic want to wander off
into dubious fantasy?

Several answers are possible, based on the aims which William
sets himself in the *Gesta*. First, there is no reason why a Latin epic
hero should not be brought in contact with the Otherworld. On the
contrary, Aeneas travels among the dead and glimpses the far
future. Statius describes in technicolour the descent to Avernus of
the prophet Amphiarius (*Thebaid* VII.1-211). Even Gautier
considers an otherworld scene obligatory (X.25-216). Shall Arthur
fear to treat a similar path? However, were Gautier inspired solely
by classical precedents, we should expect to find Arthur in Hades,
or at best in the Elysian fields. Is William bowing to the pressure
of Breton, that is Celtic, tradition by putting him on a Fortunate
Isle which, while having obvious 'otherworld' characteristics, is a
land of the living rather than of the dead? This is, I think, part of
the answer. The 'regia virgo' (4224) and the mysterious 'King
Avallo' (4232) point us towards the confused mass of material
about Morgan and Avalon to be found in Celtic sources and
derivatives,[48] though it is impossible to trace William's exact
affiliations with them. It would not be surprising, however, if
William were unwilling to eliminate the idea of Arthur's survival
which was so dear to his countrymen. (It seems unlikely that he

[47] See e.g. R. Barber, *King Arthur in Legend and History* (Cardinal edn,
London, 1973), pp. 58-63.
[48] See L. A. Paton, *Studies in the Fairy Mythology of Arthurian Romance* (2nd
edn, New York, 1960), pp. 1-24 and *passim*.

had not heard of the 'discovery' of Arthur's bones;[49] indeed, his emphasis on the rival account may be a protest against that 'discovery'). He does not, however, commit himself absolutely to the story, drawing back with a prudent 'si credere fas est' (4234). Nor, significantly, does he mention the hope of Arthur's *return*, at this or any other point in the *Gesta*. Doubtless he hoped that this omission would redeem him in the eyes of the academic establishment – or the political one! Like Wace, William treads a narrow path between two beliefs; William goes further along the path than Wace, but he does not step off it.

Other factors were also at work. William's description is not 'purely' Celtic. Howard Patch, interpreting it in the light of his vast knowledge of medieval otherworld literature, found it to be a disappointing tissue of commonplace.[50] One feature, however, is striking because William has used it before. In Arthur's paradise there is 'proprium nichil ... communia queque' (4222). Arthur's earthly paradise mirrors the same ideal as his court. Indeed, with its absence of old age and sickness and its perpetual innocent dalliance of man and maid, William's paradise is not unlike the ideal of a high medieval court; it reminds us of the courtly garden of the *Roman de la Rose*. Is William saying that war and ambition make impossible the realisation, in this harsh world, of the ideal which the peacetime Arthur represented? That Arthur's fall into sin robbed Britain of its chance to become and remain an earthly paradise? The idea, if it is present, is not explicit, but it would provide a further explanation for this strangely conspicuous passage.

The final reason, I think, is literary rivalry. William obviously believes that his verse *Gesta* is an improvement on the *Historia* (which he never acknowledges as his source). However, in his other major work, the *Vita Merlini*,[51] Geoffrey too had proved himself to be a competent hexameter poet, and there he had given all the details of Arthur's passing which verisimilitude had forced him to exclude from the *Historia*. In the *Vita*, Arthur is ferried to the 'Insula Pomorum que fortunata vocatur' (908), which has virtually the same characteristics as William's paradise, and which is presided over by Morgen. The only essential difference is that

[49] Barber, *King Arthur*, p. 64, thinks that the tradition of Arthur's survival was 'still current on the Continent in William's time'; but this does not mean that the rival account had not been heard.

[50] *The Otherworld According to Descriptions in Medieval Literature* (Cambridge, Mass., 1950), p. 287.

[51] Ed. Basil Clarke, Cardiff, 1973. See ll. 906-40.

Geoffrey's island does not confer immortality, only long life (915). Even this, however, does not amount to a proof that Arthur must by now be dead, for Taliesin, who describes the island, is speaking only a few years after Arthur's passing, and is unqualified to say just how long the latter's life may yet last. If Geoffrey the poet can confer such poetic distinction on Arthur, then certainly William must go one better. He is inspired by Geoffrey and borrows from him, and he finds that the borrowing chimes in with his other ideas about Arthur. Unfortunately, he does not pause to reflect that it does not harmonise with the tone of the rest of the *Gesta* (as it does with the fantastical tone of the *Vita*). Rather than rising to great poetic heights, William seems to the reader to be lapsing from sobriety. It is no excuse to say that he is following a theme important in Arthurian literature generally. Romancers can rush in where chroniclers must fear to tread.

Having followed Wace and William thus far, we must now step back and compare their overall performance. By using the metre of the nascent romance, by showing human sympathy, by his use of colloquialism, Wace brings Arthurian story close to his readers' own experience. It is this closeness which will persist in the great romances and allow them to express the deepest concerns of medieval Man. In comparison, William's tone is elevated, distant and (in both the favourable and the unfavourable senses of the word) artificial. He is a better *poet* than Wace, and an even more conscious artist with words. At his best he combines eloquence with precision. He would have been disgusted at Wace's easy familiarity with an epic subject. Dignity, stateliness and power are his aims: he wants to give greatness to a modern theme, not modernity to a great one. Which approach should we prefer?

Wace succeeded in his aims. He successfully combined two genres which had the greatest appeal and the greatest prestige in his time. He was swimming with the literary tide: the exhilaration of that experience can still be felt by modern readers. William went against the tide. It is always dangerous to re-create a genre which once expressed the literary identity of another people, another time. The problem is worse in Latin epic because it was artificial from the beginning, imitating the Greek in both form and context. Only Virgil ever made a complete success of the transfer. Medieval poets, unaware of the true origins of the genre and far removed even from the world of its Latin practitioners, could hope to impress only those minds which had been prepared by scholarly appreciation of those Latin originals. Such minds were – and are – impressed by the *Alexandreis*; they may be by the *Gesta*. But it was

Wace who had successors, not William, and it was Wace's successors – especially Malory, the last and greatest of them – who made Arthur's story move the heart.

William, however, was not indulging in a pure literary exercise. If he failed to touch the universal human heart, he could still touch the hearts of those to whom the story was a matter of ardent faith and hope: the British. We cannot judge William fairly until we have considered him as a national poet.

William and the British tradition

William, who sets out to be Virgil to Arthur's Aeneas, has, like Virgil, a nationalistic as well as a literary aim. Virgil describes the overcoming of human passions and weaknesses which makes possible the founding of a great empire; William laments the passions and weaknesses which brought a great nation low. This theme was fully worked out by Geoffrey,[52] but it is re-expressed with unequalled fervour and eloquence by William. The right of the British people to liberty and (within just limitations) to power inspires most of his digressions and breathes life into what might otherwise become a sterile literary exercise. But what exactly did William understand by 'the British'? How do his opinions compare with those of other continental and insular 'Britons' of his time? Can he be clearly designated a 'Breton' and not a 'Briton' writer?

It is notoriously difficult in medieval writings to distinguish between Brittany and Britain. In some circumstances, as when reading certain *lais*, it may not be necessary to do so.[53] Dark Age Brittany probably had more contacts with south-west Britain, whence the Breton settlers came, than with France. Even in the high Middle Ages, the Welsh, the Cornish and the Bretons were aware of sharing a common language, a common identity, and something of a community of interests.[54] After the Conquest, both Wales and Brittany (Cornwall having long since succumbed to the

---

[52] See Hanning, *Vision of History*, pp.137-71. Hanning denies that Geoffrey's work has any moral dimension. Certainly he is not a moraliser, but his work cries out for a moral interpretation, and the connection between British sinfulness and British downfall is made amply clear.

[53] E. Hoepffner, 'La géographie et l'histoire dans les lais de Marie de France', *Romania* LVI (1930), pp.1-32, especially p.4.

[54] See J. Piette, 'Yr agwedd llydaweg ar y chwedlau arthuraidd', *Llên Cymru* 8 (1965), p.188.

Saxons) were under pressure from the same powerful eastern neighbour: the Norman – later the Angevin – monarchy. Brittany had in addition to contend with Capetian ambitions, and was in permanent danger of becoming a battleground for French and English monarchs. This common threat, however, could tend to make continental and insular Britons aware of their differences as well as their likenesses. Wales had to take account first of England; Brittany could not ignore France. Neither could claim independence; both had undergone repeated partial conquest. Nor was either strongly inclined to preach consistently the gospel of British unity. On the contrary, whatever time Welsh or Bretons had to spare from fighting invaders they usually devoted to fighting amongst themselves.[55] Under such circumstances it would take a writer of considerable vision to reconcile British and Breton interests in a unified interpretation of either past or future.

Geoffrey of Monmouth (who had imagination if not vision) did envisage British unity, but the *Historia* also has a strong inclination to separate out British (later, Welsh), Cornish and Breton interests. In fact, the work shows exactly the dual vision we should expect from an alert writer of the mid-twelfth century. But is also shows a marked favouritism towards the Bretons – so marked that Geoffrey himself has often, on no definite evidence, been claimed as a Breton.[56] Of course, if Geoffrey was really using a Breton source, we might expect such a bias, but there is no way of proving that he did. (It would be a very seductive hypothesis that William of Rennes was using not Geoffrey but that same Breton source; unfortunately, the verbal resemblances of *Gesta* to *Historia* are so close as to prove beyond doubt the dependence of the former on the latter.) Be that as it may, the fact that Geoffrey keeps or introduces a Breton bias means that he approved of it. As soon as Brittany is settled (p.159) and a distinction becomes possible, the Bretons become the best of the British, and are repeatedly asked to pull the islanders' chestnuts out of the fire for them. Arthur himself is of Breton origin, so that the apogee of British power is reached under a continental Breton. The present day insular British are treated with disdain as being 'degenerati a britannica nobilitate' (p. 303). There is no confusion of Briton and Breton in the *Historia*, where in any case 'Armorica' is the term for Brittany.

[55] For the detail behind this overview see Saint-Sauveur, *Histoire de Bretagne*; J. E. Lloyd, *History of Wales to 1282*, 2 vols (3rd edn, London, 1939).
[56] For a sharp correction to this view see O. Padel, 'Geoffrey of Monmouth and Cornwall', *Cambridge Medieval Celtic Studies* 8 (Winter 1984), pp.1-5.

Clearly, to Geoffrey the last surviving memory of British splendour is to be found there. It is deeply ironical that this author, who so scorned the Welsh, should have been enthusiastically adopted (and adapted) by them over several hundred years. It is particularly ironical that Geoffrey should apparently have been writing his gloomy concluding words in the late 1130s, a time of vigorous Welsh revival which was to profit from English division and restore effective independence to large areas of the country.[57] Bede, Geoffrey's model here, could justly speak of a cowed and retreating British race;[58] Geoffrey could not. Brittany presented, if anything, a less hopeful picture. There was an independent Breton duke, Conan III, but large tracts of the peninsula refused his sway; he was at odds with his own family and faced with rebellion by the powerful count Eon de Porhoet. Geoffrey could not imagine that praise of Brittany would particularly please his Norman patrons, for they themselves had only recently lost effective suzerainty over it.[59] Only a strong personal preference can explain the very favourable treatment given to Brittany in the *Historia*. We may well imagine that such a preference would make Geoffrey's work irresistible to a Breton Latinist already impressed with its narrative and stylistic excellences. Will not William enthusiastically develop the *Historia*'s Breton bias?

William does not give us an immediate answer. His *proemium* does not announce a Breton history (or epic), though it does announce the story of a people, not a land or a line of kings: 'Unde genus Britonum ... qualiter amisit infelix natio regnum' (12-15). The allusion to a lost *regnum* points to the insular Britons, and certainly this introduction shows that we must not expect an out-and-out reworking of the *Historia* so as to bring the Bretons into prominence. However, Geoffrey himself makes his preferences clear while never declaring them overtly, so we may legitimately expect William to follow suit. This means that we must look first at his narrative of the divergence of Breton from Briton.

In the *Historia*, the conquest of Brittany from the Gauls (pp.159-64) is a shameless act of unprovoked aggression. The ensuing settlement is a cynical piece of horse-trading between Maximianus of Britain and the erstwhile rebel, Conan. Geoffrey himself does not judge the matter in exactly that light, however.

[57] Lloyd, *History of Wales*, II, pp. 462-80.
[58] B. Colgrave and R. A. B. Mynors, ed., *Bede's Ecclesiastical History* (Oxford, 1969), p. 560: 'qui quamuis ex parte sui sint iuris, nonnulla tamen ex parte Anglorum sunt seruitio mancipati'.
[59] H. Poisson, *Histoire de Bretagne*, 4th edn (Rennes, 1966), pp. 68 ff.

Throughout the *Historia* he takes the convenient (and still familiar) view that aggression against his own side is damnable, while aggression by his own side meritorious – God being with it, of course, in both cases.[60] William, as we have already seen in the matter of Arthur's last battles, disagrees. The idea that each nation should remain within its natural boundaries (see 3890-1) is at the root of the *Gesta*. This conviction, so close to genuine 'patriotism', is by no means unexpected in a Celtic writer. Much insular Celtic literature from earliest times is imbued with an attachment to the Land so strong that its origins are felt to be magical.[61] Often this attachment expresses itself through fanatical opposition to an invader, and William never denounces a character for defending his own land. But William himself is no fanatic, and he fully recognises the right of other peoples to their own lands. The idea that Brittany was born out of bloody aggression must therefore distress him. Out of his distress comes an unbridled address to Conan, one of William's vigorous apostrophes of reprobate characters:

> O regnum minime felix! o sanguine fuso
> optentum regale decus! Conane, resi[g]na
> hoc jus injustum. Prescriptio nulla tueri
> te poterit, [quoniam] dum visceris intus habebis
> accusatricem que te[que] tuosque nepotes
> semper mordebit.

(1922-7)

The sins of the Breton fathers will, in fact, be visited on the children. William elaborates on the notion (1935-41). Here, he clearly identifies the Bretons as a separate nation, defined by geography – by their Land. Because they usurped that land, they are accursed, condemned to punish themselves eternally by their own inconstancy:

> Inconstans Britonum populus constanter in ipsa
> mobilitate viget; nunquam Ramissia virgo [Fortune]
> mobiliore rota fertur quam spes eius.

(1943-5)

A glance at the troubled history of early Brittany reveals the basis of William's denunciation. The Bretons (like the Welsh) were indeed perpetually quarrelsome; they would resist any invader heroically, only to turn on one another when the invader retreated.

---

[60] An aspect of what Tatlock calls the book's 'primitive male appeal': *Legendary History*, p. 305.

[61] See P. Mac Cana, *Celtic Mythology* (new edn, London, 1983), pp. 117-21.

William does not only speak in general, however. He ends his diatribe with a summary of the present situation:

> O regio! tibi nunc rex presidet, ante ducatus
> aut comitatus ejus; non regnum sive ducatus
> sed comitatus eris tu qui ducibus dominaris.
> Cum servis domino continget te dominari.
> Ecce dies venient quibus ad sua jura reducti,
> tristia sub pedibus Galli tua colla tenebunt.

(1946-51)

The circumstances evoked are those of the mid-1230s. Brittany was once a *regnum*, though only for a few years under Nominoë and Erispoë; readers of the *Historia* could believe in a more solid and ancient claim. It had been a dukedom since 942, when Alain Barbetorte reconquered it from the Normans and did homage for it to Louis IV. Until the time of Henry II it had been ruled by native dukes; in 1181 it was taken over by Henry's third son, Geoffrey Plantagenet, husband of the last duke's only daughter. Geoffrey and his son Arthur did homage either to the French or the English King according to the political dictates of the moment. After Arthur's murder, Brittany came into the hands of the French baron Pierre 'Mauclerc' of Dreux. Mauclerc exercised full ducal powers, though strictly speaking he held the duchy in trust for his son John, whose right to it came from his mother Alix, daughter of Constance of Brittany. In 1234, after having tried once too often to play off the French King against the English, Mauclerc surrendered to Louis IX. He was allowed to retain the duchy, but only under the strict supervision of the King, who 'presided' over Breton affairs until John came of age in 1137.[62] The distinction between 'ducatus' and 'comitatus' was, as William says, uncertain in Mauclerc's time. He called himself 'dux' or 'comes' more or less indifferently;[63] the former title was a courtesy one in his case, though his son was duke in his own right. Extrapolating from the humiliation of 1234, William foresees that Brittany will eventually lose its independence. He was right, of course, though the event was delayed for longer than he could have expected – until the marriage of Ann of Brittany to Charles VIII in 1491.[64] Soon or late, however, the bitterest aspect of Brittany's collapse, to William, is

---

[62] Saint-Sauveur, pp.105-32, 194-210; J. L. Montigny, *Essai sur les institutions du duché de Bretagne* (Paris, 1961); S. Painter, *The Scourge of the Clergy* (Baltimore, 1937); N. Chadwick, *Early Brittany* (Cardiff, 1969), pp. 230 ff; Michel, *Gesta*, p. xiv.

[63] Montigny, *Essai*, p. 22.

[64] J. Markale, *Anne de Bretagne* (Paris, 1980), p.176.

the fact that it will be merited. The trampling Gauls will be but taking back their own. Such is the conclusion which William drew from an unprejudiced reading of Geoffrey's text. It would have horrified Geoffrey.

Having thus annihilated Breton pride, William is rather in a quandary. How is he to deal with the *Historia*'s subsequent proofs of Breton superiority, and how is he to deal with questions of pan-British, Breton or insular nationalism? This inquiry throws up some interesting answers, which reveal a complex attitude to the problem.

William – who never tampers with the narrative sequence of the *Historia* – retains all the British appeals for Breton help. He does not give Brittany any greater prominence than it had in the *Historia*, but neither does he give it any less. He does not gloss over the cowardice of the remaining insular Britons (see 2091-21), or over the Bretons' success in helping them. This is not surprising, however. When the Bretons come over, they are helping the British to defend their own Land. There is nothing immoral about that. Nor is it inconsistent with William's interpretation that the Bretons should be militarily more competent than the Britons; they were only too competent in conquering Armorica unjustly. Prowess is not, in William's eyes, identical with virtue. There is virtue in it, nevertheless, if it is rightly used; William can rejoice in his countrymen's good deeds as sincerely as he castigates them for their sins. Towards the end of the *Gesta*, however, he introduces a shift of the *Historia*'s evidence which tends to restore the equilibrium of Breton and Briton. This is done through King Salemon's response to the final plea for aid (*Historia* 291-2, *Gesta* 4470-547). In the *Historia* Salemon is contemptuous and supercilious. In the *Gesta* he uses some hard words ('de stirpe leonum/ egressi lepores', 4479-80). But whereas in the *Historia* he castigates the Britons in the second person plural, in the *Gesta* he uses the first, associating his own half of the nation with the general decline. Instead of ending with a boast about Breton success, he exhorts Britons everywhere to equal their ancestors: 'Veteres didicere Britanni/ vincere, nec vinci;/ norunt dare terga Britanni' (4496-7).It is the Briton Cadwallo who admits that the best of the Britons are now settled on the continent (4501-7). Salemon's evocation of their common origin restores William to the pan-British viewpoint which he rejected in his address and denunciation of Conan. At the end of the *Gesta*, I believe, we are to consider William's comments on the Britons to be applicable to both branches of the race. If we do so, an interesting notion emerges. Geoffrey ends his book by showing how the sinfulness of the insular Britons, after the Breton migration and the glories of Arthur, brought about their downfall. To emphasise this sinfulness, the wickedness of the Saxons, heartily endorsed in the middle books, is toned down. In part, this shift of emphasis reflects a change of sources: from Nennius (heartily pro-British) to Gildas (hating the Saxons, but despising the British for their sins) to Bede (a Saxon for whom the British are a deservedly defeated enemy). It suits Geoffrey's own plan, nevertheless; and by balancing harsher criticism of the British by a calmer appreciation of the Saxons, he is able to end with something like a historian's impartiality. The British have retreated to Wales, the Saxons are in control, and that is that.

William appreciates Geoffrey's pattern, but puts it to a different final use. He has already paralleled it once, for the fate inflicted by Geoffrey on the Britons is the fate foretold by William for the Bretons, who thus become a microcosm of the British race. At the end of the *Gesta*, William again accepts the notion of British sinfulness. Indeed, he extends it, in a very striking way. Geoffrey begins it after the migration. William traces it back to the origin of the whole British race:

> Regni cepisti nomen habere
> vi gladii; tua cepta tenes, tua cepta tenebis,
> dum poterunt Britones et Saxones arma tenere.

(4859-61)

They have inherited corruption from the Trojans, 'progenies Priami, fera gens' (4862), who always loved discord and war. This goes for the Bretons as well. William, we are tempted to say, must feel this corruption in his own flesh. Does he see the whole history of the Britons as a record of evil? Is he another Gildas?

To some extent he is. We know that he detests unjust aggression, which must mean all conquest of land. No doubt he is appalled at the quarrelsomeness of his countrymen, on both sides of the Channel. One can denounce the sins of one's country, however, and still wish it well, and this is William's case. He does not speak those final, denunciatory words *in propria persona*, as he spoke to Conan and many others. He attributes them to wise and aged British people after the death of Cadwaladr, at the nadir of British fortunes. At such a dismal time people are inclined to see the worst side of everything, to lapse into defeatism, even as William himself was tempted to do when discussing present-day Brittany. William remains detached from the tirade, and after it he changes the tone. Whereas Geoffrey had accepted the Saxon

103

conquest, William, speaking for himself this time, attacks it with a fusillade of sibilants and plosives:

at genus Anglorum, stirps impia, natio fallax,
gens in marte fugax, in agendis fraudibus audax,
turba bibax, soboles mendax, poplusque bilinguis,
excedit numero Britones

(4868-71)

Michel comments with justice that such sentiments might be expected from a Welshman rather than a Breton.[65] But William is making no distinction between the two at this point. Moreover, a Breton of William's time would have reason to abominate the 'English'. (Note that William says 'Anglorum', not 'Saxonum'; thirteenth-century chroniclers called the supporters of the Angevin Kings 'Angli' regardless of their geographical origin.) The 'English' King Henry II had forced the last truly Breton duke to abdicate. The English King John had murdered the next heir, the fatefully named Arthur. Henry III had invaded Brittany with a particularly rapacious army, drawn down the wrath of the French, and then left the Britons in the lurch. There was more than ancient history for William to remember as he dipped his pen in the acid.[66] He continues his diatribe by claiming that the Britons excel the Angles in probity, though they are inferior in numbers (4871-2). Considering what he has recently been reporting about British wickedness, this inevitably makes the Angles into limbs of Satan (4081). His last words before the formal conclusion are 'contra foedera juris/ acephali [sc. kingless] Britons spoliantur jure paterno' (4892-3). This claim, made *in propria persona*, must outweigh the denunciations of the aged Britons – who, after a lifetime of plague, famine, fire and sword, can be expected to show a certain prejudice. William achieves his own balance: compared with the Saxons or 'Angles', the Britons are entitled to possession of the Land, to which they have a hereditary, though not an absolute and unsullied, right. How exactly this right is to be exercised we shall consider later (below, pp.108-11). The positive endorsement which William gives to it in his peroration confirms his rejection of Geoffrey's final bias and turns the *Gesta* into a political document. The ending is not artificial or contradictory, for it takes up a second major theme of the work, the mirror-image of unjust conquest: the theme of freedom.

---

[65] *Gesta*, p. xvi.
[66] Saint-Sauveur, *Histoire*, pp.122-32, 194-210; Painter, *Scourge*, pp. 60-85.

Like British sinfulness, the theme of freedom was already present in the *Historia*. That work begins with the Trojan's escape from a slavery in Greece, and ends with the Britons' enslavement to the Saxons. William adds little save eloquence to the former story (the Greeks are of no contemporary concern); he modifies the latter as we have seen. It is in between, however, that he makes his most notable contribution to the theme of freedom, in connection with the third great enemy to the British in the *Historia*, the Romans:

> Roma manus rodens, thesauri dedita tanti
> ydroppisi, quam nulla phisis tibi tollere novit,
> quid tibi nobiscum? Cur nos tibi subdere temptas?
> Ardor avaricii, quo naturaliter ardes,
> te stimulat census mundique sitire metalla.

(1229-33)

The words are put in the mouth of Cassibelanus, Rome's first British victim. They develop a phrase of Geoffrey's ('quicquid est auri vel argenti sitiens', p.127), but their resonance is all of the thirteenth century. It is the Curia, not Caesar, whose exactions provoke such passionate denunciation. William adds his voice to a chorus which could be heard everywhere in Western Europe,[67] but was particularly vociferous in Brittany, where Pierre Mauclerc had long been disputing with the Pope about ecclesiastical revenues. (He was, as his nickname suggests, no friend to the local clergy either, but some of them must have applauded his resistance to Rome.)[68] William sees Rome as the universal robber, so bloated with ill-gotten gains that her sack by Brennius and Belinus was positively healthful (1070). The Parthians' execution of Crassus by molten gold was symbolically apt (1235-6). In pursuit of this theme William, through Cassibelanus, contrasts British (and Breton) resistance to Rome with Gaulish complaisance:

> Quam bona libertas! quam detestabilis auri
> argentique fames! Que libera debuit esse
> et potuit, corrupta datis gens Gallica servit.

(1297-9)

In context, this refers to Caesar's having stifled a Gaulish rebellion by buying off its leaders. Geoffrey used this reference to gibe at Caesar, forced to put off the lion and assume the lamb (p.130). William's gibe is at those who were – and are – bought. He is thinking of the excellent relations enjoyed (on the whole) with the

---

[67] G. Barraclough, *The Medieval Papacy* (London, 1968), p.122.
[68] Montigny, *Essai*, 186-206; Painter, *Scourge*, 90-100.

Papacy by the contemporary Capetians.[69] He does not rejoice at French subjugation, past or present. Freedom is the inalienable right of all nations.

William's detestation of Rome leads him to reject Geoffrey's interpretation of Britain's 'Roman' period. Geoffrey, as is well known,[70] inverts the natural meaning of Caesar's conquest so that it redounds to British credit: 'O admirabile tunc genus Britonum, qui ipsum bis in fugam propulerat, qui totum orbem sibi submiserat!' (p.127). Like Roland in the *Chanson*, the Britons can be defeated only by treachery. It is on this treachery that William focuses. Its author, Androgeus, joins William's personal role of infamy:

> servire laboras
> qui fueras dominus ...
> non tu, sed Caesar curru victore vehetur
>
> (1375-6, 1378)

Androgeus is bidden to remember Brutus the liberator, founder of his race: a reminder that the theme of freedom runs through the whole book. Cassibelanus, too, is castigated, for surrendering: 'Pax Caesaris omni/ est nece deterior' (1422-3). William seems to be thinking of classical histories, of Calgacus or of Vercingetorix, and their sentiments combine with his own to annihilate Geoffrey's. William, in any case, must have known his Roman history well enough to recognise Geoffrey's cover-up for what it was.

The identification of Rome as the greatest enemy has important implications for the story of Arthur. In the climax to this story, William's twin themes, freedom and conquest, come together. In Geoffrey, Arthur's whole career is a series of conquests. This ought to make him loathsome in William's eyes, but it does not, because he sees Arthur as an epic hero. To justify his view, he takes some trouble to make Arthur's early conquests irreproachable. This is easy with the Saxon wars. Saxons have no saving graces and may be exterminated. In dealing with Ireland and Scandinavia, William carefully throws into relief the factors which justify Arthur's conquests, especially Arthur's support of Loth as rightful heir (3288-90). The next stage is France. The Bretons were castigated for invading French territory; must not Arthur be castigated also? The answer is easy: Arthur comes to France not as a conqueror, but as the liberator of an oppressed Roman province.

---

[69] Louis IX had not yet manifested the independent spirit of his mature years; Philip Augustus's marital complications belonged to the past. See Hallam, *Capetian France*, pp.196, 239.
[70] Hanning, *Legendary History*, pp.164-9.

He has no quarrel with the Gauls, who are forced to fight by Frollo (329-300). Before leaving Arthur restores all rights and customs (3360-1). The only 'freedom' which is suppressed is the Gascon custom of eating human flesh; the Breton King is given the satisfying duty of imposing civilisation on these, in William's eyes disagreeable, neighbours at the sword's point (3350-3)![71] Arthur's liberation of France is contrasted with Caesar's suppression of it, so that the theme of freedom runs smoothly on.

If Rome is seen as the universal oppressor, *any* attack on it is justifiable. This supposition leads William easily into Arthur's council of war (*Historia* 247-51; *Gesta* 3425 ff), but induces him to tone down the aggressiveness of the opinions there expressed. Arthur calls Rome 'violentus predo' (3476); his refusal of tribute echoes William's own opinion of Roman rapacity. Auguselus, bloodthirsty in the *Historia*, becomes legalistic:

> Roma tumet, fastusque parit, sacramque recuset,
> fasque nephasque sibi licitum facit; omnia credit
> que jubet aut statuit vim sacrae legis habere;
> omniaque esse putat Romani propria fisci,
> serviciumque sibi partes debere remotas
>
> (3506-10)

Again the resonance is modern. This time we are facing not papal taxes but the Papacy's claim to universal hegemony. This was to be a vital political issue of the late thirteenth and the fourteenth century, and there were plentiful adumbrations of it in the earlier years. England in particular, a papal fief under John and Henry III, exemplified Rome's secular ambitions.[72] William, certainly a church-man and possibly a canon lawyer, exemplifies the robust independence of many contemporary French and Breton ecclesiastics.[73]

Auguselus goes on to distinguish between *lex* and *ius* (3509-16). Rome has built her power on unjust *leges*, and now *ius*, the fundamental justice acknowledged by all humanity,[74] demands that her *leges* should be overthrown by force, as she has forfeited all

---

[71] This curious belief about the Gascons is traceable to Juvenal, XV.93-4. Montaigne alludes to it in 'Des Cannibales'.

[72] R. W. Southern, *Western Society and the Church in the Middle Ages* (Pelican, 1970), pp.130, 148; M. J. Wilks, *The Problem of Sovereignty in the LaterMiddles Ages* (Cambridge, 1963), especially pp.15-84.

[73] Michel, *Gesta*, p. vi; Hallam, *Capetian France*, pp. 236-9.

[74] Wilks, pp. 210-11; Pollock and Maitland, *History of English Law*, 2nd edn, 2 vols (Cambridge, 1968), I, p.175. *Lex* and *ius* were not always distinguished in practice, but Justinian's definitions were known.

rights. The Britons' action is therefore justified by the highest authority perceptible to human intellect. To intellect, Auguselus adds emotion. His peroration takes up the freedom theme (3523), which is immediately echoed by William in the narrative:

[omnes] arma movere monent pro libertate tuenda
Utheriden

(3530-1)

The ideological momentum of William's anti-Romanness seems now to demand that Arthur should score a glorious military and moral triumph. Alas, this could not be, because the source forebade it. Fortune is to turn against Arthur. Now, this is a problem for William. If the Britons have *ius* on their side, if they are animated by the sole desire for freedom, if they symbolise the political yearnings of thirteenth-century Europe, then their downfall is the humiliation of those ideals. Since the downfall is a historical fact (in so far as the *Historia* is accepted as history), then William must show that at that point the Britons are no longer just: that they have joined the detestable ranks of the conquerors. It is, I think, possible to pinpoint the moment when this happens. It is in Arthur's hortatory speech at Siesia (3832 ff). He still talks of liberty, but it is a liberty which must be bought by pitiless bloodshed. He exults over the helplessness of the entrapped enemy, promises to meet treachery with treachery, and looks forward to world domination. Most of these ideas are in Geoffrey, but they do not worry Geoffrey, for whom ferocity is a necessary item of regal equipment. William brings them out, and condemns them. Fortune, for him, is not an arbitrary goddess, but synchronises her wheel with the turnings of morality. It is time that she brought Arthur down. The scene is set for the horrific last battle which we examined above (pp. 71-7).

This condemnation of Arthur in no way exonerates the Romans. Nor does it brand Arthur as evil. As soon as he returns to defend his own Land, he becomes just again, and the condemnation is transferred to Mordred. The story is a reminder that all men are subject, under God, to a universal moral law. Arthur, as the 'hero' of the *Gesta*, inevitably synthesises the two themes, of freedom and conquest, which dominate it. It is round these two themes that William constructs his personal patriotism: my country, my people, but never when they are in the wrong. In the *Historia*, William sees events which echo his modern preoccupations and can be used to express them. He sees elements which help to explain the character and circumstances of his race, and which therefore merit

108

urgent attention from its present-day representatives. It is when such elements are in play that the *Gesta* ceases to be the plaything of a scholar and becomes a committed work. That is not to say that it is a political work. William does not forget that he is writing an epic. He values great deeds for the light they throw on human nature in its extremes, good and bad. But as epic is a 'social' genre, and social man is a political animal, its explorations must have a political dimension; and in most great epics that political dimension is the one with which the author is most concerned. Roland speaks for France as well as himself; his sins are hers, as is his redemption. William's Arthur, and William's poem, speak in the same way for Britain. If they do not have the greatness of Roland and his Chanson, that is Britain's great misfortune.

If William claims to speak for the British race, how do his words compare with those of other British writers of the time? If we consider him first as a Breton, we find that his uneasy, critical attitude is in fact outstandingly favourable in contrast to others'. It seems that the finest sight a medieval Breton scholar could see was the high road which led him to France. Abelard, Marbod, Baudri de Dol, the Chronicler of Nantes, vie with one another in casti-gating their countrymen. Abelard's wails of lamentation at being exiled to his homeland are particularly well known. Baudri and Thierry 'of Chartres' could not get out of their native Brittany quickly enough.[75] To write such a poem as William's would doubtless have seemed to them a self-condemnation to vain parochialism. There is a sole Breton writer who might be thought to challenge William for his laurels. This is Guillaume le Breton, verse historiographer to Philip Augustus. As a Breton writing a Latin hexameter poem (*Phillippis*)[76] in praise of a conquering hero, Guillaume is obviously analogous to William. There are internal similarities in the works, too. Guillaume, like William, sees himself as a rival to Gautier de Châtillon, over whom Guillaume openly claims superiority. Like William, Guillaume sets his hero over those of Virgil, Homer, Lucan and Statius ('Nuncupatio', 7-15, 11-13, 20-1; *Gesta*, 2976-85). It is quite probable that William deliberately set out to outdo Guillaume. Their rivalry, however, has no nationalistic basis. Guillaume's fervour is all for Philip Augustus and the Franks; he considers his Breton origin as a geographical accident. He does take an interest in Breton affairs,

---

[75] Saint-Sauveur, pp.173-84; Abelard, *Historia calamitatum*, ed. J. Monfrin (Paris, 1962), p. 98.
[76] Ed. H. F. Delaborde, Société de l'Histoire de France (Paris, 1885).

but no more, it seems to me, than is necessary for an account of Philip's reign. His political vision is Philip's: not a united British race, but a united France. His final hope is that 'si fastidit extranea natio mecum,/ Francigenum nobis sit satis in ore legi' (p.385) – a remark which may even have nettled William into 'excluding' all but the British (and most particularly the French) from reading his *Gesta* (4913-14).

William, then, is the sole Breton Latinist of the time to show national concern. We may imagine that native Breton voices spoke in similar vein, but as no Breton literature of the time survives, we cannot prove it. Echoes of Breton story may survive in French *lais* and romances, but the latter consider Brittany as a neutral 'dreamland',[77] not as a political entity. Did the indifference of the literary establishment on the continent encourage William to emphasise the links between Brittany and Britain? It is possible, though this was certainly not the whole reason. What is certain is that the Welsh literary scene would have been far more congenial to William. It is to Wales that we must turn if we wish to judge William in context as a British writer.

By adapting the Latin epic medium, William declares an intention to speak for Brittany on the international scene. Wales already had such a spokesman, a Latin prose writer with eloquence and inventiveness to match any poet: Giraldus Cambrensis.[78] Giraldus, like some contemporary Breton scholars, had studied in Paris (p.12), but this produced in him no inclination to disparage his homeland. On the contrary, Wales was to him what Arthur was to William and Philip Augustus to Guillaume le Breton: a subject superior to Homer's, Virgil's or Statius's (p.212). He was equipped to consider her objectively: he was three-quarters Norman by descent (p.10), he was a scholar, and he was a pragmatist. Nevertheless, he was prepared to identify Wales's interests with his and to fight resolutely for both, as he showed in the long battle for St David's (pp.16-21). *Engagé* but not uncritical, he shows a marked similarity of attitudes to William of Rennes.

The similarity may be pursued in detail. In his *Description of Wales* (c.1191), Giraldus, like William, accepts from the *Historia* the idea that the Welsh lost Britain through their sins. Like William again, Giraldus traces the sinfulness back to Troy (pp.264-6). Giraldus specifies a single sin, homosexuality, but

---

[77] H. Baader, *Die Lais*, Analecta Romanica 16 (Frankfurt, 1966), p.152.
[78] All references to Giraldus are to Lewis Thorpe, ed. and trans., *Journey through Wales and Description of Wales* (Penguin, 1978).

generously backs it up with 'a deep abyss of every vice' (p. 265). Still with an eye to Geoffrey, Giraldus adds that the Welsh

> boast, and confidently predict, that they will soon reoccupy the whole island of Britain. It is remarkable how everyone in Wales entertains this illusion. According to the Prophecies of Merlin [*Historia*, p.194], the foreign occupation of the island will come to an end and the invaders will be destroyed. The Welsh will then be called Britons once more and they will enjoy their ancient privileges. (p. 265)

Compare that with William's peroration:

> solis hec scribo Britannis
> ut memores veteris patriae jusisque paterni
> exiliique patrum, proprii que pudoris, anhelent
> vocibus et votis ut regnum restituatur
> antiquo jure, que [sic] possidet Anglicus hostis.
>
> (4914-18)

There is the same pride in (illusory) ancestral glory, the same attachment to the Land, the same outrage at foreign usurpation, in both passages. This is not to say that William knew the *Description*, no MS of which seems to have reached the continent (pp. 49-50). Rather does it show the similar reaction of similar minds to similar circumstances, as they compare the *Historia* data with contemporary reality. Giraldus does not share his countrymen's belief in a reconquest of the whole island; indeed, he paints a gloomy picture of their political subjection, only admitting at the end that recently 'they have been able to raise their heads a little higher, recover their lands and cease to bear the yoke which once weighed so heavily upon them' (p. 167). The recovery of which he speaks was in fact very striking. In the 1190s, most of South Wales was under the firm rule of the Lord Rhys, and the North, while missing the strong hand of Owain Gwynedd, was still substantially under Welsh control.[79] Giraldus knew his volatile countrymen well enough to realise that this independence was unstable, that it was partly owing to English political dissensions, and that it was not a basis for reconquest of the whole island. He could, however, see in it an encouragement for the Welsh 'illusion', and he could see how that illusion fostered national pride and the will to resist, as the famous concluding words of the *Description* show:

---

[79] Lloyd, *History of Wales*, II, pp. 536-72.

> Whatever may come to pass, I do not believe that on the Day of Direst Judgement any race other than the Welsh, or any other language, will give answer to the Supreme Judge of all for this small corner of the earth (p. 274).[80]

William's peroration endorses the hope of reconquest which Giraldus only reports. Its exact impact is notable. William seems to advocate that Briton and Breton join forces against *all* their enemies. This peroration, however, must be interpreted as envisaging the reconquest of the *Island* of Britain by a reunited British race. The island alone can be described as 'vetus patria'. The 'exilium patrum' could mean the expulsion of the Welsh from lands now held by Saxons or English, but it could refer equally well to the self-imposed exile of the Breton settlers. 'Proprius pudor' could be the shame of the Welsh at their defeat, or the shame of the Bretons at their unjust occupation of Gaulish land. The land to be regained is not Brittany but Britain, 'que [sic] possidet Anglicus hostis'. William is saying that the independence of Brittany is a lost cause; contemporary political reality supported him. But contemporary Welsh reality was far more encouraging. Since Giraldus's time a brilliant new ruler had built on the successes of the Princes and united the whole of Wales. The noble achievement of Llewelyn ap Iorwerth was not to survive his death in 1240, but in the 1230s his independent British kingdom was a reality.[81] Depression at the downfall of Brittany would be lifted if William looked across the Channel. Even so, he realises that there is no real prospect of ever reconquering the whole island. He says 'anhelent vocibus et votis', not 'pugnent ferro et incendio'. The aspiration must serve to keep the British nation alive and conscious of its single identity. As Giraldus, so William.

So far we have considered only Latin writers, whose sameness of view could partly be attributed to a similar intellectual training. Would William find himself in sympathy with vernacular Welsh writers, were he ever to meet them? the answer is emphatically 'yes'. The notion that the Island of Britain belonged to the British race, that it had once been united under them and that it ought to be so again, is fundamental in early Welsh literature. Geoffrey of Monmouth's success was partly due to his realisation of the power of that theme. It can be traced back at least as far as the tenth-

---

[80] This 'I' is not Giraldus, but a Welsh renegade addressing Henry II. Despite the implied irony, I do not believe that Giraldus would have ended with these words if he did not intend to endorse them.

[81] Lloyd, *History*, II, pp. 655-91.

century *Armes Prydein*.[82] This prophecy urges all the Celtic peoples to unite and repossess the land 'from Manaw [Man] to Brittany, from Dyfed to Thanet, from the Wall to the Forth' (ll.1711-14). The same impulse is perceptible in the Triads, which record the essentials of Welsh tradition in a form which reminds us incessantly of the integrity of the Land: 'the three ... of the Island of Britain'. That tradition also formed the 'literary' background for the court poets of William's time, whose confidence in the destiny of all things Welsh rose with the political fortunes of their princely patrons.[83] It was from the same background that much of the material for the *Historia* must have come,[84] so that William and the Welsh bards were drawing inspiration from the same ultimate source. There is no direct literary relationship between them, but they would have understood each other.

Closer to William's literary world are the contemporary Welsh chronicles, of which the most important is *Brut y Tywysogion*.[85] The work purports to continue the annals of the British race begun by Geoffrey in the *Historia*. William, too, has this sense of continuity, as his relating of *Historia* events to contemporary concerns makes clear. In describing the 'national awakening' of the later twelfth century, the *Brut* acquires a sudden sense of urgency and purpose.[86] We hear how in 1164 'all the Welsh united together to throw off the rule of the French' (p. 63). In 1197 the chronicler laments the mighty Lord Rhys in terms which William might well have applied to Arthur: 'the glory of battles and the shield of knights, the defender of his land, the splendour of arms, the arm of prowess, the hand of generosity, the eye and lustre of worthiness, the summit of majesty, the light of reason, the arm of Hercules!' (p. 77) Undaunted by this loss, the next year Gwenwynwyn of Powys 'gathered a mighty host to seek to win for the Welsh their original rights and to restore their bounds to their rightful owners, which they had lost through the multitude of their sins' (p. 79). Again we see the power of Geoffrey's interpretation of 'history', together with the conviction that his judgement is not final, that the Land can be regained. The rise of Llywelyn is charted, and we hear how 'all the Welsh gathered together in unity with their

---

[82] Ed. I. Williams/R. S. Bromwich (Cardiff, 1972).
[83] On the Court Poets see J. E. Caerwyn Williams, *The Poets of the Welsh Princes* (Cardiff, 1978).
[84] Bromwich, *Trioedd*, p. xcvi.
[85] Ed. Thomas Jones (Cardiff, 1952).
[86] Cf. Caerwyn Williams, *Poets*, p. 4.

113

prince' to repulse Henry III in 1228 (p.101). These notes of confidence and unity are embedded in a complex account of strife and deceit, practised as much among the Welsh as against the English. William would not be surprised at that. He was fully aware of the Celtic tendency to disunity even while he hoped for unity, and the *Historia* itself contains many incidences of civil strife. What the two works, the *Brut* and *Gesta*, have in common is a commitment to the cause of British renaissance, and a conviction of the unity of past and present.

Behind *Brut y Tywysogion* is the original *Brut*, the *Historia*. Welsh acceptance of this work seems to have been rapid, enthusiastic and uncritical. There are at least six Welsh translations, extant in about sixty MSS.[87] Thus no one Welsh author could claim the sole glory of adapting the work for his countrymen's especial benefit, but together the translations achieve a success comparable to that of the prose *Lancelot* or the *Roman de la Rose*. To no other readers of the *Historia* – except the Bretons – could it speak as urgently and personally as to the Welsh. It took elements already familiar to them from vernacular legends and codified them as no vernacular writer had ever attempted to do. It told the world what the Welsh had always told themselves: that whatever their present sorrows, their ancestors had been a great nation. At the same time, however, Geoffrey's Latin had slightly alienated the characters of the story. The Welsh translators undertook to remove that alienation by restoring traditional Welsh nomenclature whenever possible, and by making links with familiar legendary material which Geoffrey had not used. Geoffrey had introduced British prestige on the international scene. The Welsh were pleased with this, but nonetheless they wanted to reclaim Geoffrey for their own, to make the *Historia* once again into an integral part of the tradition from which it had sprung.[88] It is obvious that William of Rennes was not doing anything of the sort for the Bretons. (If anyone did, then his work has fallen into the oblivion which has swallowed all the native literature of the time). Nonetheless, William, like the Welsh writers, certainly felt that he was dealing with material that belonged to his nation. His attitude was therefore quite dissimilar from that of a Wace or a Layamon. And he does address himself to a British audience, even if his true ambitions are obviously wider. It is therefore worth comparing his

---

[87] See B. Roberts, *Brut y Brenhinedd* (Dublin, 1971), pp. xxvii-xxxix.
[88] *Ibid.*, p. xxix. On the absorption of *Historia* material back into Welsh literature see Bromwich, *Trioedd*, xcvi-xcviii and *passim*.

work with the *Bruts*, in order to show what each author thought would appeal to 'Britons' of his time.

In making this comparison, we shall be concerned with translation rather than free adaptation. Despite their occasional references to native legend, the Welsh authors are most reluctant to contradict Geoffrey or reshape his narrative. Some MSS make one major interpolation, the story of Llud and Llevelys.[89] It involves no adaptation of Geoffrey's data, though it does modify the *Historia* in that no indication is given of a new source being used. William (alas!) adds no new stories. On the other hand, it is William who adds detail to Geoffrey's peculiarly bald account of Arthur's passing (see above, p. 94). Here, if anywhere, we should expect the Welsh, with their enthusiasm for Arthur and their stores of Otherworld lore, to make some comment. Often, indeed, we are frustratingly aware that the translators know more about Arthur's passing than they are prepared to say, for they express surprise that the *Historia* says no more.[90] It may be that the translators' extra knowledge was not (like William's and Geoffrey's in the *Vita Merlini*) otherworldly, but related to the 'discovery' of Arthur's 'grave', news of which seems to have spread quite rapidly through Wales.[91] Their surprise would then be a reaction to apparently needless mystification by Geoffrey. Alternatively, they may be believers in Arthur's return – for his survival legend persisted long in Wales[92] – who do not wish to commit themselves too firmly to that belief in an 'historical' work. William, as an epic poet, did not need to share that inhibition. We must admit, however, that at key points such as this neither William nor the *Bruts* ever do much to assuage our thirst for Celtic Arthurian material.

Common to both translations is a care for stylistic excellence in their own medium.[93] In each case, this was a medium whose maturity and stylistic resourcefulness permitted the maximum of expressiveness. Like William, the *Bruts* condense the *Historia*

---

[89] *Trioedd*, pp. xciv-xcv.

[90] *Brut Dingestow*, ed. Henry Lewis (Cardiff, 1942), p.185; J.J. Parry, *Brut y Brenhinedd* (Cambridge, Mass., 1937), pp.193, 224.

[91] For the latest investigation of the grave-story, see the article by R. Barber in *Arthurian Literature* IV, pp. 37-63.

[92] See T. Gwynn Jones, *Welsh Folklore and Folk-custom* (reprinted Cambridge, 1979), pp. 87-9.

[93] Welsh prose of the twelfth and thirteenth century had achieved a maturity not to be matched in French or English before the Renaissance. See T. Parry, trans. Bell, *History of Welsh Literature* (Oxford, 1955), pp. 67-98, especially 84-5.

narrative, except in the most significant episodes. Whereas William's verse is often ornamental, however, the Welsh prose is rapid, economical and unadorned. The effect of each may be gauged by their adaptations of a short, exciting episode of the *Historia*, the murder of Constans by Vortigern's Pictish assassins (*Historia*, pp.173-4; *Gesta*, ll.218-45; Parry, *Brut*, pp.109-9). In the *Gesta* the episode becomes a study in rhetoricised emotion. First comes the maudlin devotion of the Picts, 'imbutos munere Bacchi' (2118), for Vortigern. Vortigern responds to it with false tears, feigned emotion, and a feigned intention to act which (as he intends) acts as a trigger to real action by the Picts. He declares that he can no longer afford to remain at court, so will retire forthwith: 'Discedo, valete' (2127). The Picts, hurrying off to murder Constans, channel their drunken indignation into a tidy antithetical speech culminating in 'Rex miser occubat, regnet dux imperia' (2133). Finally there is another bout of feigning by Vortigern – feigned anger as the murderers present him with Constan's head, leading to the murderers' (genuine) execution. In William's patterning of stimulus and reaction, and in his sonorous verse, the foxy cunning of Vortigern and the viciousness of the Picts are muted into ritualised gestures which proceed in slow motion, like the exaggerated actions in a miracle play. In contrast, the Cleopatra Welsh text has a brutal immediacy. William's characters declaim; the Welsh ones whisper. The swift conversation between Vortigern and his Picts (p.109) is redolent of small dark rooms and conspirators huddled round a lamp or brazier. Once the idea of the murder has been planted in the Picts' fuddled heads, they act instantly, with no time for speech, let alone rhetoric: 'Sef a wnaethant wy, rwng medawd a geirieu Gorthern: dyrchy y stawell y brenhyn a llad y ben a dyvot hut yn lle ydoed Gorthern a bwrw yr pen yn y arffet. "Hwde!" heb yr wynt, "a byd vrenhyn weithion o's mynne!"' ('This is what they did between drunkenness and Vortigern's words: they went to the king's chamber and cut off his head and came to the place where Vortigern was and flung the head in his lap. "Here!" said they, "and be king now if thou desire it."' My translation and punctuation). Here is no ritual, no fictional elaboration: it is like the terse account of an eye-witness. It convinces us that such a thing could happen. (Indeed, from what we know of the savage feuds of medieval Wales, such things frequently did). It also convinces us, better than William's rhetoric, of the utter lack of conscience of both Vortigern and the Picts, to whom the murder of an anointed king is all in a night's work. This urgent immediacy must have been part of the appeal of the *Bruts*. The events they describe lack the extravagance of the native tales, but have the same headlong excitement. In contrast, William's Latin seems stately, but at times lifeless. In striving after poetic dignity, he sacrifices the taut immediacy which Welsh readers obviously appreciated. This may have been the main reason (apart from the language difficulty) why William's work did not appeal to the Welsh, although (as we have seen) he is in sympathy with them at so many points. The fault is not all his. Neither medieval Welsh nor medieval Irish literature ever produced an epic, though they did produce characters – Pryderi, Arthur, Cuchulainn, Finn – with epic potential. Quarrelsome, inconsistent, exuberant, individual, these characters are; but so are those of the *Iliad* and the French Guillaume cycle, both of which manage to fit the characters into a tight structural and ideological discipline. The trouble with the Celtic characters is that the authors who handled them were also quarrelsome, inconsistent, exuberant and individual. They lacked the discipline to make an epic, and though the Welsh *Brut* authors received discipline from Geoffrey, it was of the wrong kind. William had, if anything, too much discipline. Perhaps if one could combine his controlled dignity with the exuberance of *Culhwch and Olwen* and the economy of the *Bruts*, one would at last have a Celtic epic!

Conclusion

If literary success is measured by the popularity and influence of a work, then William's *Gesta* was a failure. Only three MSS survive. It was the *Alexandreis* that became a new 'classic'; Wace who set his stamp on Arthurian vernacular literature; the Welsh court poetry and the *Bruts* which nourished British independence. No author, Breton or otherwise, cites the *Gesta*, as far as I know. But enough authors now considered great – especially medieval authors – have been ill-considered in their own time to make us mistrust the judgement of contemporaries. Having investigated the *Gesta*, should we now hail it as, if not a neglected masterpiece, at least as an unjustly neglected work?

Considered purely as a *Historia* derivative, the *Gesta* scores highly. It is infinitely superior to any of the innumerable other Latin versions. In the vernacular, only Wace, Layamon and (for their effective prose style) the Welsh *Bruts* can challenge it. We have seen that on his own ground, William can outrank Wace. Layamon, though far removed from William's literary sphere, deserves some consideration here because his powerful, occasionally savage narrative does occasionally bring us close to an epic world, that of *Beowulf* and the heroes of the North.[94] Like William, and like all epic poets, Layamon treats his matter with intense seriousness. Both of them have *gravitas*. Geoffrey does not. Despite the credibility which he widely gained, it is possible to sense in his writing the detachment of a puppet-master, arranging his artificial figures in dramatic but repetitive attitudes. It is, of course, possible to treat genuine historical characters in this way; the difference is one of literary conviction. To Layamon, Arthur is real as Beowulf would be real; to William, he is real as Aeneas is real. To Wace, he is an odd compromise between historicity and the 'fables' which Wace is inclined to mock. He is not 'real'. This is a vital distinction. If Wace had treated Arthur with epic solemnity, the whole course of medieval Arthurian development might have been different. As it is, vernacular writers after Wace use the Arthurian legend to speculate on every topic under the sun, including themes of immense *gravitas*; but there is an inexorable tendency in their work to lighten the burden on the central figure, to dissipate the interest, to lower Arthur's stature. This is by no means a negative development; it is a difference of genre. Arthur becomes a figure of romance. The pity of it is that the genre became so fixed, that it became almost impossible to think of Arthur in epic terms. If Layamon or William had had any influence, the possibility might have been realised. Unfortunately, both were using the wrong medium. English was not yet a literary language fit to challenge the domination of French and Latin. And thirteenth-century Arthurian writers, imbued with Chrétien and Wace, evidently did not think to look for their hero amongst the champions of Latin epic.

Considered as a *Brut* author and as an inspiration, then, William has always been unjustly neglected, possibly to the great impoverishment of Arthurian literature. He himself aimed higher. As the only writer consciously to treat Arthur on an epic plane, he must be judged on that plane. What do we expect of an epic? A substantial narrative work concerning a single, great, complete action, with a distinguished hero who, like the action itself, is of concern to the audience; a serious style and an intention to affirm values essential to the collectivity of which author and audience form a

---

[94] For an appreciation of Layamon in this light see Tatlock, *Legendary History*, p. 484: 'the poem is the nearest thing we have to a traditional racial [sc. English!] epic'.

part: such might be a working definition of the genre. It is usual, but not essential, for there to be a single hero (The *Iliad* has many). It is usual, but not essential, for the action to occupy a relatively short period of time, or, rather, that the audience's perception of time should be concentrated. Rarely does an epic cover a longer period than one man's life, and that often cut short by a violent death (but Odysseus's and the Cid's are not). How many of these points does the *Gesta* answer?

There is undoubtedly a single, great, and complete action: the rise and fall of British royalty. William did not invent this schema, but took it over from Geoffrey. Does this mean that we should first ask ourselves whether the *Historia* is an epic? We should of course reply that it is not, and is not intended to be. Geoffrey, for all his stretching and condensing of various event, thinks basically in terms of the linear progression of the annalist. Like all story-tellers, he manipulates his readers' perception of time, but not consistently. He is constantly returning them to 'real' time by pegging his narrative to a familiar Biblical and historical chron-ology: '... at this time Eli ruled the Jews and Silvius Italicus reigned in Italy'. Such an approach is lethal to the autonomous concentration of time-perception demanded by epic. The sheer length of time covered by the *Historia* does not matter: the central theme could concentrate it into a 'légende des siècles' in which the passing of time became a dynamo, driving the story forward. Unfortunately, William does not realise this. He is not willing to abandon the annalistic structure, or even the chronological pegs. Even Arthur, at the climax of the whole work, must pass away 'anno quingeno quadragenoque secundo' (4229) while the hex-ameter creaks under the strain. William is aware that certain moments in the story are decisive and must be poetically em-phasised: this is what he does in his personal denunciations of delinquent characters, in his encomium of Arthur, and in the fine lines which hail the coming of Christ (1454-82), so one hesitates to accuse him of simple laziness in following Geoffrey's schema. He makes enough changes to show that he has thought hard about the nature of his adaptation. He must, nonetheless, be convicted of artistic ineptitude. He tried to work in two genres at once, and achieved only a set of uncomfortable juxtapositions.

The need for a distinguished hero is met by Arthur. As a beloved and all-conquering hero who is himself conquered by hubris, by the treachery of those he loves, and by Heaven's decree, he invites comparison with Roland and Alexander. Obviously he is not present throughout the work, but this would not matter if he

119

were felt to dominate it conceptually. To a considerable extent he does. He is mentioned at the beginning as the high point of the work (l.14); he raises Britain to its greatest glory; he has a unique destiny, yet is the quintessence of British royalty. William describes him in stately metaphors, gives him magnificent gestures and weighty speeches. But after that, his talent fails him. He does not let us into Arthur's mind because he has formed no conception of it, and a hero without a mind is a puppet. To bring him to life, there is no need of sophisticated psychological understanding and advanced vocabulary. We know the mind of Roland or Beowulf without either: a word, a tear, a gesture can give us the whole man. We know what he is; on what he is depends what he does, and our understanding of what is done to him. William's Arthur (like Geoffrey's) is an entirely public figure – save in his fight with the giant, and in that episode William concentrates on the spectacular terror of the adversary and the combat. Even Arthur's emotions are public, and always consonant with the situation. Events which invite a personal reaction – marriage, Guinevere's and Mordred's betrayal, the deaths of Kay, Beduer and Gawain – are skimmed over. Arthur is never called upon to face death, which affords so many epic heroes their noblest and most intimate moment of self-realisation. William shows us how Arthur could be made into an epic hero, but he does not do this himself.

Dominant as Arthur is, it is possible to look elsewhere for a 'hero' of the *Gesta*. There is one character who always remains in view; who has a complex and unique range of good and bad qualities; who climbs to greatness, and falls through self-betrayal and the weight of destiny; who admits to his fatal flaw in the end; who is passionately loved or hated by others in the story; and by whom the author is personally involved and moved. That character is the British people. If individuals in the *Gesta*, including Arthur, remain subordinate to the action, the action is always subordinated to the portayal of a nation. Even Virgil, an immeasurably greater poet, did not portray the individuality of a nation which such concentration and conviction. Many a reader has preferred Dido and Turnus to the remorseless abstraction of Roman destiny which eliminates them. William's readers must prefer Britain to the two-dimensional figures of Arthur and Brutus, but this preference causes no conflict: the glory of the state reflects that of the human heroes. The *Gesta* is not the epic of Arthur, but it can claim to be the epic of Geoffrey's Britain.

As such, the poem is indeed of concern to poet and audience, so long as the audience is British. Any epic worth considering as literature, however, must have a transcendent human interest, a theme of perennial concern. William proposes three such themes: human sinfulness, political freedom, the attachment of a race to its Land. In handling them, alas, he again falls short of greatness. He makes them relevant to his own time but not transcendent. We are never sure whether he values them for their own sake, or only insofar as they touch the fate of Britain. We are not convinced, as we are when reading the greatest epics, that all the surface detail is held in place by the force of the author's understanding of the human condition. Geoffrey piles up detail for the sake of historical verisimilitude; William piles up detail for the sake of detail, and the reader is immediately aware of it. We may agree to be bored occasionally by a chronicle, which exists to inform and commemorate. Epic exists for, and through, a committed and consenting audience. They will not endure boredom.

William's work conforms, perhaps too well, to the demand for a serious style. Michel (p. xvii) praises his style for its variety in comparison with Wace's. Certainly Wace can exasperate by his limited syntax and his small, remorselessly exploited stock of rhetorical devices. William has a perfect literary language at his disposal, but if he varies it, it is within a narrow compass. There is no humour, unless the passion for word-play can be so described. There is the occasional whimsical conceit, as when Britain's virgin soil marvels to find itself penetrated and fecundated by agriculture (468-70). There is little lyricism. William's eye is no more delighted by a fair landscape than Geoffrey's, which looks only for agricultural or military potential. Women cause no more reaction. All William's heroines surpass the rest of their sex as the moon the stars, as the sun the moon (see e.g. ll.2900-1), but the same similes are used of the galumphing Corineus (ll.447-9). The birth of Christ is hailed with fervent devotion (1453-31), and the imagery of it is elegantly woven in the manner of a Latin hymn. Even here, however, William cannot suppress his love of word-play, antithesis and ratiocination. He destroys the tension between stillness and exultation which characterises the best Latin religious lyrics. The description of Arthur's enchanted island (4213-22) is little more than an itemisation of necessary features. Many medieval writers are matter-of-fact about otherworld lore; they are far less concerned than is often supposed to convey a 'frisson de l'inconnu'. Nonetheless we should expect better of an aspiring poet who has followed Aeneas through Hades and Daphnis through the Italian vales. Vigour is found in William's set speeches, but they never advance from virtuous indignation into understanding or tenderness. William's greatest stylistic strength is his mastery of metaphor. None of his comparisons is new, and many are repeated in recurrent contexts: the river of blood, the cloud of spears, the warrior like a raging lion, the descent of souls to stygian darkness. Yet this very repetition, when combined with more highly wrought metaphor corresponding to unique events, has value. It becomes a coherent subtext, formed from the classical poetry which William knew so well, and it enriches the poet's vision. Through it, William's characters taste of some of the dignity of classical heroes. It is the reverse of the medievalising process which we observe in the *romans antiques* and the Alexander romances. Because William is so much at home with the great Latin poets, his classicising seems as natural as the modernising of vernacular writers. He knows when to stop: he does not (like Camoẽs, for example) attempt to convey active intervention by the classical gods. He does, I think, convince us that Geoffrey's militaristic Arthur is as capable of inhabiting Latin epic as Quintus Curtius's Alexander. Sadly, no Latin author of genius came after William to create a Latin Arthur great enough to rival the Arthurs of vernacular writers.

In our final judgement, we must assess William as a highly meritorious failure. Too interesting for a chronicler, too dull for an epic; too creative for an imitator, too cautious for a literary genius; too learned for a patriotic propagandist; too committed for an intellectual commentator; perhaps he should be set down as the epic chronicler of Britain! Our analysis cannot, at the last, eliminate our first reservation: that only by ruthless excision could William have found himself a worthy subject for Arthurian epic. William is not the only Arthurian writer to have missed this lesson. The whole of medieval Arthurian development is marked by two processes, ruthless selection and inexorable accretion. From the *Chevalier de la Charrete* there grows the prose *Lancelot*. From Wace springs the alliterative *Mort Arthure*, which comes closer than any other Arthurian work to a Homeric concentration of theme. At last, from the whole immense creation comes the work of Malory. Malory is a romancer to the core, but it is in his most piteous tale of the Morte Arthure sanz Guerdon that we hear, for the only time in Arthurian literature, the tone of high tragedy which marks the greatest epic. We cannot claim that William showed Malory the way, but we can say that he was the first to recognise the epic potential of the theme.

What does a modern scholar gain from the reading of the *Gesta*? In it, we see the meeting of three cultural currents: classical literature, Celtic fervour and medieval heroic narrative. Separately and together, these currents directed vast areas of medieval writing and thought. William of Rennes was no genius, but he was ingenious. As he contemplates his material, chisels out his hexameters, and projects his convictions into the story, he reveals to us the working of a scholar's mind, a mind perhaps similar to our own. Through it we perceive something of the intellectual passions of the thirteenth century.

IV

MOUVANCE AND REVISIONISM IN THE TRANSMISSION OF THOMAS OF BRITAIN'S *TRISTAN*: THE EPISODE OF THE INTERTWINING TREES

Merritt R. Blakeslee

It is the thesis of this study that the episode of the intertwining trees preserved in the Old Norse translation of Thomas's *Tristan*, *Tristrams Saga ok Ísöndar*, existed originally in Thomas's work, from which it was subsequently excised. The primary obstacle to the adoption of this apparently simple and self-evident proposal is, however, a singularly thorny one. Only fragments of Thomas's poem have survived, but its manuscript tradition is most authoritative in the last thousand lines of the romance, where two manuscripts, Bodleian Library MS. Douce d.6 [Douce] and Bodleian Library MS. Fr. d.16 [Sneyd], exhibit a high degree of uniformity in recounting its final episodes. As no trace of the episode of the intertwining trees is found here, it has been assumed that it is the invention of Thomas's translator, Brother Robert. Recently, it has been proposed that it is a late interpolation by a copyist. However, a close comparison of the two manuscripts suggests that the episode originally existed in Thomas's poem.

The second Sneyd fragment [Sn²], which contains 828 lines,[1] follows the longer Douce fragment [D] faithfully for almost 800 lines (Sn² 1-782, D 1047-1815) from the episode of Tristan's last wound to the account of his death and Iseut's arrival at his side. Sneyd² then diverges radically from Douce, presenting a fifty-seven line passage (Sn² 783-839) that contains an expanded version of Iseut's lament (Sn² 783-808), the final embrace of the lovers, Iseut's death (Sn² 809-19), and Thomas's *envoi* (Sn² 820-39).

---

[1] Wind has misnumbered the lines of Sneyd², which comprises 769 lines that parallel the text of Douce (D 1047-1815), two lines inserted after D 1812, and 57 lines that have no counterpart in Douce (Sn² 783-839).

Douce, on the other hand, closes with a three-line ending recounting Iseut's embrace and death that offers a coherent, if extremely abrupt, conclusion to Thomas's romance:

> Dejuste lui va dunc gesir
> Embrace le e si s'estent
> Sun espirit a itant rendit. (D 1816-18)

A comparison of the abbreviated conclusion of Douce with the fuller, more measured ending of Sneyd[2] indicates clearly that Douce has been truncated.[2] The alternative hypothesis – that the final fifty-seven lines of Sneyd[2] are an interpolation – is far less likely; for it is here, in his *envoi*, that the poet names himself for a second time (Sn[2] 820, the first occurring at D 826). It is most improbable that a highly self-conscious artist like Thomas, given as he is to frequent authorial intervention, should close a work of some thirteen thousand lines without an *envoi* of the sort found in Sneyd[2]. Nevertheless, the three-line conclusion to the Douce manuscript would, in the absence of the contrary evidence furnished by Sneyd[2], make it impossible to demonstrate the existence of a lacuna in the text of Douce. Yet, the comparison of the two manuscripts proves that such truncation has indeed taken place in Douce at precisely the point where the episode of the intertwining trees would have appeared.[3]

The discovery of a lacuna in the otherwise apparently authoritative Douce manuscript raises the possibility that other examples of truncation may have occurred in the extant manuscripts of Thomas's poem – lacunae not discernible by a comparison of Douce and Sneyd[2] but readily apparent once those two manuscripts are compared with *Tristrams Saga*. The presence of the episode of the intertwining trees in *Tristrams Saga* and the evidence of truncation in Douce strongly suggest that Sneyd[2] was subjected to similar, if less extensive, truncation serving, as in Douce, to remove the episode of the intertwining trees.

[2] It was Fourrier's failure to recognize this fact that led him to conclude: 'Il est impossible de décider si Thomas le [i.e. le motif des arbres entrelacés] donnait aussi, car, d'une part, le texte que nous avons de lui ne comporte pas ce récit, mais, d'autre part, il figure dans la *saga* et dans la *Tavola ritonda*, dérivée, elle aussi, de Thomas. Est-ce une lacune dans notre fragment? Il n'y subsiste cependant aucune trace de coupure et comme nous avons vu souvent le poète anglo-normand éviter le merveilleux, une suppression de ce genre lui serait parfaitement imputable' (95).

[3] The truncation in Douce is not the result of the accidental loss of a leaf from that manuscript; for Thomas's work ends on the twenty-fifth line of fol. 12va and the *Folie d'Oxford* begins at the top of fol. 12vb.

A comparison of the earliest manuscript fragments of *Tristrams Saga*, the later, integral manuscripts of that work, and the surviving fragments of Thomas's romance reveals only one example of the interpolation in the *Saga* of narrative material not found in Thomas: Ísönd's prayer over the dead Tristram (Ch. 101). While Eilhart's *Tristrant* and the MS. B.N.fr. 103 variant of the French prose *Tristan* recount the final episodes of the romance in similar terms, their accounts of the episode of the miraculous plants differ fundamentally, with MS. B.N.fr. 103 incorporating narrative elements found in *Tristrams Saga* and absent from Eilhart. Since it can be shown that MS. B.N.fr. 103 elsewhere incorporates material found only in Thomas's romance, it follows that Thomas's poem originally contained a version of the episode of the intertwining trees, which was copied by *Tristrams Saga* and which coloured the version of the episode given by MS. B.N.fr. 103. This study speculates that, because Thomas's romance generally and the episode of the intertwining trees in particular were perceived in the late twelfth and early thirteenth centuries to be subversive, the episode was suppressed in the extant manuscripts of his work.

I

THE EPISODE OF THE INTERTWINING TREES
IN THE MEDIEVAL TRISTAN CORPUS

The reincarnation of lovers as plants is a widespread motif in world folk-lore (Psichari-Gaidoz; Child 1: 94-99; Thompson E631; Vàrvaro 1060-63; Gallais). Such episodes are numerous and widely distributed in the medieval Tristan corpus.[4] Versions of the episode survive in the *Tristrant* of Eilhart; in the works of the continuers of Gottfried von Strassburg's *Tristan*, Ulrich von Türheim and Heinrich von Freiberg; in the variant version of the French prose *Tristan* preserved in MS. B.N.fr. 103 and in the late fifteenth- and early sixteenth-century French imprints that reproduce it; in the Italian *Tavola Ritonda*; and in the Old Norse *Tristrams Saga* and

[4] Arboreal and vegetative symbols of love existed both in classical texts known in twelfth-century France and in French texts from the first two thirds of that century. The motif of the metamorphosis of lovers into plants occurs in Ovid's *Metamorphoses* in the episodes of Narcissus (Bk. 3), Pyramus and Thisbe (Bk. 4), and Baucis and Philemon (Bk. 8), and in the variant of the twelfth-century French *Pyramus et Tisbé* given by the *Ovide moralisé* (de Boer 51-52). Zingarelli (52-53) and Delpino (331) imply that Thomas, whose romance is heavily coloured by Ovidian reminiscences, borrowed the motif of the resurrection of the lovers in the form of plants from Ovid's *Pyramus and Thisbe*. Vàrvaro contests this conclusion, arguing that the motif as found in Eilhart and MS. B.N.fr. 103 derives from popular, oral sources and was suppressed by Thomas 'il razionalista' (1062-63). Perhaps the most extensive development of the motif in twelfth-century French literature is found in the 'aristocratic' version of *Floire and Blancheflor*, composed around 1150 (Leclanche 11) or in 1160-61 (Delbouille, 'A propos'), which Delbouille suggests was the source of the episode in the French Ur-Tristan ('Premier roman' 432). It contains the motif of love as a tree that grows in the heart of the lover (377-90), of the (false) tomb of the beloved shaded by precious trees (551-666), of a tree of love (2045-92), and of a lover (Flore) who rejoins his captive beloved by hiding in a basket of flowers and who is explicitly compared to a flower (2288-440). Nor was the motif unknown in Celtic literature. In the Irish tale of 'Baile and Ailinn' a yew tree grows over Baile's grave and an apple tree over Ailinn's. When the trees are cut down and a poet's tablet made from the wood of each, the two tablets come together and are joined 'like honey-suckle about a branch' (Carney 223-25). The tale was composed at the latest in the tenth or eleventh century, but it is probable, as Carney suggests (224), that the motif of the miraculous trees is a secondary accretion.

its Icelandic descendants, the *Saga af Tristram ok Ysodd* and the ballad, *Tristrams Kvæði*. In addition, Marie de France's *Chevrefoil* contains an echo of the motif, while yet another idiosyncratic rendering of the motif is found in a Spanish romance of the thirteenth century and in its fifteenth-century Portuguese adaptation.[5]

Two distinct thematic traditions may be distinguished among the earliest versions of the episode of the miraculous plants in the medieval Tristan corpus. In that represented by Eilhart and his imitators, Ulrich and Heinrich, the lovers are buried with honour by a repentant Marke in a single grave, from which the miraculous plants spring and intertwine. The version of Eilhart gives the following account:

> Ich sag üch wärlich:
> Man legt sie bayde in ain grab.
> Man sagt dar ab,
> Und ward mir gesagt alsuß zwar,
> Der kunig ainen rosenbusch dar
> Ließ setzen uff daß wib
> Und ainen stock uff Tristrandß lib
> Von ainem winreben.
> Die wŏchsen ze samen eben,
> Daß man sie mit kainen dingen
> Mocht von ain ander bringen
> – Für wăr hort ich daß sprechen –,
> Wenn wölt sü dann ab brechen:
> Daß macht deß tranckß kraft so.
> Nu ist eß alleß vol schriben jo,
> Daß ich west von Tristranden,
> Dem künen wŷganden. (9508-24)

In the tradition preserved by *Tristrams Saga* and its Icelandic derivatives and by MS. B.N.fr. 103, the lovers are deliberately separated in death by a jealous spouse (Ísodd in the *Saga*, Mark in the prose romance) who orders that the lovers be interred in separate graves on either side of a chapel, the better to disunite them. A plant or plants grow(s) across the chapel, miraculously reuniting the lovers. The narrative given in *Tristrams Saga* is as

---

[5] Neither, however, is associated directly with the account of the death of the lovers. In Marie's *Chevrefoil*, the miraculous plants serve as a metaphor for the lovers' passion during their lifetime; it is said that the lovers are like the honeysuckle and the hazel tree that intertwine and that, if separated, wither and die. The Spanish/Portuguese episode recounts that Tristan, wounded by his uncle's lance, was visited by Iseo. Weeping, the two embraced, and from the spot where their tears fell there sprang a lily that possessed the virtue of impregnating maidens. Indeed, at that very moment, Iseo became pregnant with Tristan's son. See F. Michel 1: xvii, 2: 298-302; Sudre 550.

follows:

It is said that Ísodd, Tristram's wife, had Tristram and Ísönd buried on opposite sides of the church so that they would not be close to each other in death. But it came to pass that an oak tree or other tree grew up from each of their graves, so high that their branches intertwined above the gablehead of the church. And from this it could be seen how great had been the love between them. (Ch. 101)

The version of MS. B.N.fr. 103 is as follows:

Lors commanda [Marc] que les corps soient portés a la chappelle et soient illeuc enterrés si richement comme il appartient a si haulte gent. Le roy fait faire deux sercleux, ung de calcedoine et l'autre d'un beril. Tristan fu mis eu calcedoine et Yseult ou beril, et furent enfouys a plours et a lermes, l'un d'une part de la chappelle et l'autre de l'autre part. . . . De dedens la tombe Tristan yssoit une ronche belle et verte et foillue qui aloit par dessus la chappelle, et descendoit le bout de la ronche sur la tombe Yseult et entroit dedens. Ce virent les gens du pais et le compterent au roy. Le roy la fit par trois fois coupper: a l'andemain restoit aussi belle et en autel estat comme elle avoit esté autrefois. Cest miracle estoit sur Tristan et sur Yseult. (393-94)

What then was the source of the episode of the intertwining trees found in *Tristrams Saga*? Certainly, the motif of the miraculous plants procedes logically from that of the potion, which also depends on the magical properties of plants.[6] As the potion prolonged the lovers' passion during their lives, so did the miracle of the plants after their death.[7] If Thomas's poem did contain an episode of the intertwining trees, it formed a part of a larger thematic fabric. Since the death of Tristan's parents, Kanelangres and Blanchefleur (*S* Ch. 15), prefigures that of the lovers, the poem would have been framed by symmetrically disposed death scenes, each containing a vegetative motif (Blanchefleur's name and the intertwining trees). Moreover, the image of the two trees that grow from the graves of the lovers would replicate another arboreal image that stands at the centre of the poem, the single tree that grows above the subterranean grotto where the lovers lie entwined in one another's arms (*S* Ch. 64).

Unfortunately, the evidence of the other two texts which, like *Tristrams Saga*, derive directly from Thomas's poem, the Middle

[6] The *Saga* says, 'The queen prepared a secret potion with minute care and cunning craft with many kinds of blossoms and grasses' (Ch. 46). Beroul terms the potion 'li vin *herbez*' (2138), and the *Folie de Berne* poet declares:

Cil boivre fu fait a envers
De *plusors herbés mout divers*. (318-19)

[7] Both Thomas (Sn[2] 805) and MS. B.N.fr. 103 (393) allude to the potion at the moment of the lovers' deaths, although the reference in Thomas is oblique.

English *Sir Tristrem* and Gottfried's *Tristan und Isolde*, is incapable of resolving the question. The first is fragmentary, the last leaf of the single manuscript having been lost, while the second was left uncompleted by its author. Gottfried's continuers, Ulrich and Heinrich, who modeled their continuations on Eilhart's narrative, did not know Thomas's poem. However, the existence of such an episode in Eilhart's *Tristrant* (the only other extant twelfth-century Tristan text to recount the death of the lovers), in MS. B.N.fr. 103 (that elsewhere shows traces of the influence of Thomas's romance), and in *Tristrams Saga* (the only text deriving directly from Thomas that preserves the conclusion of the romance) strongly suggests that a version of the episode existed in the common source of the poems of Eilhart and Thomas, as well as in the latter's romance.

II

BROTHER ROBERT'S FIDELITY TO HIS SOURCE

The history of the literary relations between Norway and Western Europe in the thirteenth century constitutes a fascinating chapter of medieval literary history (Leach, 'Relations,' *Angevin Britain*; Johnsen; Helle; Knudson; Kalinke). From the eleventh to the fourteenth century, scribes in Norway produced translations of Latin and, less frequently, of English and German texts for the edification and delectation of the Norwegian court (Halvorsen 247). However, under the reign of King Hákon IV Hákonarson, who ruled from 1217 to 1263, there was a momentary proliferation of translations from the French and Anglo-Norman. Before Hákon ascended the throne, there had been almost no translations from the French-speaking world, as there would be none after his death (Togeby 183-85). Described by Matthew Paris, the erudite English monk and traveler who visited Norway in 1248, as *'bene litteratus,'* Hákon worked tirelessly to further commercial and cultural contacts with the South. The monarch looked to England and continental Europe, and in particular to the Angevin court of Henry III, for models of courtly practice and for literary texts that, in translation, might serve to refine the minds and manners of his court (Leach, *Angevin Britain* 153-54; Helle 108-09; Barnes;

Halvorsen 251; Zink 92). The name of one of King Hákon's translators has survived, that of an individual who, in his prologue to *Tristrams Saga*, which he claims to have translated in 1226, identifies himself as 'Brother Robert' and who, in the conclusion to *Elis Saga*, refers to himself as 'Abbot Robert,' saying in each case that he undertook his translation at the behest of King Hákon.[8]

The episode of the intertwining trees has traditionally been ascribed to Thomas's translator. However, an examination of the habits of Brother Robert reveals that there exists in *Tristrams Saga* only one instance of the interpolation of non-canonical narrative material, Ísönd's prayer (Ch. 101). Since it was not Robert's habit to interpolate narrative material, it may be assumed that he was not the inventor of the episode of the intertwining trees.

Certain generalizations may be made concerning Robert's practices as translator and adaptor of Thomas. First, it must be cautioned that *translation*, unless understood in its medieval sense – a sense closer to adaptation than to the modern meaning of literal, undeviating fidelity to an original – is an inappropriate term to describe Brother Robert's literary production. Essentially he is an abridger, although the figure given by Bédier (*Thomas* 2: 75, 93-4), who estimates that Robert reduces Thomas's poem to one half of its original 17,000–20,000 lines, is perhaps excessive; for the majority of those passages of Thomas's romance that have survived

---

[8] The question of the authenticity of Robert's prologue, and hence of its date and patron and the name of its translator, has recently been examined by Sverrir Tómasson, who argues that the prologue, which is preserved only in manuscripts of the seventeenth century, imitates the style of sixteenth- and seventeenth-century booktitles. However, he notes that three of the four data contained in the prologue, Robert's name, his clerical state, and the patronage of Hákon, are echoed in the colophon to *Elis Saga*, preserved in a thirteenth-century Norwegian manuscript (MS. De la Gardie nr. 4-7 fol.). This early confirmation of the factual contents of Robert's prologue suggests their authenticity, even if, as seems likely, the prologue was rewritten at a later date. He concludes: '.. the passage is probably originally a colophon which the 16th or 17th century cop[y]ist has modernised in the fas[h]ion of booktitles of his times. ... The following features are shown to be from mediaeval times: the name of the translator, the naming of the patron, the description of the translator's language and possibly the date. It is also stressed that it is unthinkable that the cop[y]ist invented these features. ... It is hardly possible to cast any doubt on [the prologue] as a valid source for literary history; *Tristrams Saga* was originally translated during the reign of Hákon Hákonarson the Old. But from this fact it does not necessarily follow that the existing *Tristrams Saga* should be regarded as a 13th century Norwegian prose-romance' (78). See also Kalinke 3-4.

to permit comparison with Robert's translation show the Anglo-Norman poet at his most prolix. Such passages would consequently have been condensed most heavily by the Old Norse adaptor.[9] Robert tends to economize in descriptive passages, to minimize monologue and dialogue, to suppress passages of psychological analysis, especially those treating love, and to eliminate authorial interventions and references to his source. Yet he is faithful in his fashion to the text that he renders. While he omits much narrative material, he translates with accuracy those details of plot that he retains. His additions are few and with one exception, Ísönd's prayer (Ch. 101), touch only the surface of a work whose *narrative* content they do not significantly modify (Bédier, *Thomas* 2: 64-75; Gunnlaugsdóttir 212-20, 329-32; Shoaf 21-54). His originality, such as it is, resides in his skilful use of rhetorical and metrical embellishment at the level of the word or phrase (Schach, 'Style'; Gunnlaugsdóttir 212-13, 216).[10]

Robert's additions, all minor, fall into four categories. A number arise from his penchant for providing occasional explanations not found in his model, either to recapitulate, to clarify, or to instruct. Thus, where Thomas's text has none, Robert will frequently invent an explicative detail (Gunnlaugsdóttir 213). For example, as Tristram takes leave of Ísönd after their discovery in the garden, he tells her, ' "I cannot remain here any longer, *for those who hate*

---

[9] Halvorsen 251. Schach estimates that Robert's translation is about two-thirds as long as his source ('Observations [1957-59]' 115). It is perhaps possible to come to a more accurate estimate of the length of Thomas's original poem than that arrived at by Bédier. The Sneyd manuscript in its present form consists of fourteen parchment leaves of the original manuscript, numbered in this century from 4 to 17, as well as fly-leaves and binding papers of more recent date. (Folios 1 and 2 consist of modern preliminary material; folio 3, also modern, has been removed.) Each of the two Sneyd fragments is contained in a quire of four bifolia from which a single leaf is missing. The sewing holes and folds in folio 21, a notarial document dated 1366 that served at one time as a limp-vellum cover to the book, show that the codex originally contained approximately thirteen quires of eight leaves each. Assuming that the manuscript contained only Thomas's poem, it would in its original form have contained approximately 13000 lines of text (13 quires of 8 leaves x 4 columns per leaf x 32 lines per column = 13312 lines). My statements here and below (note 32) concerning the manuscript are based on information generously communicated to me by Dr Bruce Barker-Benfield, Assistant Librarian in the Department of Western Manuscripts of the Bodleian Library.

[10] This is not to imply that Robert does not substantially alter his model. In fact, as Shoaf has shown, he effects important changes in the theology and ideology of his source. However, his tool in doing so is omission and not addition, for he respects the letter of his model while markedly altering its spirit (Shoaf 15).

us will soon be here" ' (Ch. 67; cf. C 35). Robert also adds details that would hold a special interest for a Scandinavian audience. Hence, he is generally assumed to have expanded the list of Norwegian exports (Ch. 18) and the itinerary of countries visited by Róaldur in his search for the kidnapped Tristram (Ch. 19) (Leach, *Angevin Britain* 40; Bédier, *Thomas* 1: 32, n. 1).[11] His predilection for using alliterating word pairs for stylistic effect leads him to add words not found in his model. In Thomas Tristan ascribes his impotence to ' "le grant travail qu'ai eü" ' (Sn[1] 633); in *Tristrams Saga* to ' "vásum ok vokum" ' ('hardships *and sleepless nights*,' Ch. 70). Iseut characterizes Cariado as a 'huan' (Sn[1] 865); Ísönd calls Maríadokk an ' "**úlfr** ok **ug**la" ' ('an owl *and a wolf*,' Ch. 72). Elsewhere, Robert simply exaggerates, presumably to retain the interest of an audience used to the action-filled narratives of the native sagas. Thus, the doldrums that becalm the ship bearing Iseut to Tristan last for five days in Thomas (D 1697) but *ten* in Robert's account (Ch. 98). While there exist numerous examples of such minor alteration of narrative detail, none (with the exception of Ísönd's prayer) is important enough to change the plot significantly.

However, Brother Robert does alter his original in one significant respect. He treats quite differently from Thomas passages where he perceives questions of morality and religion to be at issue. One is left with an impression of the unease of a literal-minded provincial cleric confronted with the embarrassing doctrinal freedom of his cosmopolitan colleague.[12] For example, in Thomas's poem the scene of the *eau hardie* takes place while Kaherdin, Iseut, and Tristan are on the way to 'une feste por jüer' (T[1] 198), a detail that Robert alters to 'a certain holy place to say their prayers' (Ch. 82).[13] In Thomas Tristan le Nain requests that Tristan help him regain his 'bele amie' (D 939), that is, his paramour (a detail consistent with the analogous scenes in the versions of Eilhart, MS. B.N.fr. 103, and the account that Thomas

---

[11] The corresponding enumerations in Gottfried are less detailed (2198-209, 3757-803). Schach has speculated that the list of exports was further expanded by an Icelandic copyist (*Saga* 21, n. 1), while Gunnlaugsdóttir has observed that it is not impossible that the lists were found in Thomas (245). Cf. in this regard similar enumerations at D 1310-13 and 1533-38.

[12] Geraldine Barnes has asserted that the *riddarasögur* were intended 'as textbooks of chivalric conduct and of Christian morality' (157). Gunnlaugsdóttir observes that 'Robert, ante este tema [love], adopta una actitud de reserva que calificaríamos de actitud moralizadora' (215).

[13] Wind (T[1] 198) rejects Bédier's emendation of *iuer* to *urer* (*Thomas* 1: 1138).

133

rejects). However, as if to suppress the reference to extra-marital love, Robert twice insists that the lady in question is Tristram the Dwarf's *wife* (Ch. 94). In order to palliate certain particularly troubling passages, he repeatedly causes his characters to invoke the Deity in circumstances in which His name is not mentioned by Thomas's. Hence, as Tristram prepares to take leave of Ísönd in the garden, he says, ' "Now kiss me farewell, *and may God guard and protect us"* ' (Ch. 67; cf. C 36). Bringvet declares to Ísönd: ' *"God knows* that I [gave up my virginity] for the sake of your honor" ' (Ch. 89; cf. D 8-9), and Ísönd, who persuaded Bringvet to sacrifice her honour to conceal her own transgression, later says to her companion: ' *"God knows* that I have always regretted what I have done against you" ' (Ch. 93; cf. D 694).[14] Kardín says that he will abduct Ísönd from her lawful husband and return with her to Brittany, ' *"if it be God's will"* ' (Ch. 96; cf. D 1170). In the same episode Tristan, appealing for Iseut's aid, puns at length on *salu* ('greeting,' 'salvation'; D 1195-1210). Robert suppresses this irreverent word play and instead has Tristram urge his friend 'to bear repeatedly *God's and* his own greetings to Queen Ísönd' (Ch. 96). Certain of Robert's omissions appear motivated by a similar sentiment of shocked religious zeal. In the Cambridge fragment Thomas describes the discovery of the sleeping lovers by the king and the malevolent dwarf. Mark, says Thomas:

> Prendre les cuidoit a l'ovraine,
> Mes, *merci Deu*, bien i demorerent. (5-6)

Thomas's editorial *merci Deu*, which suggests God's complicity in the lovers' escape from danger, is resolutely suppressed by Robert in a passage that he translates more closely than any other in the surviving fragments of his model.

In place of Thomas's benevolent if distant God, Robert substitutes a condemnatory Deity to whom the lovers must appeal for aid and grace. In place of Thomas's conception of a fatality of love grounded in the human frailty of his protagonists, Robert substitutes that of a relentless, impersonal destiny that impels the lovers toward their fate. In summarizing in a brief half-paragraph the one hundred and ninety-four lines of Tristan's monologue and Thomas's authorial commentary on the situation of the four protagonists and

---

[14] Although Robert condenses to a single paragraph Iseut's plaintive lament during the storm, a monologue that extends over eighty lines in Thomas (D 1615-94), he still manages to retain two of her six appeals to the divinity (D 1616, 1627, 1636, 1664, 1675, 1692).

Tristan's obligation to pass the nuptial night with his new bride (Sn¹ 395-588), Robert places in Tristram's mouth the untoward observation: ' "Nevertheless, what is destined must come to pass" ' (Ch. 70). In describing the clandestine departure of Kardín and Ísönd from Mark's court, Robert indulges in a bit of foreshadowing that likewise evokes the Nordic conception of an implacable fate carrying the lovers to their doom:

> They were all merry and cheerful, and looked forward to something quite different from what was in store for them.   (Ch. 96)

The interpolation of Ísönd's prayer, whose tone and intent are alien to Thomas's poem, is explicable only in light of Robert's attempts to modify the theological perspective of his model:

Sneyd²	*Tristrams Saga*
Ysolt vait u le cors veit,	Queen Ísönd now went to where Tristram's body lay on the floor,
774 Si se turne vers orient,	and turning to the east
Pur lui prie pitusement:	offered up her prayer with these words: 'I beseech Thee, almighty God, be merciful to this man and to me inasmuch as I believe that Thou wast born into this world of the Virgin Mary for the redemption of all mankind, and inasmuch as Thou didst help Mary Magdalene and endure death for us sinful people and that Thou didst suffer Thyself to be nailed to the cross and to be pierced with a lance in the right side, and didst go harrying to Hell, whence Thou didst redeem all Thy people into eternal bliss. Thou art our Creator. Eternal, almighty God, look with mercy on our sins inasmuch as I will believe all this. And I will gladly believe and I will gladly praise and worship Thee. And grant, I pray Thee, my Creator, that my sins be forgiven, one God, Father, Son, and Holy Ghost. Amen.'

135

	'Tristram,' she said, 'I love you deeply.
776 'Amis Tristran, quant mort vus vei,	And now that I see you dead, it is
Par raisun vivre puis ne dei.	not fitting for me to live any longer,
778 Mort estes pur l'amur de mei	for I see that you died for my sake.
Par raisun vivre puis ne dei.'	And therefore I shall not live after you.'

In Thomas the lovers die unshriven and unrepentant, their attention entirely focused on one another. Tristan, who, in a passage that Robert omits, appeals in passing for God's mercy for himself and his beloved (D 1760), reserves his dying breath for the evocation of a higher good:

> 'Amie Ysolt' treis feiz dit,
> A la quarte rent l'esprit.   (D 1769-70)

Iseut gives no thought to her Maker; her final act is to embrace the body of her dead lover. Robert's long prayer is clearly intended to save the souls of his protagonists and with them the *bienséances* of his work.[15] On the other hand, the episode of the intertwining trees, with its overtones of pagan animism, signifies not the lovers' spiritual salvation but the perfection and perpetuation of their earthly love; it could scarcely have been composed by the earnest moralizer Robert, who reduces to a minimum the love element in the romance (Gunnlaugsdóttir 215) and whose narrative additions to his source are negligible.

[15] Similarly, the prayer that opens the lament of the castaway Tristram (Ch. 20), 'the longest prayer, and one of the longest speeches, in the whole work,' was in all probability expanded to its present dimensions by Robert (Shoaf 129, n. 2); for the corresponding prayers in Gottfried (2487-532, 2586-619) and *Sir Tristrem* (390-96) incorporate much less theological detail.

III

THE FIDELITY OF THE MODERN MANUSCRIPTS
OF *TRISTRAMS SAGA*

A recent article has raised points that, if correct, demonstrate that the episode of the intertwining trees in *Tristrams Saga* was a late interpolation that existed neither in Thomas's romance nor in Robert's thirteenth-century translation of it. M. F. Thomas has recently advanced the theory that in its extant form *Tristrams Saga*, which survives in its entirety only in manuscripts of the seventeenth and eighteenth centuries,[16] does not accurately represent the translation of Thomas's romance made in the thirteenth century but is a version contaminated at a later date by narrative material from other sources, notably Eilhart's *Tristrant*, the fourteenth-century Icelandic *Saga af Tristram ok Ysodd*, and the fifteenth-century Icelandic ballad *Tristrams Kvæði*. She suggests that the episode of the intertwining trees, given by all of the modern manuscripts of *Tristrams Saga*,[17] is a late interpolation derived from *Tristrams Kvæði* and ultimately from the *version commune* represented by Eilhart and MS. B.N.fr. 103 (73-74). While in its general lines her thesis is an engaging one, neither the evidence that Ms Thomas cites in support of her hypothesis nor other, more pertinent evidence that bears on this question demonstrates that the three modern manuscripts of *Tristrams Saga* contain interpolated narrative material.[18]

A comparison of the oldest manuscript fragments of *Tristrams Saga*, three fifteenth-century vellum leaves preserved in manuscript AM 567 4to and one in the fifteenth-century Reeves

---

[16] For a discussion of the manuscript tradition of *Tristrams Saga*, see Gunnlaugsdóttir 14-18.

[17] While the episode has been lost from MS. ÍB 51 fol., which breaks off in mid-sentence (at Kölbing 112, 12), its presence in MS. JS 8 fol., a copy of MS. ÍB 51, confirms that it was originally present in the latter.

[18] Ms Thomas evokes the authority of Tómasson in support of her claim of the unreliability of the modern manuscripts of *Tristrams Saga*. However, in so doing, she overstates his argument, for Tómasson's study deals with *rhetorical* transformations of the *Saga* (specifically of that portion, the prologue, most susceptible to scribal alteration) and makes no claim for the interpolation of

fragment of the Library of Congress, with the two seventeenth-century and one eighteenth-century paper manuscripts (AM 543 4to, ÍB 51 fol., and JS 8 fol.) shows that the later texts consistently, if somewhat unsystematically, condense the earlier ones.[19] The abridgment eliminates passages of rhetorical *amplificatio* (e.g. the extended explanation of Tristan's naming [Ch. 16] and the condemnation of extortion and the use of force [Ch. 27]), reduces alliterating and assonancing word pairs, and, in one case, eliminates a French pun incomprehensible in Old Norse (Ch. 16).[20] However, there is no instance in which the paper manuscripts interpolate narrative material not found in the fifteenth-century fragments. Thus, if such interpolation took place, either it failed to affect the passages preserved by the four fifteenth-century folios or it took place before their redaction and hence at a period far removed from that at which the prologue presumably was recast.

In support of her thesis, Ms Thomas cites five narrative details as proof that Eilhart's *Tristrant* and the Icelandic Tristan texts hitherto assumed to have derived from Robert's *Tristrams Saga*, the *Saga af Tristram ok Ysodd* and *Tristrams Kvæði* (Leach, *Angevin Britain* 169-98; Schach, 'Scandinavian Ballad', 'Observations (1969)'), contributed narrative material to the extant manuscripts of *Tristrams Saga*. She notes that while in Thomas's poem the sails to be carried by Kaherdin are black or white, in *Tristrams Saga* they are black or blue-and-white and in *Tristrams Kvæði* black or blue (75). This detail is hardly decisive; the evolution from black and white (Thomas) to black and blue-and-white (*Saga*) to black and blue (*Tristrams Kvæði*) is surely a more natural one than that postulated by Ms Thomas. She also notes that 'the traditional ballad-image of Tristram's turning himself to the wall' (77), a detail found in *Tristrams Saga*, also occurs in *Tristrams Kvæði*, which, she suggests, is its source. In fact, this

narrative material in other portions of the text. See *supra*, note 8. She also bases certain of her conclusions on the assumption of an absolute separation between the *version commune* and the *version courtoise* (81, 88, 89), a misunderstanding of the significance accorded the terms by modern critics. The latter are in general agreement '[pour] placer en tête de la tradition une "version commune" représentée directement par Eilhart, Béroul et la *Prose*, mais remaniée profondément par Thomas' (Delbouille, 'Premier Roman' 275).

[19] For a discussion, see Kalinke 58-63.

[20] For an explanation of the treatment of word pairs and more generally of Thomas's 'court style' by the copyists of the paper manuscripts, see Schach, 'Observations (1957-59)' 104-12, 116-17, 'Unpublished Leaf' 60-62, 'Style' 66, 74, and 'Reeves Fragment' 306-08; Gunnlaugsdóttir 134-45.

image is a verbatim translation by Robert of Thomas's: 'E turne sei vers la parei' (D 1759). She further contends that the episode of Tristan's first voyage to Ireland (Ch. 30) was influenced by the version of Eilhart, with which it agrees regarding Tristan's intentions and destination when he set sail, and does not derive from Thomas, whose successor Gottfried recounts it differently (64-65, 67-68). In fact, as Aitken has cogently demonstrated, the presence in Thomas of a version of the *voyage à l'aventure* similar to that in Eilhart is confirmed by the evidence of Chertsey tile 20 and the *Folie d'Oxford*.

According to Ms Thomas (75-77), the fact that in *Tristrams Saga* (Ch. 96) the device of the colored sails is omitted from the episode where is given in Thomas (D 1289-96) and only recounted later in order to explain the mechanism of Ísodd's revenge (Ch. 99) testifies to the influence of Eilhart, in whose text Isalde does not overhear the conversation of Tristrant but later is mysteriously informed of the sail signal (9290-97, 9346-47). However, a close comparison of Robert's text with Thomas's reveals that a different process led the translator to omit the detail in question. In the first half of Chapter 96 he translates the episode of Tristan's conversation with Kaherdin and Iseut aux Blanches Mains' reaction thereto (D 1067-1366). He renders closely the opening lines of the episode, which contain the essence of Tristan's lament to his friend (D 1067-1189), eliminating the repetitions and amplifications in his source, occasionally summarizing, but suppressing only one narrative detail (D 1082-84). At this point Thomas embarks on a long *amplificatio* in which Tristan's instructions to Kaherdin become a lengthy expatiation on his suffering, his love for Iseut, the fact that she alone is capable of saving him, and the necessity that she come to his aid (D 1190-1280). Tristan concludes by touching briefly on the practical details of the voyage, announcing that Kaherdin will have forty days to accomplish his errand (D 1281) and explaining the device of the sail signal (D 1289-96). Thomas then recounts Kaherdin's departure and voyage (D 1300-22) and how Iseut overhears the conversation, improving the occasion by a digression on feminine jealousy (D 1323-66). In his haste to be done with the rhetorical excurses that open and close this long passage (D 1190-1366), Robert condenses sweepingly and undiscriminatingly, excising rhetorical and narrative material alike (including the detail of the sails) and translating with some degree of exactitude only seven of its one hundred and seventy-seven lines.[21] When he later

---

[21] D 1302-04, 1337-39, 1346.

comes to recount Ísodd's lie (Ch. 99), Robert must belatedly explain the device of the sails, concluding: 'Ísodd, Tristram's wife, had heard all this when she had concealed herself behind the wooden wall', a close rendering of Thomas's earlier statement: 'Ysolt estoit suz la parei, / Les diz Tristran escute et ot, / Ben ad entendu chacun mot' (D 1336-38). The initial failure to explain the sail signal indicates not that Robert substituted Eilhart's version for that of Thomas but that, faced with a long passage of amplification and digression, he heavily and uncritically abridged his model, discarding the grain of narrative detail with the rhetorical chaff.[22]

Finally, citing the absence of an episode of the intertwining trees in Thomas and pointing to the indications of contamination discussed above, Ms Thomas suggests that the source of the episode in *Tristrams Saga* was *Tristrams Kvæði* or the *Saga af Tristram ok Ysodd* (72-74, 78-80). However, it has been seen that none of the other examples offered by Ms Thomas in support of her theory of the unreliability of the extant version of *Tristrams Saga* can be retained. Hence her theory, which remains unproven, cannot be invoked to demonstrate the non-canonical character of the episode of the intertwining trees in *Tristrams Saga*.

IV

EILHART'S *TRISTRANT* AND MS. B.N.fr. 103

It is a basic premise of Tristan scholarship that the first generation of extant Tristan texts (Eilhart, Beroul, Thomas, and the dominant version of the French prose romance) shared a common source, although opinion has long been divided on its precise nature. One school of thought, believing that by their very nature literary cycles are fluid and that this instability was particularly pronounced in the twelfth-century Tristan matter, has held that the source of the extant Tristan poems was a diverse body of oral tales and motifs.

[22] Shoaf offers a different explanation for the initial omission by Robert of the sail signal. She suggests this is one of several examples of a stylistic device unique to Robert that she terms 'deferred suspense,' that is, the postponing of the explanation of a crisis until it has passed (76-79).

Another school has maintained that the archetype was a complete, written version of the romance composed in mid-twelfth-century France by a single poet who adopted and unified earlier source material (Bédier, *Thomas* 2: 186-87).[23] Proponents of both theories now agree, however, that the three texts of the so-called *version commune* hewed more closely to their common source(s) that Thomas also knew but substantially altered (Fourrier 35-36; Delbouille, 'Premier Roman' 275; Frappier 259).[24] While this assumption remains theoretical, no evidence has been put forward to contradict it. Thus, in principle there is no impediment to the hypothesis that the episode of the intertwining trees in Eilhart and Thomas had a common source, should it be demonstrated that such an episode was present in Thomas. Whether one assumes with Bédier that a version of the episode existed in the *estoire* (*Thomas* 2: 186-87, 301) or postulates the existence of an independent oral or written lay, it suffices to assume as the original of the very different renderings of Eilhart and Thomas a single archetype sufficiently general in nature to permit the divergent interpretations given it in the German and the French traditions.

The existence of a version of the miraculous plants in MS. B.N.fr 103 elucidates the relationship of the versions of Eilhart and *Tristrams Saga* to one another and to Thomas and serves to demonstrate by triangulation that a similar episode existed in Thomas's poem. Composed between 1340 and 1450 (Baumgartner 83) and preserved only in a single late fifteenth-century manuscript and in eight early printed editions that derive from it (Curtis, *Tristan en prose* 1: 16-17), MS. B.N.fr. 103 presents a version of the final episodes of the romance similar to that given by Eilhart

---

[23] Delbouille, who has argued most recently in favour of this thesis, maintains that Eilhart's poem is a close and reliable translation of this lost archetype ('Premier Roman'). Yet, even the staunchest proponents of the theory of a single archetype admit the possibility of the later interpolation by the first-generation texts of material not found in the archetype. Delbouille, for example, contends that the episodes of the Irish harper and the ambiguous oath, traces of which are found in all of the first-generation texts save Eilhart, are not canonical ('Premier Roman' 277-82, 419-23).

[24] A most persuasive explanation of the reasons that led Thomas to depart from his source has recently been advanced by Tony Hunt ('Significance'). Most scholars who have treated the question of the genesis and evolution of the Tristan matter in the twelfth century have failed to give proper weight to the wide divergences within the *version commune*, prominently those dividing Eilhart from Beroul and those separating the dominant French prose *Tristan* and MS. B.N.fr. 103 from one another and from Eilhart and Beroul.

and, in certain details, to that given by Thomas.[25] MS. B.N.fr. 103, which contains 383 folios, gives generally an abridged version of the narrative of the French prose *Tristan* from fol. 1 to fol. 374 (including the episode in which Tristan's death at Mark's hands is prepared and predicted [Löseth §191]). At this point, it diverges to follow a narrative close to that of Eilhart in recounting the episodes of Runalen's adulterous liaison with Gargeolain and Tristan's last wound, suffered at the hands of her cuckolded husband Bedalis,[26] a narrative that Thomas also knew and that he rejected as an inferior rendering of the legend (D 852-58). It intercalates in the middle of this episode another in which Tristan leads an army against the Count of Nantes[27] and a second recounting Tristan's madness.[28] The independent testimony of Thomas to the existence of an archetype of the Gargeolain episode suggests that a common source existed for the versions of Eilhart and MS. B.N.fr. 103 rather than that the former served as the source of the latter (Bédier, 'Mort' 491).

Following the episode of Tristan's last wound, the narratives of Thomas (D 1054-Sn[2] 819) and Eilhart (9235-9438) converge to give a generally similar account of Tristan's suffering, his summons to Iseut, and the death of the lovers.[29] The account of MS. B.N.fr. 103 hews more closely to that of Eilhart (e.g. the young girl who reveals the sail device to Yseult/Isalde: MS. 103, 388-89; Eilhart 9346-67) but adds two details found only in Thomas. In both French texts Iseut aux Blanches Mains acts out of jealous anger in her lie concerning the sails (*T* D 1323-49, 1739-56; MS. 103, 389), and Tristan descends to the shore to watch for Iseut's return (*T* D 1557-60; MS. 103, 388). The account in B.N.fr. 103 of the aftermath of the lovers' deaths conflates material found in *Tristrams Saga* (and hence presumably in Thomas) and in Eilhart (and hence

---

[25] The dominant version of the prose romance, the earliest portions of which were composed around 1230-1235 (Baumgartner 40), differs profoundly from all of the twelfth-century versions of the legend, most notably in its account of Tristan's death. Tristan is fatally wounded by Mark (§546) with a poisoned lance given him by Morgain (§191). It contains no version of the miraculous plants and, as in Eilhart, Mark repents his persecution of the lovers and supervises their burial (§550).

[26] Fols 374ra-374vb, 377rb-378va; Bédier, *Thomas* 2: 372-74, 380-82; cf. Eilhart 7865-8134, 9033-9234.

[27] Fols 374vb-375rb; Bédier, 'Mort' 497-98; cf. Eilhart 8135-8200, 8553-657.

[28] Fols 375rb-377rb; Bédier, *Thomas* 2: 374-79; cf. Eilhart 8658-9032. For a comparative analysis of the episode as given by MS. B.N.fr. 103, Eilhart, and the *Folies Tristan* of Bern and Oxford, see Lutoslawski.

[29] For a comparative analysis, see Bédier, 'Mort'.

presumably in his French source). The bodies of Tristan and Yseult, together with a letter composed by the dying Tristan, are sent to Mark, who declares first that his nephew will not be buried in his kingdom (391-93). However, upon the plea of his subjects, he relents. After reading Tristan's letter explaining the circumstances of their love and of the potion, he repents (393; cf. Eilhart 9465-501) and has the lovers richly buried (393-4; cf. Eilhart 9502-07). Here MS. B.N.fr. 103 and Eilhart diverge. In the former, the lovers are buried: 'l'un d'une part de la chapelle et l'autre de l'autre part' (394; cf. *Tristram Saga*: '... on opposite sides of the church so they would not be close to each other in death' [Ch. 101]); in Eilhart: 'bayde in ain grab' (9509). When a briar grows from Tristan's tomb into Yseult's, Mark thrice causes it to be cut down, while Eilhart specifically rejects the notion that the plants can be separated by force (9516-20). The account of MS. B.N.fr. 103, which fails to explain the inconsistency between Mark's forgiveness of the lovers and his subsequent efforts to separate them and to sever the vine, conflates elements similar to those found in Eilhart and *Tristram Saga*. From a version similar to that of Eilhart (presumably the latter's French source), the author retained the details of Mark's repentance and supervision of the burial of the lovers. From a version similar to that of *Tristrams Saga* (presumably the latter's source, Thomas), he retained the details of the separation of the lovers in death and of their reunion through a marvelous vegetative reincarnation in spite of the efforts of a spouse to disunite them, details at odds with those derived from Eilhart's source.

The author of MS. B.N.fr. 103 knew Thomas's text and incorporated into his own narrative details given only by Thomas. It has been amply demonstrated that the dominant version of the prose romance borrowed material from Thomas, and, to the extent that MS. B.N.fr. 103 reproduces that version, it also relies on Thomas.[30] However, it can also be shown that the author of MS.

---

[30] Vinaver has argued most strongly for the influence of Thomas both on the dominant version of the prose romance and on MS. B.N.fr. 103. He lists among other points the etymology of Tristan's name, the unlimited duration of the potion, the fact that the Tristan and Yseult fall in love before consuming the potion, the episode of the Irish harper, and Tristan's hesitation before his marriage as elements derived by the dominant version from Thomas (*Etudes* 11, 20, n. 1; 'Love Potion' 78-83; 'Prose Tristan' 340-41) and Yseult aux Blanches Mains' jealousy as a detail borrowed by MS. B.N.fr. 103 (*Etudes* 18). Baumgartner is more cautious in assessing the extent of Thomas's influence, but she accepts all but Vinaver's third and fourth points (102-09). To these she

B.N.fr. 103 utilized Thomas in composing his idiosyncratic conclusion to the prose romance. In addition to the points of contact noted by Baumgartner (116), MS. B.N.fr. 103 adopts another detail given only by Thomas. When Iseut's ship is in danger of sinking in a violent storm as she hastens to Tristan's aid, she laments that her desire to be buried in a single tomb with him will not be realized:

> 'Amis, jo fail a mun desir,
> Car en voz bras quidai murrir,
> *En un sarcu enseveiliz*,
> Mais nus l'avum ore failliz.'   (*T* D1649-52)

MS. B.N.fr. 103 contains a clear echo of this scene. As Yseult is taking leave of Tristan at the end of the madness episode, she imagines their death in the following terms:

> '[Je] vous prendray entre mes bras et vous beseray que ja pour nully ne le leisseray, et puis mourray, si que *nous serons tous deux ensembles enfouys*; car, puis que l'amour est si joincte a la vie, elle ne doit pas estre dessevree a la mort.'   (379)

In view of these examples of Thomas's influence, there can be little doubt that the account of the miraculous plants in MS. B.N.fr. 103 was coloured by a corresponding episode in Thomas. The divergence of Eilhart and MS. B.N.fr. 103 and the agreement of MS. B.N.fr. 103 and *Tristrams Saga* concerning the reaction of the spouses after the lovers' deaths and the manner of the lovers' interment furnish the most persuasive demonstration of the existence of an episode of the intertwining trees in Thomas.

---

adds the depiction of the life in the forest and the absence of guilt on the part of the lovers (111). She lists ten possible points of Thomas's influence on the dominant version (115) and three on MS. B.N.fr. 103 (115-16).

V

THE SUPPRESSION OF THE EPISODE
OF THE INTERTWINING TREES

How then did it come about that both the episode of Iseut's prayer and that of the intertwining trees are missing from the two extant Anglo-Norman manuscripts that give the end of Thomas's *Tristan*? It would appear that the audience of the late twelfth and early thirteenth centuries, or, at the very least, an influential portion of that audience, was profoundly alarmed and deeply threatened by the content of Thomas's *Tristan*, and most especially so by the concluding episode of the intertwining trees. For this reason, the episode of the intertwining trees was suppressed in the extant manuscripts of Thomas's poem.

Thomas is responsible for two important innovations with respect to his source, the *version commune*. Unlike their counterparts in the versions of Beroul and Eilhart, his lovers are seldom prey to guilt or remorse concerning the morality of their love (Frappier 451; Payen, *Motif* 354-55). Unlike the situation in Eilhart's work and in the dominant version of the prose romance, the conflict between Thomas's lovers and the legal and religious institutions of their society is not resolved at their deaths but is prolonged beyond the grave. I propose that the original conclusion to Thomas's poem, which contained the text of the Sneyd manuscript *and* the episode of the intertwining trees but omitted Iseut's prayer, was profoundly shocking to certain of its readers, who perceived it to be a blasphemous exhaltation of an unlawful passion in which God Himself helps the adulterous lovers to contravene the laws of Church and State.

(1) At the final moment of their lives, a moment that marks the culmination of their adulterous passion, the attention of each of the lovers is focused on the other, rather than on the preparation for the next life and the expiation of the sins of this one. They die

145

unshriven and unrepentant, if we except the apocryphal prayer placed in Iseut's mouth by Friar Robert.[31]

(2) The highly eroticized love-death, in which the final embrace of the lovers is a transparent simulacrum of sexual intercourse, outrages numerous taboos, Christian and otherwise. The image of the intertwining trees, like that of the phallic briar of MS. B.N.fr. 103, serves as an objective correlative for the dead lovers lying entwined 'cors a cors, buche a buche' (Sn^2 812).

(3) The episode of the intertwining trees is the last in a long series of tricks designed to permit the lovers to enjoy sexual union (Blakeslee, 'Trickster'). This trick, by which the lovers outwit the vigilance of the civil and ecclesiastical orders, despite the efforts of the slighted, lawful spouse to separate them and in symbolic defiance of the Church (whose physical structure is used to enforce that separation), represents a double violation of temporal and spiritual law. The lovers' post-mortem reunion signifies their permanent alienation from and ultimate triumph over social and religious morality.

(4) The lovers' death and reincarnation, or better, resurrection, in the form of intertwining trees constitutes either an example of pagan magic or a divinely ordained miracle worthy of the highest hagiographic tradition. The latter implies that God has actively intervened on behalf of the lovers.

In sum, Thomas is a theoretician of a religion of love whose values supercede or subvert those of feudal and familial obligation, chivalric honour, social convention, and religious orthodoxy.

In contrast, Eilhart's poem, the only other twelfth-century text to contain an account of the lovers' death, treats the scene quite differently (Buschinger, 'Iseut aux Blanches Mains'). As has been noted, the lovers' memory is rehabilitated and the episode of the miraculous plants merely translates the forgiveness and approba- tion accorded the lovers in death. The jealousy of Tristrant's wife has vanished and her lie concerning the colour of the sail is treated as an unintentional and momentary lapse (9378-83) that is followed immediately by remorse and grief:

> Do der her tod waß,
> Vor laid kom genaß
> Sin wip, dü daß wort sprach,

---

[31] Payen expresses a somewhat different view of the subversive character of the romance: 'Le vrai scandale est que Tristan et Yseut aient été capables de s'aimer à ce point que la mort devînt la seule issue possible, et que, dans un contexte de civilisation chrétienne, des auteurs aient pu faire une telle apologie d'une passion idolâtre et désespérée' (*Motif* 363).

Da von im sin hertz brach.
Über lüt sü do schraÿ:
'O we, ach und we,
Daß mir ÿe so geschach!'
Selber sü daß wol sach,
Daß er von iren schulden starb.   (9391-99)

Likewise, when Marke is told that the passion of Tristrant and Isalde was involuntary, a result of the accidental consumption of the potion, he laments his persecution of the lovers (9465-9501) and orders their bodies to be brought back to England. There he has them buried with splendour in a single grave upon which he plants with his own hand the vine and the rose that symbolically wed the couple and commemorate their love. His choice of plants represents a variant on the traditional marriage topos of the vine and the elm (Demetz), the rose planted above Isalde symbolizing the purity of their love, the vine above Tristrant its immortality.[32]

Jean-Charles Payen has described the process of the *conjuration* of the dangerous content of the texts of the Tristan verse corpus and the transmutation of that content in the dominant version of the French prose *Tristan*, which retained the exterior form of the verse romance, while replacing its menacing content with the paraphernalia of chivalric romance, a disconnected fabric of quests, jousts, and adventures prolonged *ad libitum* ('Conjuration'). His theory offers a solution to the enigma of the exceedingly corrupt manuscript tradition of the verse corpus. A number of texts of the early verse corpus have been lost entirely, including perhaps the *estoire* and the numerous hypothetical versions postulated by genealogists of the legend, as well those ascribed to Chrétien, La Chievre, and Breri. The surviving texts of the French verse corpus are in ruinous condition. Only two poems, *Chevrefoil* and *Tristan ménestrel*, survive in more than a single manuscript (each is preserved in two). *Tristan rossignol* and the *Folies Tristan* of Bern and Oxford have each survived only in a single manuscript (although a short fragment of the *Folie de Berne* has recently come to light). The condition of the two full versions

---

[32] In the dominant version of the French prose romance, Tristan writes to Mark from his deathbed, explaining the potion and forgiving his uncle. As in Eilhart, Mark has the lovers buried side by side with great pomp and lamentation. The tone of this account, in which there is no trace of the version of the intertwining trees, contrasts sharply with that of the subversive accounts of MS. B.N.fr. 103 and Thomas. In the versions of Ulrich and Heinrich, Marke, who perceives in the intertwining plants a miracle signifying God's pardon of the lovers, causes a monastary to be built in their honour.

147

of the legend, those of Beroul and Thomas, is the worst of the corpus. Beroul's poem exists in a single manuscript fragment that lacks a beginning and an end but that is integral. Thomas's text, which is both fragmentary and discontinuous, is contained in fragments of five different manuscripts. The picture of devastation offered by the verse corpus is to be contrasted with the case of the far longer French prose *Tristan* that exists in seventy-eight different manuscripts, many complete and in excellent condition, as well as with that of Chrétien's *Cligés*, an 'anti-Tristan' that survives in seven complete and five fragmentary manuscripts. This disparity between the manuscripts of earlier and later stages of legend demands an explanation. Payen has suggested that the verse corpus was the object of a deliberate conspiracy of silence that manifested itself in the refusal on the part of scribes (undoubtedly under instructions of their superiors) to reproduce its manuscripts ('Conjuration' 632). This *de facto* censorship, which may have gone as far as the deliberate revision or even destruction of texts, culminated in the substitution of the prose for the verse version ('Conjuration' 629-31).

Payen's theory offers an explanation for the discrepancy between the texts of the Douce and Sneyd manuscripts and between those two texts and the *Tristrams Saga*. The reaction against the supposedly blasphemous character of the conclusion of Thomas's poem may reasonably be assumed to have taken four different forms. In one instance, without otherwise altering the narrative of the original, a transmitter of a manuscript of the poem (presumably Brother Robert) interpolated Ísönd's prayer in a pious attempt to palliate Thomas's conclusion by suggesting that the resurrection of the lovers was a consequence of her petition for God's grace. A second form of reaction against Thomas's 'blasphemous' ending was practiced independently elsewhere. In this instance, a copyist took upon himself to omit offending material in the conclusion of the poem. This technique of suppression was applied with varying degrees of severity to the Douce and Sneyd manuscripts. In the case of Douce, the entire conclusion of the poem, including the episode of the intertwining trees and Thomas's *envoi*, was excised and a three-line conclusion clumsily substituted. In the case of Sneyd[2], only the episode of the intertwining trees was suppressed.[33] A third type of reaction against Thomas's poem

---

[33] Another hypothesis might be offered to explain the disappearance of the episode of the intertwining trees from the Sneyd manuscript. The Sneyd[2] fragment (fols 11-17 of MS. Fr. d.16) is a quire of four bifolia, the last of which

was its non-transmission, a phenomenon testified to by the paucity of Tristan manuscripts, which were not recopied as they deteriorated,[34] and a fourth was its replacement by the prose romance.

Thus, each of the extant conclusions to Thomas's poem, those of Douce, Sneyd[2], and *Tristrams Saga*, presents a different version of a text that, in its original form, recounted Iseut's lament on the death of Tristan (Sn^2 775-808; D 1810-15; S Ch. 101), the final embrace of the lovers and Iseut's death (Sn^2 809-15; D 1816-18; S Ch. 101), Thomas's commentary on their death (Sn^2 816-819; S Ch. 101), the episode of the intertwining trees (S Ch. 101), and Thomas's *envoi* (Sn^2 820-839), but omitted Iseut's prayer (S Ch. 101), the work of an interpolator. Robert, who worked from an intact original containing the episode of the intertwining trees,

has lost its second leaf. A notarial document dated 1366 served as a limp-vellum cover to the manuscript until it was bound more sturdily in this century. The text of Sn^2 as given in the Wind edition concludes with line 839 at the bottom of the second column of fol. 17^r. However, the text would appear to be continued on the verso, for the first column of fol. 17^v contains ten lines in a hand very like the main script, followed by two lines, possibly an *explicit*, in a different hand. These twelve lines (as well as material at the top of the second column in another, rather later hand), having been badly rubbed, are illegible even under ultra-violet light. There is no indication that the bottom half of the page was ever written on. While it may be that the contents of fol. 17^v were obliterated deliberately, it is more likely that the erasure was accidental, 'the result of heavy wear [of the sort that would have been produced] if this were the last page of an unbound manuscript' (Barker-Benfield). It is congruent with the facts to assume that fol. 18, which presumably remained blank, was removed for other purposes and that the exterior of the manuscript was heavily worn between that moment and the time sometime after 1366 when it received its first cover, the notarial document. That it was not bound previously is proved by the single set of sewing holes found both in the cover and the interior of the manuscript. While it is not impossible that the obliterated ten lines of fol. 17va recounted the episode of the intertwining trees, there are two difficulties with this theory. First, fol. 17rb contains only twenty-nine lines, while every other column in the Sneyd[2] fragment contains thirty-two. The last line of Thomas's text does not coincide with the bottom of the page (although it nearly does so), suggesting that his text did not continue onto the next leaf. Second, one would expect to find the episode of the intertwining trees, the last narrative portion of the romance, before and not after the concluding non-narrative *envoi*. If indeed the text at the top of fol. 17va does belong to Thomas's romance, I am inclined to believe that it was a continuation of the *envoi* and not the missing episode.

[34] It is relevant to note in this regard that all of the extant manuscripts of Thomas's poem were preserved outside of France: the Douce and the Cambridge manuscripts in England, the Sneyd and Turin manuscripts (and the manuscript of Beroul's poem) in Italy, and the Strasbourg fragment in Germany.

faithfully reproduced the narrative of his model, substantially abridging Iseut's monologue (Sn² 775-808) and omitting Thomas's *envoi*. For the latter he substituted a one-line *explicit* and probably a colophon containing the material given in the preface to the modern manuscripts.[35] The redactor of MS. B.N.fr. 103 also knew an integral version of Thomas's romance and incorporated details from it in his version of the episode of the miraculous plants.

In conclusion, the discrepancy between the two manuscripts that contain the extant conclusion to Thomas's poem permits the assumption that neither preserves the canonical form of Thomas's romance. The presence of an episode of the miraculous plants in *Tristrams Saga* and MS. B.N.fr. 103 strongly suggests that a similar episode in Thomas's romance was their common source. It was inconsistent with the practice of the translator of Thomas's romance and with that of the Icelandic copyists of that translation to interpolate non-canonical narrative material in *Tristrams Saga*. The perception of Thomas's poem as subversive was responsible for the suppression of the episode of the intertwining trees in the Sneyd and Douce manuscripts, a specific instance of a generalized effort to suppress the French Tristan poems. These conclusions, taken together, indicate that the episode of the intertwining trees that is present in the Old Norse *Tristrams Saga* was composed by the poet Thomas.

---

[35] This omission is consistent with Robert's practice. In his preface he identifies his work as a translation but says nothing of his source nor of its author, nor does he mention his source in the colophon to *Elis Saga*, where he also names himself and his patron. Similarly, Robert suppresses entirely Thomas's long and highly personal digression on the versions of the legend (D 835-84) where Thomas names himself (D 862) as he will again in the *envoi* (Sn² 820), and as, in all probability, he did in the lost prologue to the poem (see Sn² 829). Thus, Robert's action in omitting Thomas's *envoi* is consistent with his practice elsewhere of supressing references to his source, of omitting extra-narrative material contained in his source, and of suppressing lengthy monologues on the subject of love, be they pronounced by Tristan, by Iseut, or by the *persona* of the author.

WORKS CITED

Primary Texts

A. Thomas's *Tristan*

Thomas. *Les Fragments du roman de Tristan, poème du XIIe siècle.* Ed. Bartina H. Wind. Textes Littéraires Français 92. Geneva: Droz; Paris: Minard, 1960.

B. Brother Robert's *Tristrams Saga*

Die nordische und die englische Version der Tristan-Sage. I. *Tristrams Saga ok Ísondar mit einer literar-historischen Einleitung, deutscher Uebersetzung und Anmerkungen zum ersten Mal herausgegeben.* Ed. Eugen Kölbing. Heilbronn: Henninger, 1878.
The Saga of Tristram and Ísönd. Trans. Paul Schach. Lincoln: University of Nebraska Press, 1973.

C. The B.N.fr. 103 Variant of the French Prose *Tristan*

Le Roman de Tristan par Thomas, poème du XIIe siècle. Ed. Joseph Bédier. Société des Anciens Textes Français. Paris: Firmin-Didot, 1905, 2: 321-95.

D. The Dominant Version of the French Prose *Tristan*

Le Roman en prose de Tristan, le roman de Palamède et la compilation de Rusticien de Pise. Analyse critique d'après les manuscrits de Paris. Ed. Eilert Löseth. Paris: Bouillon, 1891. Rpt. New York: Burt Franklin, 1970.

E. Eilhart von Oberge's *Tristrant*

Eilhart von Oberg. Tristrant. Edition diplomatique des manuscrits et traduction en français moderne avec introduction, notes et index. Ed. Danielle Buschinger. Göppinger Arbeiten zur Germanstik 202. Göppingen: Alfred Kümmerle, 1976.

F. Other Texts

Beroul. *The Romance of Tristran by Beroul. A Poem of the Twelfth Century.* Ed. Alfred Ewert. 2 vols. Oxford: Blackwell, 1939, 1970.
Le Conte de Floire et Blancheflor. Ed. Jean-Luc Leclanche. Classiques Français du Moyen Age 105. Paris: Champion, 1980.
La Folie Tristan de Berne. Ed. Jean-Charles Payen. *Tristan et Yseut. Les Tristan en vers. 'Tristan' de Béroul, 'Tristan' de Thomas, 'Folie Tristan' de Berne, 'Folie Tristan' d'Oxford, 'Chèvrefeuille' de Marie de France. Edition nouvelle comprenant texte, traduction, notes critiques, bibliographie et notes.* Paris: Garnier, 1974, 247-64.
Gottfried von Straßburg. *Tristan und Isold. Text.* Ed. F. Ranke. 7th edn. Berlin: Weidmann, 1963.
Piramus et Tisbé, poème du XIIe siècle. Ed. C. de Boer. Classiques Français du Moyen Age 26. Paris: Champion, 1921.
Sir Tristrem. Ed. George P. McNeill. Scottish Text Society 8. 1886. Rpt. New York: Johnson Reprint Corp., 1966.

Secondary Sources

Aitken, D. F. 'The "Voyage à l'aventure" in the "Tristan" of Thomas'. *Modern Language Review* 23 (1928): 468-72.
Barker-Benfield, B. C., Assistant Librarian, Department of Western Manuscripts, Bodleian Library, Oxford University. Letter to author. January 28, 1985.
Barnes, Geraldine. 'The *Riddarasögur* and Mediaeval European Literature'. *Mediaeval Scandinavia* 8 (1975): 140-158.
Baumgartner, Emmanuèle. *Le 'Tristan en prose'. Essai d'interprétation d'un roman médiéval.* Publications Romanes et Françaises 133. Geneva: Droz, 1975.
Bédier, Joseph. 'La Mort de Tristan et d'Iseut, d'après le manuscrit fr. 103 de la Bibliothèque Nationale, comparé au poème allemand d'Eilhart d'Oberg'. *Romania* 15 (1886): 481-510.

————. *Le Roman de Tristan par Thomas, poème du XIIe siècle*. Société des Anciens Textes Français. 2 vols. Paris: Firmin-Didot, 1902, 1905.

Blakeslee, Merritt R. 'Tristan the Trickster in the Old French Tristan Poems'. Forthcoming in *Cultura Neolatina* 44.3-4 (1984).

Buschinger, Danielle. 'Tristan et Iseut aux Blanches Mains dans la tradition de Tristan en France et en Allemagne au moyen âge'. *Actes du 14e Congrès International Arthurien. Rennes, 16-21 Août 1984*. 2 vols. Rennes: Presses Universitaires de Rennes 2, 1985. 1: 142-57.

Carney, James. 'The Irish Affinities of Tristan'. *Studies in Irish Literature and History*. Dublin: Dublin Institute for Advanced Studies, 1955. 189-242.

Child, Francis James. *The English and Scottish Popular Ballads*. 5 vols. Boston and New York, 1882-1898. Rpt. New York: Cooper Square Press, 1965.

Curtis, Renée L. *Le Roman de Tristan en prose*. I. Munich: Hueber, 1963.

————. 'Bédier's Version of the *Prose Tristan*'. *Tristan Studies*. Munich: Fink, 1969. 58-65.

————. 'The Manuscript Tradition of the *Prose Tristan* (Part I)'. *Tristan Studies*. Munich: Fink, 1969. 66-91.

Delbouille, Maurice. 'A propos de la patrie et de la date de *Floire et Blanchefleur* (version aristocratique)'. *Mélanges de linguistique et de littérature romanes offerts à Mario Roques*. Paris: Didier, 1952. 4: 53-98.

————. 'Le Premier *Roman de Tristan*'. *Cahiers de Civilisation Médiévale* 5 (1962): 273-86, 419-35.

Delpino, Marcella. 'Elementi celtici ed elementi classici nel "Tristan" di Thomas'. *Archivum Romanicum* 23 (1939): 312-36.

Demetz, Peter. 'The Elm and the Vine: Notes Toward the History of a Marriage Topos'. *PMLA* 73 (1958): 521-32.

Fourrier, Anthime. *Le Courant réaliste dans le roman courtois en France au Moyen Age*. I. *Les Débuts (XIIe siècle)*. Paris: Nizet, 1960.

Frappier, Jean. 'Structure et sens du *Tristan*: version commune, version courtoise'. *Cahiers de Civilisation Médiévale* 6 (1963): 255-80, 441-54.

Gallais, Pierre. 'Les Arbres entrelacés dans les romans de Tristan et le mythe de l'arbre androgyne primordial'. *Mélanges de langue et de littérature médiévales offerts à Pierre Le Gentil*. Paris: SEDES, 1973. 295-310.

Gunnlaugsdóttir, Álfrún. *Tristán en el Norte*. Reykjavík: Árna Magnússonar, 1978.

Halvorsen, Eyvind. 'Problèmes de la traduction scandinave des textes français du Moyen Age'. *Les Relations littéraires franco-scandinaves au Moyen Age. Actes du colloque de Liège, avril 1972*. Ed. Maurice Grave. Paris: Les Belles Lettres, 1975. 247-74.

Helle, Knut. 'Anglo-Norwegian Relations in the Reign of Håkon Håkonsson (1217-63)'. *Mediaeval Scandinavia* 1 (1968): 101-114.

Hunt, Tony. 'The Significance of Thomas's *Tristan*'. *Reading Medieval Studies* 7 (1981): 41-61.

Johnsen, Arne Odd. 'Les relations intellectuelles entre la France et la Norvège (1150-1214)'. *Le Moyen Age* 57 (1951): 247-68.

Kalinke, Marianne E. *King Arthur North-by-Northwest. The matière de Bretagne in Old Norse-Icelandic Romances*. Bibliotheca Arnamagnæana 37. Copenhagen: C. A. Reitzels, 1981.

Knudson, Charles A. 'Les Versions norroises des romans de Chrétien de Troyes: le cadre'. *Mélanges de langue et de littérature du Moyen Age et de la Renaissance offerts à Jean Frappier*. Publications Romanes et Françaises 112. 2 vols. Geneva: Droz, 1970. 2: 533-41.

Leach, Henry Goddard. 'The Relations of the Norwegian with the English Church, 1066-1399, and their Importance to Comparative Literature'. *Proceedings of the American Academy of Arts and Sciences* 44.20 (May 1909): 531-60.

————. *Angevin Britain and Scandinavia*. Harvard Studies in Comparative Literature 6. Cambridge, Mass.: Harvard UP, 1921. Rpt. Millwood, NY: Kraus, 1975.

Lutoslawski, W. 'Les Folies de Tristan'. *Romania* 15 (1886): 511-33.

Michel, Francisque. *Tristan. Recueil de ce qui reste des poëmes relatifs à ses aventures, composés en françois, en anglo-normand et en grec dans les XII et XIII siècles*. 3 vols. London: Pickering; Paris: Techener, 1835-38.

Muret, Ernest. 'Eilhart d'Oberg et sa source française.' *Romania* 16 (1887): 288-363.

Payen, Jean-Charles. *Le Motif du repentir dans la littérature française médiévale (des origines à 1230)*. Publications Romanes et Françaises 98. Geneva: Droz, 1967.

————. 'Lancelot contre Tristan: la conjuration d'un mythe subversif (Réflexions sur l'idéologie romanesque au Moyen Age).' *Mélanges de langue et de littérature médiévales offerts à Pierre Le Gentil*. Paris: SEDES, 1973. 617-32.

Psichari, Jean, and H. Gaidoz. 'Les Deux Arbres entrelacés'. *Mélusine* 4 (1888-89): cols. 60-62, 85-91.

Schach, Paul. 'Some Observations on *Tristrams Saga*'. *Saga-Book of the Viking Society* 15 (1957-59): 102-29.

——. 'Tristan and Isolde in Scandinavian Ballad and Folktale'. *Scandinavian Studies* 36 (1964): 281-97.

——. 'An Unpublished Leaf of *Tristrams Saga*: AM 567 Quarto, XXII, 2'. *Research Studies (Washington State University)* 32 (1964): 50-62.

——. 'The Style and Structure of *Tristrams Saga*'. *Scandinavian Studies. Essays Presented to Dr. Henry Goddard Leach on the Occasion of his Eighty-Fifth Birthday*. Eds. Carl F. Bayerschmidt and Erik J. Friis. Seattle: University of Washington Press, 1965. 63-86.

——. 'The Reeves Fragment of *Tristrams Saga ok Ísöndar*'. *Einarsbók. Afmæliskveðja til Einars Ól. Sveinssonar. 12. desember 1969*. Eds. Bjarmi Guðnason, Halldór Halldórsson and Jonas Kristjánsson. Reykjavík: Prenthús Hafsteins Guðmundssonar, 1969. 296-308.

——. 'Some Observations on the Influence of *Tristrams saga ok Ísöndar* on Old Icelandic Literature'. *Old Norse Literature and Mythology: A Symposium*. Ed. Edgar C. Polomé. Austin: University of Texas Press, 1969. 81-129.

Shoaf, Judith P. 'Thomas's *Tristan* and the *Tristrams Saga*: Versions and Themes'. Diss. Cornell University, 1978.

Sudre, Léopold. 'Les Allusions à la légende de Tristan dans la littérature du Moyen Age'. *Romania* l5 (1886): 534-57.

Thomas, M. F. 'The Briar and the Vine: Tristan Goes North'. *Arthurian Literature* 3 (1983): 53-90.

Thompson, Stith. *Motif-Index of Folk Literature: A Classification of Narrative Elements in Folk Tales, Ballads, Myths, Fables, Medieval Romances, Exempla, Fabliaux, Jest-Books and Local Legends*. 6 vols. 1932-36. Rpt. Bloomington: Indiana University Press, 1955-58.

Togeby, Knud. 'La Chronologie des versions scandinaves des anciens textes français'. *Les Relations littéraires franco-scandinaves au Moyen Age. Actes du colloque de Liège, avril 1972*. Ed. Maurice Grave. Paris: Les Belles Lettres, 1975. 183-91.

Tómasson, Sverrir. 'Hvenær var Tristrams Sögu Snúið?' *Gripla* 2 (1977): 47-78.

Vàrvaro, Alberto. 'L'utilizzazione letteraria di motivi della narrativa popolare nei romanzi di Tristano'. *Mélanges de langue et de littérature du Moyen Age et de la Renaissance offerts à Jean*

Frappier. Publications Romanes et Françaises 112. 2 vols. Geneva: Droz, 1970. 2: 1057-75.

Vinaver, Eugène. *Etudes sur le 'Tristan' en prose. Les sources; les manuscrits, bibliographie critique*. Paris: Champion, 1925.

———. 'The Love Potion in the Primitive Tristan Romance'. *Medieval Studies in Memory of Gertrude Schoepperle-Loomis*. New York: Columbia UP; Paris: Champion, 1927. 75-86.

———. 'The Prose *Tristan'. Arthurian Literature in the Middle Ages. A Collaborative History*. Ed. Roger S. Loomis. Oxford: Clarendon, 1959. 339-47.

Zingarelli, Nicola. 'Tristano e Isotta'. *Studi Medievali*, n.s. 1 (1928): 48-58.

Zink, Georges. 'Les Poèmes arthuriens dans les pays scandinaves'. *Les Relations littéraires franco-scandinaves au Moyen Age. Actes du colloque de Liège, avril 1972*. Ed. Maurice Grave. Paris: Les Belles Lettres, 1975. 77-95

UPDATE

V

THE MANUSCRIPTS OF THE WORKS OF
GEOFFREY OF MONMOUTH:
A NEW SUPPLEMENT

Julia Crick

One of the objectives of the Geoffrey of Monmouth Research
Project is the publication of a Summary Catalogue of the Manuscripts of Geoffrey of Monmouth's *Historia Regum Britanniae*. Having undertaken this task as well as full-time research on the textual
history of the *Historia*, I have inherited from David Dumville the
regular reporting of adjustments to the list of known manuscripts.
Some further additions and corrections can be made to the lists
published by Dr Dumville in *Arthurian Literature* III (1983), 113-
28, IV (1985), 164-71 and V (1985), 149-51. References to further
witnesses continue to be found. In what follows
I proceed in the order established in the previous listings. The
members of the Research Project would be glad to continue to
receive corrections or supplementary information: any such matter
may be sent to the Editor of *Arthurian Literature* at the office of
Boydell and Brewer Ltd.

SHELFMARKS

ENGLAND

London, British Library
It should be noted that MSS. Arundel 319 and 409 are parts of the
same manuscript, as correctly indicated by H. L. D. Ward, *Catalogue of Romances in the British Museum* I (London, 1883), pp. 232-3.
MS. 319 (fos 16r-97v) contains the text of *Historia Regum Britanniae* to the beginning of § 163, 'Alphatina'. The first fifteen folios are
codicologically distinct, fos 1-7 being scrappy leaves containing a
variety of notes, and fos 8-15 bearing an abridged copy of the *De*

157

Vita Contemplatiua of Iulianus Pomerius in an earlier hand and narrower format than the rest of the book. MS. 409 contains the remainder of Geoffrey's History from § 163, 'rex Hispanie', with no loss of text (fos 1r-23r), followed by the prophecies of Merlinus Siluestris (fos 23r-24r). The total number of manuscripts (including the three listed abridgments) therefore stands at 215.

MANUSCRIPTS NOT KNOWN TO GRISCOM

FRANCE

30. Colmar, Bibliothèque municipale, MS. 448 (14)　　　*s*. xii
Historia (fragmentary) on fos 1r-72v.
This manuscript, of which Geoffrey's History is the sole surviving content, bears a fifteenth-century *ex libris* of the Augustinian abbey of Marbach, near Colmar (diocese of Basel, later Strasbourg). A description by Pierre Schmitt may be found in *Catalogue général des manuscrits des Bibliothèques Publiques de France*, t. LVI (Paris, 1969), pp.166-7.

31. Paris, Bibliothèque de l'Arsenal, MS. 982 (7.H.L)　　*s*. xiv
Historia on fos 168v-188r.
This copy of the First Variant Version, discovered only shortly before completion of the new edition of that text, concludes a substantial historical miscellany. The *Historia* is immediately preceded by the *De Excidio Troiae* of Dares Phrygius (fos 165r-168v). Interpolated into the text of the *Historia*, between § 178 and § 179 on fo 186r/v, is a copy of the *Vera Historia de Morte Arthuri* (of which an account will be given in a future volume of *Arthurian Literature*). A description of this large-format historical miscellany, perhaps written in southern France in the third quarter of the fourteenth century, is given by Henry Martin [and F. Funck-Brentano], *Catalogue des manuscrits de la Bibliothèque de l'Arsenal* (9 vols in 10, Paris, 1885-94), II. 205-7. An important witness to the text of the First Variant Version, it will be fully treated in Neil Wright's forthcoming edition of the First Variant Version.

32. Paris, Bibliothèque nationale, MS. latin 13935　　　*s*. xiii
A reference to another copy of the *Historia* in Paris is currently under investigation. L. Delisle, 'Inventaire des manuscrits latins de Saint-Germain-des-Prés', *Bibliothèque de l'École des Chartes*

29 [6th S., 4] (1868), 220-60, at p. 250, lists among the manuscripts of small format '13935 Histoire de Geoffroi de Monmouth, XIII s.'.

UNITED STATES OF AMERICA

33. Notre Dame (Indiana), University of Notre Dame Library, MS.
    40   s. xv
    Historia on fos 13r-35v.
    For details of this complete copy, apparently written after 1414,
    see James A. Corbett, *Catalogue of the Medieval & Renaissance
    Manuscripts of the University of Notre Dame* (Notre Dame,
    Ind., 1978), pp. 177-81. I owe my knowledge of it to Dr Richard
    Barber.

ABBREVIATED VERSIONS OF GEOFFREY'S HISTORY

4. Paris, Bibliothèque nationale, MS. latin 11107
   This manuscript should be removed from the list of complete
   witnesses, for it contains extensively abbreviated passages interspersed with chapters in which the usual text is followed.

LOST COPIES OF GEOFFREY'S HISTORY

Surviving manuscripts which can be shown, whether by a contents-list or other evidence, once to have contained more than their present complement of texts may occasionally provide evidence for another copy of the *Historia*. Occasionally this may enable the missing copy to be identified among known manuscripts.

1. Bern, Burgerbibliothek, MS. 392   s. xii
   In her investigation of the migration of books from Parisian
   college-libraries, Elisabeth Pellegrin ('Manuscrits de l'Abbaye
   de Saint-Victor et d'anciens collèges de Paris à la Bibliothèque
   municipale de Berne, à la Bibliothèque Vaticane, et à Paris',
   Bibliothèque de l'École des Chartes 103 [1942] 69-98) discussed
   the only book from Saint-Victor found in the Burgerbibliothek.
   It bears the Saint-Victor mark 'BBB 7' and an *ex libris* inscription. The contents were listed in a fifteenth-century hand on the
   verso of the first folio, from which they were printed by Hermann Hagen, *Catalogus Codicum Bernensium (Bibliotheca Bongarsiana)* (Bern, 1875), pp. 360-1: Bede's prose Life of

159

St Cuthbert; *Translatio sancti Cuthberti*; 'Quedam de cronicis'; Dares Phrygius; 'Quedam ex Ysidoro Ethimologiarum' (*sic*); *Hystoria regum Britannie Maioris ab eorum exordio*. The details of the entry confirm that this last work was indeed Geoffrey's History. The extent of the work (fos 56-95) is stated. Details are then added about fos 75-77: 'Ubi folio 75 et duobus sequentibus habetur de Merlino et eius prophetia. A sedet me, B cum nauigio, C 95 et usque 97'. The *Prophetiae Merlini* would be in their usual position, mid-way through the work. However, the second sentence is puzzling: it is possible that *sedet me* is a misreading of *Sedente*, the opening word of §111, but I have not found such a variant elsewhere; also, the phrase *cum nauigio* does not occur in the *Prophetiae* or in the 'Merlinus iste' chapter which follows in the Second Variant Version. The manuscript is now imperfect, having only fos 1-23 and 36-52. The last item is now the copy of Dares Phrygius, ending on 52v, which indicates the loss of the Isidore excerpts and Geoffrey's History. The fifteenth-century list indicates that *Vita Cuthberti* (now mutilated at the end) concluded on fo 34 and the *Translatio* (now acephalous) began on fo 35.

Bern 392 has been studied for its other contents. Bertram Colgrave, *Two Lives of Saint Cuthbert* (Cambridge, 1940), p. 36, listed it as no. 33 of the manuscripts of Bede's prose Life, suggesting that it was written in England: he pointed to associations with Durham suggested both by the style of the initials and textual similarity to a group of copies of Durham origin. Although all the parts of the book were of similar date, they were not originally sections of a single manuscript, however. G. V. Scammell, *Hugh de Puiset* (Cambridge, 1956), pp. 158-60, noted that seven copies of Bede's writings about Monkwearmouth-Jarrow and St Cuthbert were made at the instigation of Hugh de Puiset during the campaign of the Durham Cathedral Chapter for free elections. The later history of the manuscript was investigated by B. Colgrave and I. Masson, 'The *editio princeps* of Bede's prose Life of St Cuthbert, and its printer's XIIth-century "copy"', *The Library*, 4th S., 19 (1938), 289-303 see especially pp. 290 and 302 on the origin and physical features of this composite manuscript. The *Vita* was still complete in 1563 when Hervagius used it for the Basel *editio princeps* of Bede's works: the printer's ink- and chalk-markings can still be seen. The book came via Jacques Bongars and Jacques Gravisset to the Bern library.

160

COPIES OF GEOFFREY'S 'PROPHETIAE MERLINI'

A list of independent copies of this work has recently been published: C. D. Eckhardt, 'The *Prophetia Merlini* of Geoffrey of Monmouth: Latin manuscript copies', *Manuscripta* 26 (1982), 167-76. I owe the following additions to her list to Dr David Dumville.

1. Cambridge, Fitzwilliam Museum, MS. 379, fos 4v-8v   *s.* xiv *in.*
   See Francis Wormald and P. M. Giles, *A Descriptive Catalogue of the Additional Illuminated Manuscripts in the Fitzwilliam Museum acquired between 1895 and 1979 (excluding the McClean Collection)* (2 vols, Cambridge, 1982), I. 391-4. Rubric: 'Incipit liber Merlini de regibus Anglie'. Inc.: 'Sedente'.

2. Cambridge, Trinity College, MS. R.7.23 (759), pp. 3-13   *s.* xiv
   See [James II.233-5].
   Inc.: 'Ue rubeo draconi, nam exterminacio eius festinant ...'
   Expl.: '... et cancer cum sole litigabit'.
   Cf. Ward, *Catalogue of Romances*, I.303.

3. Cambridge, Trinity College, MS. O.1.17 (1041), fos 177r-181r
   s. xiv
   See M. R. James, *ibid.*, III.16-19. This copy follows a complete text of the *Historia*. The manuscript's mediaeval provenance is Whalley: N. R. Ker, *Medieval Libraries of Great Britain. A List of Surviving Books* (2nd edn, London, 1964), p. 197.

4. London, British Library, MS. Cotton Nero D.viii, fo 175r *s.* xiv
   This is only a fragment, added in the fourteenth century to an earlier book which contains a full copy of the *Historia*.

5. Oxford, Bodleian Library, MS. Douce 207 (*S.C.* 21781), fos 40v-42r   *s.* xiii/xiv
   Incorporated in Roger Wendover, *Flores Historiarum*: see [sc IV.555].

6. Paris, Bibliothèque nationale, MS. latin 2321, fo 48   *s.* xiii
   The *Prophetiae* have been added to an Italian manuscript of *saec.* x/xi: see Ph. Lauer, *Bibliothèque Nationale: Catalogue général des manuscrits latins* II (Paris, 1940), pp. 404-5.

7. San Marino (California), Huntington Library, MS. HM 1345, fos 107r-111r   *s.* xiv *med.*

See the note by D. N. Dumville, *ante*, IV. 171. For a description of this English manuscript, see Seymour De Ricci and W. J. Wilson, *Census of Medieval and Renaissance Manuscripts in the United States and Canada* (3 vols, New York, 1935-40), I. 107.

VI

THE MANUSCRIPTS OF
THE *VERA HISTORIA DE MORTE ARTHURI*

Richard Barber

Since the update in *Arthurian Literature* II in which Michael Lapidge published a third manuscript of this text, no less than three
further MSS have come to light. His comment, 'The manuscript
evidence presented here suggests wide circulation but perhaps infrequent copying' now needs to be modified: it seems that we are
dealing with a text that was relatively common in both senses.[1]

The most interesting discovery is the insertion of the text into a
copy of the First Variant version of Geoffrey of Monmouth's *Historia Regum Britannie* in the previously unrecorded MS, Paris, Bibliothèque de l'Arsenal, MS.982, noticed by Julia Crick and examined by Neil Wright, who found that it included the *Vera Historia*.
As I commented earlier, the text 'seems to be distinctly designed to
continue Geoffrey's account of Arthur's reign, replacing the last
paragraph which sums up the results of the battle, Arthur's fate and
the handing over of the kingdom to Cador'.[2] In this MS, the piece is
simply inserted as a supplement between §178 and §179 of the
original text. In another newly discovered MS, Paris, Bibliothèque
Nationale MS Lat. 6401D, the *Vera Historia* is quoted as if it were
by Geoffrey himself at the end of an abbreviated text of the First
Variant version made for Filippo Maria, duke of Milan, by Galeaz-
zo di Correggio in the late fourteenth century. This is a partial and
corrupt text, but is fascinating for the light it sheds on the
knowledge of Arthurian literature and availability of Arthurian
texts in north Italy at this period.

The last text but one appears in a similar context to London,
British Library MS Cotton Titus D. XIX (T) in that the *De origine*

---

[1] *Arthurian Literature* II, 168, n.19.
[2] *Arthurian Literature* I, 72.

gigantum in insula Albion appears in the same manuscript, as well as a Latin version of part of *Perlesvaus*.[3] The readings of this MS, Oxford, Bodleian Library MS Digby 186, include those of the corrector in T, T[1], and it may be a direct copy of T after these corrections were made. It is an early sixteenth century MS.

In view of the number of copies of this text which have come to light in a relatively short time, it would seem prudent to delay publication of a fully revised and updated text for the moment, and to ask scholars examining late medieval Latin miscellanies similar to the Cotton and Digby MSS in which the text is found to look out for further copies. The current examination of Geoffrey of Monmouth MSS may also yield further texts, and it is possible that it may be found embedded in other Latin chronicles.

[3] A study of this will appear in *Arthurian Literature* VII.

EDITOR'S NOTE

Readers may be interested to know that a new recording of Ernest Chausson's *Le roi Artus* (discussed in *Arthurian Literature IV) is now available on Erato (discs: NUM 75271; tapes: MCE 75271; compact discs: ECD 88213) with Teresa Zylis-Gara, Gino Quilico, Gösta Winbergh, the Radio France Chorus and the New Philharmonic Orchestra conducted by Armin Jordan.*

We are always grateful for notices of recent Arthurian literature, films or music to update the lists which appeared in Arthurian Literature III and IV. Please send any information to the Editor at Boydell & Brewer Ltd, PO Box 9, Woodbridge IP12 3DF, Suffolk.

DUE DATE

BURG APR 1 1 1987			
	201-6503		Printed in USA